Sebastian Lohsse/Reiner Schulze/Dirk Staudenmayer (eds.)

Data as Counter-Performance – Contract Law 2.0?

Münster Colloquia on EU Law and the Digital Economy V

HART
PUBLISHING

Nomos

Onlineversion
Nomos eLibrary

The Deutsche Nationalbibliothek lists this publication in the Deutsche Nationalbibliografie; detailed bibliographic data are available on the Internet at http://dnb.d-nb.de

ISBN: HB (Nomos) 978-3-8487-7606-1
ePDF (Nomos) 978-3-7489-0853-1

British Library Cataloguing-in-Publication Data
A catalogue record for this book is available from the British Library.

ISBN: HB (Hart) 978-1-5099-4031-8

Library of Congress Cataloging-in-Publication Data
Lohsse, Sebastian / Schulze, Reiner / Staudenmayer, Dirk
Data as Counter-Performance – Contract Law 2.0?
Münster Colloquia on EU Law and the Digital Economy V
Sebastian Lohsse / Reiner Schulze / Dirk Staudenmayer (eds.)
284 pp.
Includes bibliographic references.

ISBN: 978-1-5099-4031-8 (hardcover Hart)

1st Edition 2020

Foreword

With ongoing digitization, data is increasingly seen as a tradable asset. Accordingly, digital content and digital services are frequently provided in return not for money but for data. The 5th Münster Colloquium on EU Law and the Digital Economy, held on 16th and 17th May 2019, brought together scholars and practitioners from across Europe for an in-depth discussion of issues surrounding this role of 'data as counter-performance'. Its impact on the economy and contract practice will be one of the central aspects in the further development of contract law and of consumer protection in the digital age. This is true, in particular, since data as counter-performance has also become a subject of European legislation with the new EU Directive 'on certain aspects concerning contracts for the supply of digital content and digital services' (whose publication in May 2019 coincided with the Colloquium).

The publication of the results of the 5th Münster Colloquium in this volume aims to stimulate the further discussion on this subject matter and to contribute to the development of modern private law. The editors kindly thank Karen Schulenberg for her role and support in the organisation of the Colloquium and in the preparation of this volume.

June 2020

Sebastian Lohsse
Reiner Schulze
Dirk Staudenmayer

Contents

Data as Counter-Performance – Contract Law 2.0? An Introduction

Sebastian Lohsse / Reiner Schulze / Dirk Staudenmayer[*]

I. Background

With the new EU Directive on certain aspects concerning contracts for the supply of digital content and digital services[1] (hereinafter 'Digital Content Directive', 'DCD'), 'data as counter-performance' has become a subject of European legislation. The Commission proposal[2] for this Directive explicitly used the term 'counter-performance' in relation to data provided by the consumer to the supplier under a contract 'in exchange' for the supply of digital content.[3] It provided that counter-performance in this form would be equivalent to counter-performance in the form of payment of a price.

The Digital Content Directive contains essentially the same assessment in this respect, even if it does not explicitly denote the consumer's performance as 'counter-performance'. Like the underlying Commission proposal, the Digital Content Directive characterises contracts falling within its scope by describing the performance to be rendered by both parties. The trader must provide or undertake to provide the consumer with digital

---

* Sebastian Lohsse and Reiner Schulze are Professors of Law, Centre for European Private Law, University of Münster. Dirk Staudenmayer is Head of Unit Contract Law, DG Justice and Consumers, European Commission and Honorary Professor at the University of Münster. The present contribution expresses only the personal opinion of the authors and does not bind in any way the European Commission.

1 Directive (EU) 2019/770, [2019] OJ L136/1. For an overview of the Directive see Dirk Staudenmayer, 'Auf dem Weg zum digitalen Privatrecht – Verträge über digitale Inhalte' (2019) 35 NJW 2497; for a more detailed explanation of its main features see Dirk Staudenmayer, 'The Directives on Digital Contracts – First steps towards the Private Law of the Digital Economy' (2020) 2 ERPL 219, and Reiner Schulze, 'Die Digitale-Inhalte-Richtlinie – Innovation und Kontinuität im europäischen Vertragsrecht' (2019) 4 ZEuP 695. For an article-by-article analysis of the Digital Content Directive see Reiner Schulze and Dirk Staudenmayer (eds), *EU Digital Law – Commentary* (Nomos 2020).

2 COM(2015) 634 final.

3 Art 3(1) COM(2015) 634 final.

content or a digital service. The consumer's performance may consist of either paying, or undertaking to pay a price, or providing, or undertaking to provide personal data to the trader. The provision of personal data in return for the provision of digital content and digital services is treated as counter-performance in the same way as the traditional form of the payment of a price. In short: personal data is regarded as payment.

The Directive, which defines its scope with this 'disruption', is one of the first legislative measures the EU is using to respond to two emerging trends in the 'digital economy'.

First of all, the digital economy has led to the appearance of new products in the form of digital content and digital services, which both constitute a fast-growing part of many retail sectors, as illustrated by the following examples: in 2018 the total amount of worldwide subscriptions to online video services for the first time surpassed the amount of cable subscriptions.[4] In the same year, paid streaming, free streaming, and downloads accounted for 59 % of the total recorded music revenues worldwide and made up more than 50 % of revenue in 38 markets.[5] The percentage of individuals aged 16–74 reading/downloading online newspapers/news magazines in the EU has, within the space of a decade, nearly tripled from 20.7 % in 2007 to 60.6 % in 2017.[6]

Secondly, this development trend on its own is combined with another visible trend in the data economy, i.e. that data is seen as a tradable asset. This has led, in B2C transactions, to the phenomenon that digital content and digital services are no longer paid for exclusively with money but also with access to data. Based on studies and an EU-wide survey, the Commission noted in the Impact Assessment of its proposal that a very large proportion of digital content provided to consumers is not paid with money but supplied against access to personal data granted by the consumer.[7] This was noted as particularly prevalent in the sectors involving audio-visu-

---

4 <https://www.mpaa.org/wp-content/uploads/2019/03/MPAA-THEME-Report-2018.pdf> 31, last accessed 28 July 2019.

5 <https://www.billboard.com/articles/business/8505270/ifpi-global-report-2019-music-sales-rise-paid-streaming> (using data from the annual Global Music Report 2019 by International Federation of the Phonographic Industry), last accessed 28 July 2019.

6 <https://stats.oecd.org/> → Information and Communication Technology → ICT Access and Usage by Households and Individuals → ICT Access and Usage by Individuals → indicator D1G: Individuals using the Internet for reading/downloading online newspapers/news magazines, last accessed 28 July 2019.

7 Impact Assessment of 9 December 2015, SWD(2015) 274 final, 15. This is confirmed for instance for Germany, where 76 % of internet users use exclusively or

al access to sports events and other audio-visual content, listening to digital music, playing online games and reading e-books.

At the same time, this trend goes hand in hand with growing consumer awareness that their data has monetary value and that they are indeed 'paying' with data when they are using online products 'for free'.[8]

The Digital Content Directive therefore includes not only digital content and digital services paid for with money[9] but also applies when such content or services are provided against granting access to personal data, such as the consumer's name, address, email address, age, gender etc. Such data is often requested if one 'registers' for supply of 'free' digital content or a digital service. The Digital Content Directive recognises thereby that data, if it is not already a 'currency' today, probably will become a *de facto* 'currency' of tomorrow.

The adoption of the Digital Content Directive by the legislator, however, is only a part of a much broader reaction to the transition towards the digital economy. Digital content and digital services are not the sole subject of consumer contracts (to which the scope of the Directive is limited[10]). Personal and non-personal data as subject of contracts are at least as important in business-to-business transactions.

The digitalisation of our economy and society, in particular, the rollout of the Internet of Things (IoT) and the datafication of business processes, has resulted in a data economy with a huge mass of processed and stored data: the so-called phenomenon of 'big data'. Big data is often characterised by the 3 Vs[11]: high *volume*, high *velocity* and high *variety*. The 'volume' aspect of 'big data' can be best illustrated by the following example:

---

above all online offers where no money is paid; cf Deutsches Institut für Vertrauen und Sicherheit im Internet (DIVSI) study 'Daten – Ware und Währung' (2014) 10, available under <www.divsi.de>,last accessed 28 July 2019.

8 This applies to three quarters of German Internet users. Cf *DIVSI* (n 7) 11.

9 Art 3(1) subpara 1, Art 2 No. 7 and Recital 23 DCD. It includes also digital representations of value such as electronic vouchers or e-coupons as well as virtual currencies, but only if the latter are recognised by national law.

10 For more detail on the scope of the Digital Content Directive see the commentary on Art 3 DCD by Dirk Staudenmayer in *Schulze/Staudenmayer* (n 1).

11 It is unclear who came up first with this very frequently mentioned characterisation. In the meantime, other Vs and characteristics without 'V' have also been added.

by 2013[12], Google was processing more than 24 petabytes[13] of data in a single day. This corresponds to thousands of times the quantity of all printed material in the US Library of Congress. Already by 2013, the global amount of stored information was estimated at 1,200 exabytes[14]. If this had been saved on CD-ROMs, the result would have created five towers of CD-ROMs reaching the moon. However, the year 2013 is, in terms of data processed and stored, the modern equivalent to the Stone Age. The rapid increase of processing and storing data is even more impressive. It is estimated[15] that in 2016 and 2017, 90 % of the data worldwide was created. In its recently published Data Strategy[16] the European Commission mentions that the volume of data produced globally is estimated to grow from 33 zettabyte[17] in 2018 to 175 zettabyte in 2025. The Commission therefore announced to look, inter alia, into possible legislative action on B2B data sharing.[18]

Moreover, it is not only the objects of contracting but also its instruments and methods that are changing considerably as a result of digitalisation. With its development, rollout and increasing use, artificial intelligence may not only decide, for instance, which contracts are concluded with which contractual partners when a contract is concluded 'machine-to-machine', but also determine the content of the contracts according to the market situation, without human intervention.[19] The implementation of

---

12 The following examples are taken from Viktor Mayer-Schönberger and Kenneth Cukier, *Big Data* (John Murray 2013) 8ff.

13 A petabyte is 10^{15} or 1 000 000 000 000 000 bytes, while 1 byte is a single character.

14 An exabyte is 10^{18} or 1 000 000 000 000 000 000 bytes.

15 www.forbes.com/sites/bernardmarr/2018/05/21/how-much-data-do-we-create-every-day-the-mind-blowing-stats-everyone-should-read/#2d35a00560ba, last accessed 28 July 2019.

16 Communication of 19 February 2020, COM 2020(66) final, 2.

17 A zettabyte is 10^{21} or a 1 with 21 zeros.

18 For an analysis of the legal problems concerning access and transfer of data, see Sebastian Lohsse, Reiner Schulze and Dirk Staudenmayer (eds), *Trading Data in the Digital Economy: Legal Concepts and Tools* (Nomos 2017). As regards the new dependencies in B2B contracts created in the Digital Economy see Dirk Staudenmayer 'Towards a European Private Law of the Digital Economy? – Trends' in André Janssen and Hans Schulte-Nölke (eds), *Researches in European Private Law and Beyond – Contributions in Honour of Reiner Schulze's Seventieth Birthday* (Nomos 2020) 74ff.

19 On questions surrounding liability for artificial intelligence see Sebastian Lohsse, Reiner Schulze and Dirk Staudenmayer (eds), *Liability for Artificial Intelligence and the Internet of Things* (Nomos 2019).

the contract and the reactions to behaviour contrary to the contract may also profoundly change through the use of 'smart contracts' in the blockchain[20]. Self-executing contracts[21], for example, can block the use of a purchased or rented item where payments under the corresponding credit of rental agreement have not been made. New applications can take care of automatic payment of compensation for airline passengers in the event of delays.

These and many other examples suggest that the far-reaching changes in contract practice resulting from digitalisation may require a corresponding adaptation of contract law. However, this in no way means that a completely new contract law or a separate *'Datenschuldrecht'* (i.e. a 'law of *data* obligations') would have to be created. Rather, the adaptability of contract law has been demonstrated in the past in the face of far-reaching technological and social changes such as the 'industrial revolution'. In view of the new challenges posed by digitalisation, it is therefore likely to be a matter above all of further developing the terminology, principles and norms of contract law in line with the changed conditions of contract practice. Similar to 'Web 2.0', which does not refer to a fundamentally new type of technology, but to a socio-technically changed use of the Internet,[22] the phrase 'Contract Law 2.0'[23] can serve to mark this new stage in the development of contract law.

II. The response of the European legislator

Digitalisation is one of the fundamental trends of this century. There is a clear political willingness in the EU to rise to this challenge, in order to

---

20 For an overview of the blockchain technology and its legal aspects cf Primavera De Filippi and Aaron Wright, *Blockchain and the Law: The Rule of Code* (Harvard University Press 2018). As to the large number of business models possible, cf Don Tapscott and Alex Tapscott, *Blockchain Revolution* (Penguin 2016) 178ff.

21 As an introduction cf Nikolas Guggenberger, 'The Potential of Blockchain Technology for the Conclusion of Contracts' in Reiner Schulze, Dirk Staudenmayer and Sebastian Lohsse (eds), *Contracts for the Supply of Digital Content: Regulatory Gaps and Challenges* (Nomos 2017) 83ff.

22 As defined (in German) by Richard Lackes in *Gabler Wirtschaftslexikon*, available online under <https://wirtschaftslexikon.gabler.de/definition/web-20-51842> last accessed 10 March 2020.

23 As used e.g. by Alexander Savelyev, 'Contract law 2.0: "Smart" contracts as the beginning of the end of classic contract law' (2017) 2 Information & Communications Technology Law 116.

harvest the economic growth potential of the 'digital economy' and the societal benefits of digitalisation. As the internal market is thought to be the most appropriate European tool for this, the European Commission's 'Digital Single Market Strategy'[24] (hereinafter 'DSM Strategy') of 2015 was a starting point for the EU to create a framework to promote and steer this transition process, among others in contract law. Making 'Europe fit for the Digital Age' has recently become an even stronger political priority.[25]

Individual legislative provisions primarily addressing other subject matters have already been adopted, reacting to the new situation in contract law brought about by digitalisation (e.g. in the context of information obligations and the right of withdrawal under the Consumer Rights Directive in its initial[26] and amended form[27]). Furthermore, the 2011 proposal for a Common European Sales Law[28] (CESL) already included provisions on the supply of digital content in a set of rules covering core contract law matters including the conclusion of the contract, restitution after termination of the contract, and prescription.[29] However, despite approval by the European Parliament, this attempt at optional harmonisation ultimately failed in Council, due to the resistance from a number of Member States.

In its 'DSM Strategy', the Commission drew the lessons from the experiences with the Consumer Rights Directive and the CESL[30] and in December 2015 put forward one of the first digital-specific legislative projects in

---

24 COM(2015) 192 final.

25 Cf Political guidelines of Commission President von der Leyen, available online under <https://ec.europa.eu/commission/sites/beta-political/files/political-guidelines-next-commission_en.pdf> 13ff., last accessed 23 January 2020.

26 Directive 2011/83/EU of the European Parliament and of the Council of 25 October 2011 on consumer rights, [2011] OJ L304/64.

27 Directive (EU) 2019/2161/EU of the European Parliament and the Council of 27 November 2019 amending Council Directive 93/13/EEC and Directives 98/6/EC, 2005/29/EC and 2011/83/EU of the European Parliament and of the Council as regards the better enforcement and modernisation of Union consumer protection rules, [2019] OJ L328/7.

28 COM(2011) 635 final. For an overview see Dirk Staudenmayer (ed.), *Proposal for a Regulation of the European Parliament and of the Council on a Common European Sales Law, Textbook* (C.H. Beck 2012) VIIff. For more details see Schulze (ed.), *Common European Sales Law – Commentary* (Nomos 2012).

29 For an explanation to what extent both the Digital Content Directive and the Sales of Goods Directive use CESL provisions as a model, see *Staudenmayer* in ERPL (n 1).

30 As to the approach of the Commission proposals see Dirk Staudenmayer, 'Digitale Verträge – Die Richtlinienvorschläge der Europäischen Kommission' (2016) 4 ZEuP 802.

this area, namely the 'Proposal for a Directive on certain aspects concerning contracts for the supply of digital content', which ultimately was adopted – after modifications during the legislative process – as the Digital Content Directive 2019/770. In December 2015 the Commission also presented a 'Proposal on certain aspects concerning contracts for the online and other distance sales of goods'[31], which formed the basis for the Sale of Goods Directive 2019/771[32], adopted in 2019, again simultaneously with the Digital Content Directive. The legislative impact of the 'DSM Strategy' is, however, not limited to these two new Directives, but rather also includes two Regulations which have already entered into force, namely the Geo-blocking Regulation[33] and the Portability Regulation[34], and the Platform Regulation[35], which will apply from 12 July 2020. Each of these Regulations deal with consequences of digital marketing and have also an effect on contract law.[36]

The Digital Content Directive is therefore part of a package of legislative measures responding to the effects of digitalisation on contract law. Although the Portability Regulation also regulates online content services provided without payment of money[37], it was only in relation to the Digital Content Directive that the discussion about data as counter-performance became, due to its significance in terms of economic impact and legal policy, very controversial. A minority in Council and in the European Parliament was reluctant to include data as counter-performance into the scope of the Directive. This minority in Council insisted on a consultation

---

31 COM(2015) 635 final.

32 Directive (EU) 2019/771 of the European Parliament and of the Council of 20 May 2019 on certain aspects concerning contracts for the sale of goods, [2019] OJ L136/28. See for an overview of the Directive *Staudenmayer* in NJW (n 1) and for a more detailed explanation of its main features see *Staudenmayer* in ERPL (n 1).

33 Regulation (EU) 2018/302 of the European Parliament and of the Council of 28 February 2018 on addressing unjustified geo-blocking and other forms of discrimination based on customers' nationality, place of residence or place of establishment within the internal market, [2018] OJ L60I/1.

34 Regulation (EU) 2017/1128 of the European Parliament and of the Council of 14 June 2017 on cross-border portability of online content services in the internal market, [2017] OJ L168/1.

35 Regulation (EU) 2019/1150 of the European Parliament and of the Council of 20 June 2019 on promoting fairness and transparency for business users of online intermediation services, [2019] OJ L186/57.

36 See for instance as to the link between the Geoblocking Regulation and the remedies under the Sale of Goods Directive *Staudenmayer* in ERPL (n 1).

37 In its Arts 6 and 9(2). On these provisions see the comments by Nils Rauer and Lea Kaase in *Schulze/Staudenmayer* (n 1).

from the European Data Protection Supervisor. The fundamental concern was, as expressed in the opinion of the European Data Protection Supervisor, that 'personal data cannot be compared to a price, or money. Personal information is related to a fundamental right and cannot be considered as a commodity'[38] or as it was put in simpler words in the discussion 'you cannot put a price tag on a fundamental right'. The counter-argument in the discussion was 'of course, one can', quoting for instance the example of the fundamental right to one's own image and its commercialisation. The minority, however, was of the opinion, as it was put by the European Data Protection Supervisor, that 'there might well be a market for personal data, just like there is, tragically, a market for live human organs, but that does not mean that we can or should give that market the blessing of legislation. One cannot monetise and subject a fundamental right to a simple commercial transaction, even if it is the individual concerned by the data who is a party to the transaction.'[39] This was countered by the argument that a huge number of these contracts happen every day and nobody thinks about treating them like trade in live organs. Not including data in the scope of the Digital Content Directive would mean that consumers who paid with their data would be without protection if the digital content or digital service in question is not in conformity with the contract.

An additional concern was that the Digital Content Directive could be interpreted as interfering with the legal grounds for data processing, which are exhaustively regulated in Art 6 of the General Data Protection Regulation (GDPR)[40]. Beside the fact that nothing in the wording of the Commission proposal or the Directive itself points to this, the argument was made that consent according to Art 6(1)(a) GDPR, and the acceptance to a contract for supply of digital content or digital services, are legally speaking two different acts even if in practice they may both take place in a single document. While the Directive would regulate the contract law aspects, the GDPR would regulate the data protection aspects.

Ultimately, the respective majority followed the Commission's proposal thus the scope of the Digital Content Directive extends to contracts where the consumer provides data to the supplier. However, this controversial

38 European Data Protection Supervisor, 'Opinion 4/2017 on the Proposal for a Directive on certain aspects concerning contracts for the supply of digital content' (March 2017), para 14, available online under <https://edps.europa.eu/sites/edp/files/publication/17-03-14_opinion_digital_content_en.pdf>, last accessed 28 December 2019.

39 *European Data Protection Supervisor* (n 38) para 17.

40 Regulation 2016/679 of 27 April 2016.

discussion had several impacts on the drafting of the relevant clauses and recitals. The Directive avoids mentioning, in contrast to the wording under the Commission proposal, that 'in exchange, … the consumer … provides counter-performance other than money in the form of personal data or any other data…'.[41] Nevertheless, the wording adopted in Art 3(1) 2nd subpara DCD, fails to disguise that in practice that is precisely the case. Recital 24 DCD recognises the main arguments of the discussion mentioned above. On the one hand, it mentions that data protection is a fundamental right and that therefore personal data cannot be considered a commodity. On the other hand, it recalls that business models where consumers provide data instead of paying a price exist and have a considerable market share. As the principal reason for the inclusion of data within the scope, it stresses that the Directive should ensure that consumers are entitled to contractual remedies. In addition, the Directive, in Art 3(8) and the Recitals 24, 37–39, emphasises that it is the GDPR[42] and not the Directive that regulates the conditions of lawful processing of data and the rights of the data subject. Compared to the Commission proposal which had already contained the same rule and explanation[43] with far fewer words, this seems to be an exaggerated emphasis, but it needs to be understood as part of the overall legislative compromise.

III. Provision of data and conclusion and performance of contract

Against the background of these developments, this volume concentrates on questions that arise in contract law with a view to the fact that 'data as counter-performance' has become a subject of European legislation. In view of the forthcoming implementation of the Digital Content Directive in the Member States, the impact of the inclusion of data in Art 3(1) 2nd subpara DCD for the regulation of conclusion, effect and performance of contracts in the law of the Member States must be considered.

Although the equal treatment of payment of a price and provision of personal data in Art 3(1) DCD serves only to determine the scope of the Directive, it is likely to be of further significance for the laws of the Member States. In particular, the relationship between the performance obligations of the parties to consumer contracts which provide for such provi-

41 Art 3(1) DCD.
42 Regulation 2016/679 of 27 April 2016.
43 Art 3(8) and Recital 22 DCD.

sion of data can in principle be characterised in the same way as in the case of contracts which, instead, stipulate a cash payment by the consumer. If the latter is a relationship of performance and counter-performance, the former contracts would in principle be subject to the provisions on reciprocal contracts, with corresponding further consequences under national law for the consumer's performance obligations and the trader's rights in the event of non-performance or non-conforming performance.

The first question to be answered, however, is whether and under what conditions a contract is concluded if a consumer does not pay a price in money, but provides or promises to provide personal data. There is no answer, or at least no immediate answer, to this question in the Directive. Rather, the conclusion and validity of contracts do not fall within the scope of the Directive, but are matters of national law.[44] Several problems may arise in this respect. It is not beyond doubt, for example, whether the traditional notion of contracts being concluded by means of offer and acceptance can be appropriately employed where 'free' online services in fact rely upon the collection of data generated by the user. From the point of view of the service provider, the use of his services may well be interpreted as an implicit offer – or an implicit acceptance of his own offer as it may be – even though the user himself may not be aware that in providing data he is indicating an intention to bind himself. However, if, and because, users may generally not think of such services as being provided on a contractual basis at all, it is doubtful whether there is an acceptance by the service provider (or an offer by the service provider in the first instance). While the binding nature of the service provider's behaviour is indeed intentional, the user may nevertheless fail to interpret the service provider's behaviour accordingly.

Comparably fundamental problems are raised with a view to questions of validity. The fact that data is provided for the use of a service that processes data does not depend on the age of the user. However, if provision of data is to be governed by contractual agreements, how can these agreements be valid where concluded by minors? Furthermore, and beyond the issue of minors and capacity in general, questions of validity may also arise from the extent of data collected from the user or their use by the service provider. Does the consent to process data, for example, automatically extend to the generation of a personality profile by the service provider? And should consent to generate such personality profile, even where explicitly

44 Art 3(10) DCD; Recital 12 DCD.

provided, be possible or should it rather be regarded as lying beyond party autonomy?[45]

Similarly, questions with a view to formation of contract and validity can arise from the interaction of contract law and data protection law.[46] Which contract law consequences, for example, arise from an agreement to transfer data where such transfer would constitute an infringement of the GDPR? To what degree are traditional concepts, such as the rule that contracts violating legal prohibitions cannot be upheld, to be adhered to in case of violations of data protection rules? Should data protection issues rather be dealt with separately from contract law?

Assuming that contract law in general, albeit with the necessity of some adaptations, is an appropriate means for dealing with the issues at stake, further questions arise in relation to performance and withdrawal from the contract. Generally speaking, the pivotal question relates to the interaction of the different legal rules regulating data and their relation to contract law. What role does, and what role can, contract law play within the spheres of these rules? Questions of this kind in particular, arise in relation to the validity of the contract where there is a conflict between contract law and data protection law. Assuming that, for example, an obligation to transfer unlawfully processed data does not render the contract void, would a transfer of such data constitute valid counter-performance?[47] There are strong arguments that the GDPR was elaborated without its relationship to contract law in mind. If provision of data by a consumer in violation of GDPR was not regarded as valid counter-performance, this would lead to the undesirable result that the consumer in turn would be barred from exerting his contractual rights against the trader supplying the service and, that the trader would thus be favoured as a result of his own non-compliance with the GDPR. Could such a result be correct?

Similarly, another problem arises from the fact that consent to processing of personal data may be freely withdrawn at any time pursuant to Art

45 For all these questions see Axel Metzger, 'A Market Model for Personal Data: State of Play under the New Directive on Digital Content and Digital Services', in this volume.

46 A detailed account is provided for by Philipp Hacker, 'Regulating the Economic Impact of Data as Counter-Performance: From the Illegality Doctrine to the Unfair Contract Terms Directive', in this volume.

47 On this question, see Philipp Hacker, 'Regulating the Economic Impact of Data as Counter-Performance: From the Illegality Doctrine to the Unfair Contract Terms Directive', in this volume.

7(3) GDPR.[48] Even if such right to withdrawal does not necessarily question the binding nature of a contract as such, it inevitably leads to complications. For example, may there be claims for damages if, due to the right to withdrawal, obligations of the data subject are not enforceable in kind? And should there be a possibility to limit the (so far mandatory) right to withdraw consent, for example by introducing an optional 'enriched consent' which would exclude such right? Furthermore, how far does the free right to withdrawal determine the consequences of withdrawal, most importantly its restitutionary aspects?[49]

Last, but by no means least, questions also arise with respect to performance and the corresponding property law issues. In particular, at present there appears to be no appropriate qualification of the right relating to data that would be transferred in satisfaction of the contract. Traditional concepts of ownership and the rules for its transfer are targeted at an unambiguous assignment of physical objects. Data, however, is fundamentally different from physical objects, not least because data is a non-rivalrous resource, which means that the use of data by one market player does not limit the availability of the same data for use by another market player. While not all assets need an owner, all assets need to be managed and the corresponding rights to control assets are very important in commercial practice. One might therefore consider potentially supplementing possible contract law amendments with a property law approach that differs somewhat from the traditional concepts centred around physical objects.[50] In any event, questions of access to data and control of data belong to the most fundamental questions of our data economy in the years to come.[51]

IV. Conclusion and outlook

With a view to the manifold implications of qualifying the provision of data as counter-performance, such qualification may well seem questionable. In particular, one has to bear in mind that such qualification is not necessarily called for under EU law: Art 3(1) DCD does not prescribe such quali-

48 See Andreas Sattler, 'Autonomy or Heteronomy – Proposal for a Two-Tier Interpretation of Art 6 GDPR', in this volume.

49 See Martin Schmidt-Kessel, 'Right to Withdraw Consent to Data Processing – The Effect on the Contract', in this volume.

50 See Sjef van Erp, 'Management as Ownership of Data', in this volume.

51 See already the contributions in *Lohsse/Schulze/Staudenmayer* (n 19) and most recently the European Data Strategy of the European Commission (n 16).

fication, but merely states that the application of the Directive requires a consumer to undertake to provide personal data to the trader. A more pragmatic approach to the subject-matter might thus be feasible even with a view to the starting point of all discussions gathered in this volume. Quite the same might be true for all follow-up questions. Independently whether the provision of data is to be qualified as counter-performance, it is important to think through the concepts necessary to make the provision of data, which is a reality in the digital economy, legally operational in practice. For this purpose it appears to be clear that in these early stages of the development one should not focus too intensively on doctrinal aspects and traditional categories and qualifications. Rather, it seems feasible to deal with specific problems on a step-by-step approach, trying to identify both the economic rationales underlying the parties' behaviour as well as appropriately balancing their interests, in order to equip the digital economy with the necessary legal tools for its transactions.

Legal Nature and Economic Value of Data in the Contractual Relationship

A Market Model for Personal Data: State of Play under the New Directive on Digital Content and Digital Services

Axel Metzger[*]

I. Data as counter-performance in consumer contracts

Article 3(1) subpara. 2 of the new Directive (EU) 2019/770 'on certain aspects concerning contracts for the supply of digital content and digital services' (DCSD) signifies a paradigm shift in the law of personal data.

According to the old paradigm, 'free services' were offered to consumers who gave their consent to the processing of their data. Both transactions were seen as being independent of each other. The leading search engines, social media platforms and many 'content' providers did not – and still do not – demand for a money consideration from the users. Those services therefore appeared as if they would be gratuitous for the consumer, whereas the service providers earned their revenues on the other side of the market by selling advertisements to business customers. The processing of the data, either based on consent or on the other legal grounds of Article 6(1) General Data Protection Regulation (GDPR), was interpreted as an ancillary unilateral legal act besides the service contract. This model was already queried in legal literature before the Proposal of the Directive was published in 2015.[1] However, those early voices did not lead to any changes in the business practices of the services which designed – and still do so – the two transactions as being split up. The 'terms of use' and the 'privacy statements' were often drafted as separate documents, the services being described as offered for free.

---

* Prof. Dr. Axel Metzger, LL.M. (Harvard), Humboldt University of Berlin.

1 See eg Peter Bräutigam, 'Das Nutzungsverhältnis bei sozialen Netzwerken – Zivilrechtlicher Austausch von IT-Leistung gegen personenbezogene Daten' (2012) 15(10) MMR 635; Benedikt Buchner, 'Die Einwilligung im Datenschutzrecht – vom Rechtfertigungsgrund zum Kommerzialisierungsinstrument' (2012) 34(1) DuD 39, 41; Patricia Maria Rogosch, *Die Einwilligung Im Datenschutzrecht* (Nomos 2013) 41 –46.

It therefore appeared as an innovative approach, when the Proposal of the new Directive, published in December 2015,[2] suggested in Article 3(1) subpara. 2 to apply the new rules on the supply and conformity of digital content and digital services both on paid services and on services where the consumer provides 'a counter-performance other than money in the form of personal data or any other data'. The idea to treat money consideration and personal data equally was already expressed in a recital of the later dropped Common European Sales Law of 2011 (CESL).[3] However, the broader public that is interested in data protection issues only took notice when the concept reappeared in the regulatory part of the DCSD. Since that time, a lively debate has arisen both in the industry[4] and among data protection officers[5] and academics.[6] It is no exaggeration to say that we are

2 European Commission, 'Proposal for a Directive of the European Parliament and of the Council on certain aspects concerning contracts for the supply of digital content', COM(2015) 634 final, 2015/0287 (COD), 09.12.2015.

3 European Commission, 'Proposal for a Regulation on a Common European Sales Law' COM(2011) 635 final, Recital 18.

4 See eg, Eurochambres, 'Reaction to the European Commission's proposal on the distance sales of digital content (COM(2015) 634 final)' (18 April 2016), <http://www.eurochambres.eu/custom/ECH_Reaction_to_DC_proposal-2016-00095-01.pdf> accessed 27 September 2019.

5 See European Data Protection Supervisor, Opinion 4/2017.

6 For academic publications during the legislative procdure see: Marietta Auer, 'Digitale Leistungen' (2019) 5(2) ZfPW 130; Hugh Beale, 'Conclusion and Performance of Contracts: An Overview' in Reiner Schulze, Dirk Staudenmayer and Sebastian Lohsse (eds), *Contracts for the Supply of Digital Content: Regulatory Challenges and Gaps* (Nomos 2017) 33; European Law Institute (ELI), 'Statement on the European Commission's proposed directive on the supply of digital content to consumers' (ELI, 2016) <https://www.europeanlawinstitute.eu/fileadmin/user_upload/p_eli/Publications/ELI_Statement_on_DCD.pdf> accessed 27 September 2019; Beate Gsell, 'Der europäische Richtlinienvorschlag zu bestimmten vertragsrechtlichen Aspekten der Bereitstellung digitaler Inhalte' (2018) 62(2) ZUM 75; Philipp Hacker, 'Daten als Gegenleistung: Rechtsgeschäfte im Spannungsfeld von DS-GVO und allgemeinem Vertragsrecht' (2019) 5(2) ZfPW 148; Niko Härting, 'Digital Goods und Datenschutz – Daten sparen oder monetarisieren? Die Reichweite des vom DinhRL-E erfassten Geschäftsmodells' (2016) (11) CR 735; Ruth Janal and Jonathan Jung, 'Spezialregelungen für Verträge über digitale Inhalte in Theorie und Praxis' (2017) 32(9) VuR 332; Axel Metzger, 'Data as Counter-Performance – What Rights and Duties do Parties Have?' (2017) 8(1) JIPITEC 2; Axel Metzger et al, 'Data-Related Aspects of the Digital Content Directive' (2018) 9(1) JIPITEC 90; Andreas Sattler, 'Personenbezogene Daten als Leistungsgegenstand – Die Einwilligung als Wegbereiter des Datenschuldrechts' (2017) 72(21) JZ 1036; Martin Schmidt-Kessel et al, 'Die Richtlinienvorschläge der Kommission zu

facing a shift of paradigm in the law of personal data with this new approach.

The language of Article 3(1) subpara. 2 DCSD-Proposal was at the same time explicit and narrow. It was explicit that personal data or other data could be interpreted as counter-performance of the consumer[7] which provoked the severe criticism of the European Data Protection Supervisor.[8] However, the scope of application was rather narrow with regard to personal data that could qualify as counter-performance. Article 3(1) subpara. 2 only mentioned 'actively provided' data. Recital 14 excluded data automatically generated and collected by cookies and also data 'necessary for the digital content to function in conformity with the contract, for example geographical location where necessary for a mobile application to function properly', and data collected 'for the sole purpose of meeting legal requirements'. These restrictions were criticised both by academics[9]

Digitalen Inhalten und Online-Handel – Teil 1' [2016] GPR Fokus 2; Martin Schmidt-Kessel et al, 'Die Richtlinienvorschläge der Kommission zu Digitalen Inhalten und Online-Handel – Teil 2' [2016] GPR Fokus 54; Martin Schmidt-Kessel and Anna Grimm, 'Unentgeltlich oder entgeltlich? – Der vertragliche Austausch von digitalen Inhalten gegen personenbezogene Daten' (2017) 3(1) ZfPW 84; Louisa Specht, 'Daten als Gegenleistung – Verlangt die Digitalisierung nach einem neuen Vertragstypus?' (2017) 72(15-16) JZ 763; Gerald Spindler, 'Verträge über digitale Inhalte – Anwendungsbereich und Ansätze – Vorschlag der EU-Kommission zu einer Richtlinie über Verträge zur Bereitstellung digitaler Inhalte' (2016) 19(3) MMR 147; Gerald Spindler, 'Verträge über digitale Inhalte – Haftung, Gewährleistung und Portabilität – Vorschlag der EU-Kommission zu einer Richtlinie über Verträge zur Bereitstellung digitaler Inhalte' (2016) 19(4) MMR 219; Friedrich Graf von Westphalen, 'Richtlinienentwurf der Kommission betreffend die Bereitstellung digitaler Inhalte und das Recht des Verbrauchers auf Schadensersatz' (2016) BB 1411; Friedrich Graf von Westphalen and Christiane Wendehorst, 'Hergabe personenbezogener Daten für digitale Inhalte – Gegenleistung, bereitzustellendes Material oder Zwangsbeitrag zum Datenbinnenmarkt?' (2016) BB 2179. For publications after the enactment of the Directive see n 13.

7 'This Directive shall apply to any contract where the supplier supplies digital content to the consumer or undertakes to do so and, in exchange, a price is to be paid or the consumer actively provides counter-performance other than money in the form of personal data or any other data.'.

8 European Data Protection Supervisor (n 5) 7: 'There might well be a market for personal data, just like there is, tragically, a market for live human organs, but that does not mean that we can or should give that market the blessing of legislation.'.

9 See European Law Institute (n 6) 15; Metzger et al, 'Data-Related Aspects of the Digital Content Directive' (n 6) paras 25–28; Gerald Spindler, 'Verträge über digitale Inhalte – Anwendungsbereich und Ansätze Vorschlag der EU-Kommission zu einer Richtlinie über Verträge zur Bereitstellung digitaler Inhalte' (2016) 19(3) MMR 147, 150.

and consumer organisations,[10] a criticism that was finally taken up by the European Parliament which requested a broader inclusion of personal data into the framework of the Directive.[11]

The final text of Article 3(1) subpara. 2 DCSD addresses both concerns. The revised text avoids the words 'personal data as counter-performance' to make clear that the European legislature does not encourage a further commercialisation of personal data.[12] All the safeguards of the GDPR remain untouched, see Article 3(8) and Recital 38 DCSD. Consent must be freely given and may be withdrawn at any time, see Article 7(1), (2) GDPR. The crucial question, if and under which conditions such a consent may be given within the framework of a contract, will be discussed in the next section of this paper. And yet, besides all these precautions, the substance of Article 3(1) subpara. 2 DCSD has not been changed during the legislative procedure. The Directive remains applicable both for consumers who pay money and for consumers who provide personal data.[13] Whether the personal data of the consumer should be interpreted as a synallagmatic

---

10 Verbraucherzentrale Bundesverband, 'Digitale Inhalte: Für eine zielgenaue und kohärente Gesetzgebung – Stellungnahme zum Vorschlag der EU-Kommission für eine Richtlinie über bestimmte vertragsrechtliche Aspekte der Bereitstellung digitaler Inhalte – COM(2015) 634 endg.' (1 September 2017) 16 <https://www.vzbv.de/sites/default/files/17-01-10_vzbv_stellungnahme_digitale_inhalte.pdf> accessed 27 September 2019.

11 European Parliament, 'Report on the proposal for a directive of the European Parliament and of the Council on certain aspects concerning contracts for the supply of digital content (COM(2015) 634 – C8-0394/2015 – 2015/0287(COD))' A8-0375/2017, Amendments 21 and 80.

12 See also Recital 24: While fully recognising that the protection of personal data is a fundamental right and that therefore personal data cannot be considered as a commodity, this Directive should ensure that consumers are, in the context of such business models, entitled to contractual remedies.

13 For publications after the enactment of the Directive see: Ivo Bach, 'Neue Richtlinien zum Verbrauchsgüterkauf und zu Verbraucherverträgen über digitale Inhalte' (2019) 72(24) NJW 1705, 1706; Cornelia Kern, 'Anwendungsbereich der Warenkauf- und der Digitale Inhalte-RL', in Wolfgang Stabentheiner, Christiane Wendehorst and Brigitta Zöchling-Jud (eds), *Das neue europäische Gewährleistungsrecht* (Manz 2019), 33; Axel Metzger, 'Verträge über digitale Inhalte und digitale Dienstleistungen: Neuer BGB-Vertragstypus oder punktuelle Reform?' (2019) 74(12) JZ 577; Lena Mischau, 'Daten als „Gegenleistung" im neuen Verbrauchervertragsrecht' (2020) 28(2) ZEuP 335; Thomas Riehm, 'Freie Widerruflichkeit der Einwilligung und Struktur der Obligation – Daten als Gegenleistung?' in Tereza Pertot (ed), *Rechte an Daten* (unpublished manuscript 2019) 4; Gerald Spindler and Karin Sein, 'Die endgültige Richtlinie über Verträge über digitale Inhalte und Dienstleistungen Anwendungsbereich und grundsätzliche Ansätze' (2019)

counter-performance or not, is mainly of importance for the relationship between the duties of the two contracting parties. But since the DCSD does not harmonise the duties of the consumer,[14] it can also avoid to answer this question.[15]

The DSCD in its final version is applicable irrespective of whether the consumer provides the data actively; the wording 'actively provided' in Article 3(1) subpara. 2 has been deleted. However, the Directive does not provide a clear-cut solution for data collected from a passive consumer. According to Recital 24, it suffices that personal data is 'created' with the use of the digital content or service. Even a mere collection of 'metadata, such as information concerning the consumer's device or browsing history' may suffice according to Recital 25.[16] This should also cover situations in which the service provider uses cookies to collect personal data of the consumer.[17] But this applies only if the relationship between trader and consumer 'is considered to be a contract under national law'. It is therefore up to the national level to decide about the scope of application of the new rules.[18]

22(7) MMR 415, 418; Karin Sein and Gerald Spindler, 'The new Directive on Contracts for the Supply of Digital Content and Digital Services – Scope of Application and Trader's Obligation to Supply – Part 1' (2019) 15(3) ERCL 257; Dirk Staudenmayer, 'Auf dem Weg zum digitalen Privatrecht – Verträge über digitale Inhalte' (2019) 72(35) NJW 2497. For earlier publications see n 6 and n 1.

14 With the exception of Article 17.

15 See with more details Axel Metzger, 'Dienst gegen Daten: Ein synallagmatischer Vertrag' (2016) 216(6) AcP 817, 833–835.

16 See also Recital 38 at the end.

17 But see Gerald Spindler and Karin Sein, 'Die endgültige Richtlinie über Verträge über digitale Inhalte und Dienstleistungen Anwendungsbereich und grundsätzliche Ansätze' (n 13) 418.

18 See also Gerald Spindler and Karin Sein, 'The new Directive on Contracts for the Supply of Digital Content and Digital Services – Scope of Application and Trader's Obligation to Supply – Part 1' (n 13) 263ff.; See also Metzger, 'Verträge über digitale Inhalte und digitale Dienstleistungen: Neuer BGB-Vertragstypus oder punktuelle Reform?' (n 13) 579; Mischau, 'Daten als ´Gegenleistung` im neuen Verbrauchervertragsrecht' (n 13) at III.1 and V.3; Zohar Efroni, ''Gaps and Opportunities: The Rudimentary Protection for 'Data-Paying Consumers' under the New EU Consumer Protection Law' forthcoming in (2020) 57(3) CMLR.

II. Personal data and the law of contract

Consumers must conclude a contract in order to benefit from the consumer protection measures taken by the DCSD. According to Article 3(1) subpara. 1, the Directive 'shall apply to any contract (...)'. Subpara. 2 extends the scope of application to situations where the consumer provides personal data. But this also requires a contract to be concluded, as clarified by Recital 24.[19] However, the key question whether a situation in which the consumer uses a service, eg a search engine, and the service providers collects the consumer's personal data is to be qualified as a contract or not has not been regulated in the Directive. Article 3(10) determines that the Directive shall not affect the freedom of Member States to regulate aspects of general contract law, such as rules on the formation, validity, nullity or effects of contracts.

As a consequence, the law of the Member States will have to decide on the requirements of offer, acceptance and possibly further preconditions of a valid contract, eg the English consideration or the French 'cause' doctrines. The following outline is mainly based on German contract law.

1. Offer to conclude a contract

The initiative to conclude a contract (or not) will typically come from the content or service provider. In the easy case of a two-sided relationship between a content or service provider offering its service and a consumer interested in using this service,[20] it will be a matter of interpretation of the communication and conduct of the service provider and, more particularly, its general terms and conditions whether the requirements of an offer to conclude a contract are met.

According to German contract law, an objective standard of interpretation has to be to applied, § 157 BGB. The question therefore is how a rea-

19 'This Directive should, therefore, apply to contracts where the trader supplies, or undertakes to supply, digital content or a digital service to the consumer, and the consumer provides, or undertakes to provide, personal data. '.

20 The regulatory part of the DCSD ignores the fact that the supply of content or software is often not carried out by the owner of the copyright but by a trader, eg an app store, which may lead to a three-partite relationship with a supply contract and an End User License Agreement, see Recital 53. See also European Law Institute (n 6) 24–26; Metzger and others, 'Data-Related Aspects of the Digital Content Directive' (n 6) 101.

sonable consumer must understand the communication and conduct of the service provider. The terms of popular services directed to German consumers, like Facebook,[21] WhatsApp,[22] Spotify[23] or Google,[24] give a number of indications for a contract offer. They are drafted in the form of complex and lengthy standard contracts. The word 'contract' is used more or less regularly. Many of the issues dealt with in the terms and conditions are typical for contractual relationships. For a reasonable consumer, this kind of communication must appear as an offer to conclude a contract on the use of the services.[25]

This interpretation is unaffected by the fact that consumers may not pay money in exchange for the use of the service. On the contrary, users understand 'free services' as an exchange 'personal data for service'. A survey conducted by DIVSI in Germany in 2014 showed that 67% of the respondents knew personal data as one means of payment in contracts.[26] It is therefore quite conceivable that a reasonable consumer will understand a 'free service' with long terms and conditions as an offer to conclude a contract,

---

21 See N° 4 Section 2 and 6 of the German Facebook 'Nutzungsbedingungen', Facebook inc., 'Nutzungsbedingungen' (31 July 2019) <www.facebook.com/legal/terms> accessed 25 September 2019.

22 See Whatsapp inc, 'WhatsApp Business Nutzungsbedingungen' (15 May 2018) <https://www.whatsapp.com/legal/business-terms/?lang=de> accessed 25 September 2019; 'WhatsApp Inc. ist die vertragsschließende Rechtspersönlichkeit, die dir unsere Business Services bereitstellt.' (WhatsApp is the contracting legal entity, that offers you our Business Services.).

23 See Spotify AB, 'Spotify Nutzungsbedingungen' (15 August 2018) <https://www.spotify.com/de/legal/end-user-agreement> accessed 25 September 2019; see N° 1: 'Ihr Vertrag mit uns…' (Your contract with us…).

24 See Google Ireland ltd, 'Google- Nutzungsbedingungen' (22 January 2019) <https://policies.google.com/terms?hl=de&gl=de> accessed 25 September 2019; for the German terms at https://policies.google.com/terms?hl=de&gl=de, 'Willkommen bei Google': 'Die Nutzung der Dienste setzt voraus, dass Sie diesen Nutzungsbedingungen zustimmen. Bitte lesen Sie diese sorgfältig durch.' (The use of the services requires that you accept these terms and conditions. Please read them carefully.).

25 See Gerald Spindler, 'Vorb §§ 145ff BGB' in Gerald Spindler and Fabian Schuster (eds), *Recht der elektronischen Medien* (C.H. Beck 2019) para 4; more reluctant Jan Busche, '§ 145 BGB' in *Münchener Kommentar zum Bürgerlichen Gesetzbuc*h (8th edn, C.H. Beck 2018) para 13.

26 See Deutsches Institut für Vertrauen und Sicherheit im Internet (DIVSI), 'Daten – Ware Und Währung' (2014) 16 <http://www.divsi.de/wp-content/uploads/2014/11/DIVSI-Studie-Daten-Ware-Waehrung.pdf> accessed 25 September 2019.

even if he/she does not pay money as consideration.[27] A second possible interpretation would be to qualify the consumer's willingness to be exposed to advertisements as the consumer's consideration under the contract.[28] But this would not alter the fact that the reasonable consumer understands the provision of the 'free' service as an offer to conclude a contract.

2. *Acceptance by the consumer*

Acceptance by the consumer may be explicit by clicking of boxes or similar features on the service's website. It may also be implicit if the use of the service or reception of the content requires a request by the user, eg the sending of a search query or the demand for the display of a content or the streaming of an audio or a video file. But even if a mere passive use of a service or access to a content does not require an active communication by the user with the service provider, it may still be interpreted as an implicit acceptance of the contract offer. According to § 151 sentence 1 BGB, a contract comes into existence through the acceptance of the offer without the offeror needing to be notified of the acceptance, if such a declaration is not to be expected according to customary practice or if the offeror has waived it. One may well argue that the customary practice for digital services without any acceptance mechanism is to expect no kind of an explicit notification of the user of those services. Still, it should be noted that § 151 sentence 1 BGB only dispenses of the notification of the acceptance, not of the acceptance as such. The latter must be demonstrated by a clearly visible conduct or declaration of the offeree.[29]

3. *Personal data as consideration?*

European contract law instruments like the CESL, the 'Draft Common Frame of Reference' or the 'Principles of European Contract Law' deliberately refrain from requiring substantive indicia of seriousness[30] like the English 'consideration' or the French, Italian or Spanish 'cause' or 'causa'

---

27 See also Hacker (n 6) 185ff. (analysis in connection with German law of standard contracts (AGB)).

28 Riehm (n 13) 20.

29 Jan Busche, '§ 151 BGB' in *Münchener Kommentar zum Bürgerlichen Gesetzbuch* (8th edn, C.H. Beck 2018) para 9.

30 Article 30 CESL; Article II.–4:101 DCFR; Article 2:201 PECL.

doctrine.[31] But national contract laws still maintain their traditions, however often with pragmatic solutions. It is eg possible under the UK Consumer Rights Act 2015 to seek damages if a digital content supplied to a consumer causes damage to a device or to other digital content, irrespective of whether the consumer has paid money as consideration or not.[32] Still, the application of the other provisions of the Act, eg on the quality of the content, are only applicable if the consumer has paid a price.[33] It is therefore an open question for further research if and under which conditions other EU member states qualify situations as contracts in which the consumer uses a digital content or service and the provider collects the consumer's data.

4. *Contract with or without consent to data processing*

The concept of Article 3(1) subpara. 2 DCSD is based on the idea that the consumer agrees to the processing of his or her personal data. In the typical scenario, the processing of data will thus be justified by the consent of the consumer in accordance with Article 6(1)(a) GDPR. In this simple case, the scope of application of the DCSD and the requirements of the GDPR seem synchronised. But at closer scrutiny, the relationship between the DCSD and the justification of data processing under the GDPR is more complex.

Most importantly, the application of the DCSD does not require the consent of the consumer (or data-subject) to be valid under Article 6(1)(a) GDPR. Otherwise, the controller would profit from its non-compliance with the conditions of the GDPR.[34] He could disregard the requirements of the GDPR and deprive the consumer of the protection given by the DCSD. Such an interpretation of the DCSD would make no sense. Therefore, even an invalid consent may be sufficient to apply the DCSD if the other requirements are met. In this regard, it is of some importance to distinguish between the valid or invalid contractual obligations between trader and consumer on the one hand, and the valid or invalid consent by the

---

31 See on the whole Hein Kötz, 'Indicia of Seriousness'. in Jürgen Basedow, Klaus J. Hopt, Reinhard Zimmermann, and Andreas Stier (eds), *Max Planck Encyclopedia of European Private Law* (OUP 2012).

32 Section 46.

33 Section 33ff.

34 Hacker (n 6) 161; Mischau, 'Daten als „Gegenleistung" im neuen Verbrauchervertragsrecht' (n 15) at III.1.

data-subject on the other hand.[35] A possible starting point to conceptualise this question could be the so called 'abstraction principle', one of the basic principle of German civil law.[36] According to the abstraction principle, the agreement on the rights and obligations of the parties and the transactions in rem have to be separated. One may be valid, while the other may be void. Although it is obvious, that a consent in the processing of personal data is not a transaction in rem stricto sensu, it makes still sense to distinguish between the contractual promise to provide data and give consent and the performance of this promise.

The distinction between the (in-)valid consent and the contract on the supply of digital contents or digital services under the DCSD is also of relevance for the prohibition of coupling of contract and consent in Article 7(4) GDPR. According to this provision, 'when assessing whether consent is freely given, utmost account shall be taken of whether, inter alia, the performance of a contract, including the provision of a service, is conditional on consent to the processing of personal data that is not necessary for the performance of that contract'. At first glance, this sounds like an explicit prohibition of any bundling of consent and contract performance since the GDPR has primacy over the DCSD, see Article 3(8) DCSD. But the wording 'utmost account shall be taken' gives some flexibility, as emphasised by commentators.[37] Indeed, the mere framework of a contract should not be considered as an indication of coercion and defective decision-making. Other factors may be whether the consumer can use competing services or if the service is essential or dispensable for the consumer.[38] But even if consent would be invalid in a given case under Article 7(4) GDPR, this would not automatically result in the non-applicability of the DCSD as shown above.

---

35 See also Riehm (n 13) 10ff.; Specht (n 6) 765.

36 See already Friedrich Carl von Savigny, *System des heutigen Römischen Rechts Vol. 3* (Veit 1840) 312ff.; for the 'abstraction principle' under the German Civil Code see Jürgen Oechsler, '§ 929 BGB' in *Münchener Kommentar zum Bürgerlichen Gesetzbuch* (7th edn, C.H. Beck 2018) para 8 with further references.

37 Peter Schantz, 'Die Datenschutz-Grundverordnung – Beginn einer neuen Zeitrechnung im Datenschutzrecht' (2016) 69(26) NJW 1841, 1845; Sebastian Schulz in Peter Gola (ed), *Datenschutz-Grundverordnung* (2nd edn, Beck 2018) Art 7 para 26; Dirk Heckmann and Anne Paschke in Eugen Ehmann and Martin Selmayr (eds), *Datenschutz-Grundverordnung* (2nd edn, C.H. Beck 2018) Art 7 para 98; Andreas Sattler, 'Personenbezug als Hindernis des Datenhandels', ' in Tereza Pertot (ed), *Rechte an Daten* (unpublished manuscript 2019) 14ff.

38 Schulz in Gola (ed) (n 37) Art 7 para 27; Heckmann and Paschke in Ehmann and Selmayr (eds) (n 37) Art 7 para 98; Sattler (n 37) 15.

The same principles apply to a later withdrawal of the data subject's consent. According to Article 7(3) GDPR, the data subject may withdraw its consent at any time; contractual agreements may not restrict this right.[39] The withdrawal of consent does not affect the lawfulness of processing based on consent before its withdrawal. What remains unclear under Article 7(3) GDPR and the DCSD are the further consequences for the contract. Here again, the 'abstraction principle' provides a possible solution. The withdrawal of consent does not affect the validity of the contract. However, the applicable contract law provisions may allow the trader to terminate the contract.[40]

Thus, the destiny of contract and the consent may differ. But this does not mean that every use of data, legal or illegal, suffices for the application of the DCSD. According to Article 3(1) subpara. 2 DCSD the Directive is not applicable where personal data is 'exclusively processed by the trader for the purpose of supplying the digital content or digital service' or 'for allowing the trader to comply with legal requirements to which the trader is subject, and the trader does not process those data for any other purpose'. This means that the application of the DSCD cannot be based on scenarios in which the processing of the data is based on Article 6(1)(b) and (c) GDPR, eg, in case where a navigation service processes location data with the sole purpose to recommend the route to the consumer. However, the processing of data must remain limited to the mentioned purposes; otherwise the DCSD is applicable.[41]

Regrettably, the DCSD does not provide a clear-cut rule for cases in which the processing of data is based on Article 6(1)(f) GDPR, ie is 'necessary for the purposes of the legitimate interests pursued by the controller or by a third party', or on other statutory grounds, Article 6(1)(e), (2) GDPR. The issue is of growing interest, especially if one shares the criticism of consent as the commonly used basis of data processing.[42] Lengthy 'data policies' and 'privacy statements' do indeed, as put forward by the

39 See Recital 42 GDPR: 'Consent should not be regarded as freely given if the data subject has no genuine or free choice or is unable to refuse or withdraw consent without detriment.'.

40 See Hacker (n 6) 178; Metzger, 'Dienst gegen Daten: Ein synallagmatischer Vertrag' (n 13) 863ff; Riehm (n 13) 22; Specht (n 6) 768.

41 Gerald Spindler and Karin Sein, 'Die endgültige Richtlinie über Verträge über digitale Inhalte und Dienstleistungen Anwendungsbereich und grundsätzliche Ansätze' (n 13) 418.

42 See on the following Zohar Efroni et al, 'Privacy Icons: A Risk-Based Approach to Visualisation of Data Processing' (2019) 5(3) EDPL 352, 357 with further references.

critics, prevent the consumer from taking an informed decision instead of helping him. However, the politically charged follow-up question then is whether the conditions of an informed consent can be improved (liberal approach) or whether the legislature or other collective bodies or courts should define the rules (state-centered approach).[43] Two main arguments advocate for an (improved) consent-based approach, at least for the time being: First, a society should not give up too hastily the basic idea of self-determination in data protection law. The 'data subject' should have the final word on the processing of its data as long as the conditions of consent can be improved, eg by innovative information models like privacy icons.[44] Second, a consent-based approach is key to learn more about the economic value of data and the opportunities for data-subjects to participate in that value. We still do not know enough about data markets to implement an efficient regulation. But even if the law sticks to consent as the basic principle, there may still be cases where the processing of data is based on 'legitimate interests' or other statutory grounds. In these cases the application of the DCSD and its enhanced level of consumer protection are called into question. Admittedly, the DSCD does not exclude its – certainly consumer-friendly – application in these scenarios as long as the provision or processing of data can be construed in the sense of Article 3(1) subpara. 2 DCSD.[45] But the text is not clear on this matter.

5. *Obligation to provide data as counter-performance*

The main purposes of the DCSD are to secure a high level of consumer protection on the different markets for digital contents and services and to increase legal certainty and reduce transaction costs, in particular for small and medium-sized enterprises.[46] The Directive aims to achieve these goals by a one-sided harmonisation of the contractual rights and remedies of the consumer. It does not address the contractual rights of the trader at the other side of the contract (or the consumer duties as their mirror image), with the exception of some consumer duties in case of the termination of

43 In this direction Heike Schweitzer, 'Neue Machtlagen in der digitalen Welt? Das Beispiel unentgeltlicher Leistungen' in Torsten Körber and Jürgen Kühling (eds), *Regulierung – Wettbewerb – Innovation* (Nomos 2017) 269, 281ff.

44 Efroni et al (n 42).

45 Mischau, 'Daten als "Gegenleistung" im neuen Verbrauchervertragsrecht' (n 13) at III.1.c); Schweitzer (n 43) 282.

46 See Recitals 3, 5.

the contract in Article 17 DCSD. Besides Article 17, both the contractual rights of the trader and the obligations of the consumers are left to the national contract law of the member states as aspects of 'general contract law', see Article 3(10). The same holds true for the relationship between the trader's obligations and the consumer's obligations, especially to provide personal data.

If and to what extent a consumer has an obligation to provide personal data under a contract and to give its consent in the processing of that data, or whether the processing of data is a mere side-effect of the contract, is first and foremost a question of contract interpretation.[47] The data policies of popular Internet services indeed assume such a contractual obligation of the user. The career network 'Xing' states in its 'terms and conditions': 'The user is obliged (a) to provide only true and non-misleading statements along with its real name, and to refrain from using pseudonyms or pen names... '.[48] The 'Facebook' 'terms of service' provide under the headline 'Your commitments to Facebook and our community': 'You must: Use the same name that you use in everyday life. Provide accurate information about yourself. Create only one account (your own) and use your timeline for personal purposes.'[49] Comparable language may be found in Amazon's 'Conditions of Use and Sale': 'You are responsible for ensuring that the details you provide us with are correct and complete, and for informing us of any changes to the information you have provided.'[50] The cited terms and conditions clearly articulate obligations of users ('is obliged', 'must', 'are responsible') to provide accurate personal data on the basis of the used forms and dialogue boxes and, in the case of Amazon, even to proactively inform the service about any changes to the information. These obligations presuppose that the user is willing to give his or her consent to the processing of the data if it is not justified on the basis of other legal grounds. From the perspective of a reasonable consumer, these terms read

---

47 A separate question then is, whether such an obligation may be validly agreed upon regarding national contract law and the provisions of the GDPR, a question which will be dealt with in section 6.

48 See New Work SE (Xing), 'AGB' at 4.1 <https://www.xing.com/terms> accessed 2 October 2019.

49 See Facebook Inc. (Facebook), 'Nutzungsbedingungen' at 3 <https://www.facebook.com/legal/terms> accessed 2 October 2019. The validity of some the conditions has been challenged by consumer organisations, see Case 16 O 341/15 District Court Berlin, Germany (2018) = MMR 2018, 328 (appeal pending).

50 See Amazon EU Sarl (Amazon), 'Amazon.de Allgemeine Geschäftsbedingungen' at 7 <https://www.amazon.de/gp/help/customer/display.html?nodeId=201909000> accessed 2 October 2019.

as legally binding obligations under a contract, irrespective of the fact that service providers may have difficulties to enforce those duties, especially since the data subject's consent must by freely given[51] and can be withdrawn at any moment, Article 7(3) GDPR.[52]

But is this obligation to provide (correct) personal data to be qualified as the consumer's counter-performance in the sense of its synallagmatic obligation under the contract? With other words, does the provider supply digital contents or services *in order to* collect and process the consumer's personal data? Different from the initial Proposal of 2015, the DCSD does not take a position in this question. The word 'counter-performance' has deliberately been deleted.[53] If the promises and the resulting obligations under the contract may be construed as a counter-performance or not is therefore a question of national contract law. The member states' contract law is also decisive for the consequences of a possible non-performance of the consumer, eg whether the trader may refuse under § 320 BGB to supply the content or service until the consumer has provided correct data, whether he may rescind the contract under § 323 BGB if the consumer does not perform, etc. The discussion on the different types of contracts to be found in the different business models has just begun.[54]

The main parameters for an accurate qualification of the consumers obligation should be: First, is the provision or collection of data and the related consent the main benefit arising out of the contract for the trader or is it just of secondary or subordinate importance?[55] The processing of data may be of secondary interest in the framework of paid services or if the trader uses the data for a one-time selection of personalised advertisements. In the latter case, the exposure to the advertisement may be qualified as the main benefit.[56] But one should not set aside too easily the economic value of the personal data of users. At the surface, the personal data may appear as nothing more than the necessary means to offer better suited advertisements. However, it is common knowledge that providers of

51 Article 4(11), 7(4) and Recitals 32, 42, 43 GDPR.

52 Compare Riehm (n 13) 11ff.

53 See supra at I.

54 On the final text of the Directive see Metzger, 'Verträge über digitale Inhalte und digitale Dienstleistungen: Neuer BGB-Vertragstypus oder punktuelle Reform?' (n 13) 579; Staudenmayer (n 13) 2498.; on the last versions of the Draft Proposal during the legislative process Hacker (n 6) 158ff; Specht (n 6) 765ff; sceptical Riehm (n 13) 18ff.

55 See Stadler, '§ 320 BGB' in Jauernig (ed), *Bürgerliches* Gesetzbuch (BGB) – Kommentar (17th edn, C.H. Beck 2018) para 6ff.

56 Riehm (n 13).

digital services and their partner companies follow their users over different platforms with tailor-made advertisements, additional services and additional opportunities to collect and accumulate their personal data. Moreover, Internet services are very innovative in developing new business models based on the personal data of their users and creating added value besides the directly visible use of data for personalised advertisements. It would not capture the full value of the personal data provided by the consumer to qualify it as subordinate to the other interests of the service provider. Therefore, the direct payment by consumers or the exposure to advertisements may be the primary interest of the providers of some of the simpler services, but the use of personal data in a broader sense will still be the dominant motive for the more complex business models of the leading platforms. Second, even if the collection and processing of data is the main benefit for the service provider, this does not automatically lead to a synallagmatic linkage of the mutual obligations under German contract law. German law recognises different types of linkages between the obligations of the parties to a contract, the synallagmatic linkage in the sense of § 320 BGB being only one among others.[57] In this regard, it is also of importance to ask whether the provisions on synallagmatic contracts match with the interests of the parties of contracts on personal data. It may, eg, be an appropriate answer to a consumer who does not provide the correct data under a contract to give the service provider a right to refuse its own part of the performance in accordance with § 320 BGB.

6. *Validity of contract*

The DCSD does not harmonise the formation and validity of contracts, see Article 3(10). The application of the consumer's rights under the Directive is nevertheless based the conclusion of a contract as clarified in Recitals 24, 25. As a matter of principle, this will require a valid contract, irrespective of the question whether some of the provisions of the Directive may be applied mutatis mutandis to invalid contracts to provide consumers with an equivalent level of protection in case if invalidity. Contracts with the provision or collection of personal data on the consumer's side of the contract face a number of challenges regarding their validity which can only be briefly touched here. Again, the following sketch is mainly referring to

57 Hacker (n 6) 167ff; Metzger, 'Dienst gegen Daten: Ein synallagmatischer Vertrag' (n 15) 833; Riehm (n 13) 17.

German law as one instance of a member state law. As explained earlier, according to the German 'abstraction principle', the possible invalidity of the data-subject's consent under Article 6, 7 GDPR does not automatically entail the invalidity of the contract between trader and consumer. Still there are data-specific challenges for the validity of those contracts.

A first difficult and highly practical challenge for contracts covered by the DCSD is posed by the involvement of minors. Many digital contents and digital services are used by minors without parental approval. According to German contract law, contracts with minors between seven and eighteen require the authorisation of their parents (or other legal representatives) if the minor does not receive only a legal benefit from the contract, § 107 BGB. It would be simplistic to qualify 'free' digital services which do not require any payment as legally beneficial in the sense of § 107 if the service collects the minor's personal data. On the contrary, such a processing of data in the framework of a contractual relationship qualifies as legal detriment.[58] The validity of the contract is therefore subject to the authorisation of the parents. Still it should be noted that Article 8 GDPR follows different principles with regard to the consent of minors. The GDPR allows minors at the age of sixteen years to give consent without parental authorisation, Article 8(1) subpara. 1. The threshold may even be lowered by member states to the age of thirteen, Article 8(1) subpara. 2. This may lead to situations where the contract is void according to national contract law, but the given consent is valid (but may be withdrawn at any time with effect ex nunc according to Article 7(3) GDPR).[59]

Further limits of party autonomy may arise with regard to standard terms in the sense of Directive 93/13/EEC on Unfair Terms in Consumer Contracts and the national implementations, eg §§ 305–310 BGB.[60] The processing of data is often based on standardized 'data policies'. Recital 42 GDPR clarifies that the requirements of the Unfair Terms Directive apply to those policies. This means in particular, that an unclear or an unspecified purpose of data processing may be invalid since it does not meet the requirements of transparency, see Article 5 Unfair Terms Directive, § 307(1) sentence 2 BGB. Moreover, data policies may comprise 'unfair terms', see Article 3(1) Unfair Terms Directive, or 'unreasonable disadvan-

---

58 Bräutigam (n 1) 637; Florian Faust, *Verhandlungen des 71 Deutschen Juristentages Essen 2016 Bd I: Gutachten Teil A: Digitale Wirtschaft – Analoges Recht: Braucht das BGB ein Update?* (C.H. Beck 2016) 8ff.

59 On the consequences under German law see Metzger (n 13) 839ff; Specht (n 6) 768.

60 See with more details Hacker (n 6) 183ff.

tages', see § 307(1), (2) BGB. On the basis of these provisions German courts have, eg, invalidated several clauses in Facebook's data policy.[61]

As a last resort, limits of party autonomy may arise out of general clauses like eg public policy according to § 138 BGB. Public policy may be applied if a contract on digital content or services leads to an extensive commercialisation of privacy, eg by generating and exploiting personality profiles.[62] But public policy, though regularly cited in legal literature, is only rarely applied in court cases with regard to the commercialisation of personality rights, especially since most cases can either be solved by the specific legal instruments of the GDPR with regard to consent or by the control of data policies as standard terms.

III. A market model for personal data

1. Why taking the risks of a market model?

The DCSD does not open pandora's box of an unleashed marketplace of personal data. The strict limitations of any commercial use of personal data laid down in the GDPR remain untouched. Still, the DCSD tries to overcome an overly paternalistic protection of the consumers from themselves – in their own best interest.[63] From a purely factual point of view, consumers are engaged on a daily basis in the commercialisation of their personal data. The DCSD reflects the legislature's intention to accompany the consumer on the digital markets and provide him with a bundle of consumer protection instruments. A radical and dogmatic insistence on data protection principles as such does not help the consumer with regard to typical consumer contracts issues like eg conformity of the digital content or service, rights and duties in case of termination of the contract etc. In this limited perspective, the DCSD is based on a market model for personal data. This raises the question why a society should take the risk of such a market model – the alternative being to fully regulate the conditions and limits of any processing of data by the legislature. The answer lies in the very basic assumption of all models of market economies. A market model

61 Case 5 U 42/12 Court of Appeal Berlin, Germany (2014) = CR 2014, 319 = BeckRS 2014, 03648.

62 eg Hans Peter Bull, 'Zweifelsfragen um die informationelle Selbstbestimmung – Datenschutz als Datenaskese?' (2006) 59(23) NJW 1617, 1621.

63 See also Metzger et al, 'Data-Related Aspects of the Digital Content Directive' (n 6), para 14.

is better suited to maximise welfare than a state-centered regulation.[64] And indeed, one can hardly ignore that consumers benefit in many ways from the valuable services they receive over the Internet and other digital service providers, starting from contents and technology of every kind that makes their life easier, to search engines and social media platforms, which help them to keep up their social contacts, etc. Consumers would have to pay a considerable share of their income if all of these services were only available on a paid basis. But welfare maximisation becomes even more obvious when the market capitalisation of the huge companies with data-driven business models is taken into account. Each of the famous GAFA companies – Google, Apple, Facebook, Amazon, and one should add also Microsoft – has a market value which exceeds the whole German car industry.[65] It is therefore beyond any doubt, that personal data and business models which are based on personal data produce tremendous welfare – the open follow-up question being whether that welfare is distributed fairly.[66]

2. *Indications for market failure*

If a market model for personal data shall function well, the basic preconditions for such a market model must be given. Lawmakers should be attentive with regard to the indications for market failure that can be observed on the different markets for personal data of consumers. Each of the aspects dealt with in the following outline would deserve an in-depth analysis in additional full papers.

A first cause of market failure that can be observed on the markets for personal data is lack of competition. On a well-functioning market, consumers should have the choice between different services and offerings. They should have the possibility to choose between paid services and ser-

---

64 This is very basic assumption of every welfare economics model since *Adam Smith's* famous 'invisible hand' theorem, see Adam Smith, *An inquiry into the nature and causes of the wealth of nations* (The Modern Library 1937) 423.

65 Compare the current 2019 Forbes list of the World's largest companies ranked by market value, see: Forbes.com, 'GLOBAL 2000 The World's Largest Public Companies' (15 May 2018) <https://www.forbes.com/global2000/#7446c35a335d> accessed 25 September 2019.

66 On the relationship of social welfare and distribution of income see Steven Shavell, *Foundations of Economic Analysis of Law* (Harvard University Press 2004) 647–660.

vices which are based on the processing of personal data. In an ideal world, consumers should also have the choice between more or less data-intensive services.[67] However, reality proves to be different. Internet services function as platforms for their different kinds of users and have as such a natural inclination to dominance.[68] Network effects push consumers to become the customers of highly centralised communication platforms. And if services have established a dominant position in one market, they are tempted to leverage this dominant position to strengthen their position on neighbouring markets. Competition law so far has difficulties to remedy those problems, especially when service providers grow into a dominant position. The Court of Appeal of Düsseldorf just recently suspended a decision by the Federal Cartel Office to order Facebook to restrict its data collection in Germany.[69] In its decision, the Court calls into question whether the collection of personal data in an alleged violation of the GDPR may be qualified as anti-competitive in the sense of Art 102 TFEU and § 19 German Act against Restraints of Competition (*Gesetz gegen Wettbewerbsbeschränkungen*, GWB). This shows the difficulties of competition law to capture the specificities of data-driven business models.[70]

A second cause of market failure of data markets is asymmetric information.[71] In a well-functioning market for personal data, consumers must know what they consent to. Unfortunately this is hardly ever the case, in spite of overly detailed and lengthy terms and conditions or privacy statements.[72] It is well known that consumers hardly ever read terms but just tick boxes, if necessary, and continue with the use of the service.[73] The blame for the length and complexity of privacy statements does not solely

---

67 Maximilian Becker, 'Rechte an Daten – Industrie 40 und die IP-Rechte von morgen' (2017) 72(19) JZ 170, 175ff.

68 On the following see Jacques Crémer, Yves-Alexandre de Montjoye and Heike Schweitzer, 'Competition Policy for the Digital Era Final Report' (European Commission 2019) 19ff.

69 Facebook I [2019] VI-Kart 1/19 (V) (Court of Appeal of Düsseldorf, Germany) = NZKart 2019, 495.

70 See also Torsten Körber, 'Die Facebook-Entscheidung des Bundeskartellamtes – Machtmissbrauch durch Verletzung des Datenschutzrechts?' (2019) 7(4) NZ-Kart 187; Peter Georg Picht, 'Competition Law for the Digital Era – An Adventurous Journey' (2019) 50(7) IIC 789ff.; Schweitzer (n 43) 304ff.

71 See generally on asymmetric information in contracts Schäfer/Ott, Lehrbuch der ökonomischen Analyse des Zivilrechts (5th edn, Springer Gabler 2012) 80.

72 Moreover, privacy statements (as terms and conditions) show the character of 'lemon market' products, see Becker (n 67) 174.

73 Efroni et al (n 42) 355ff.

lie with the service providers but also with the European and national legislatures which have created a regulatory jungle for data subjects, service providers and public authorities. It is therefore high time to develop new information models that support the consumer in taking an informed decision instead of confusing him with overly complicated bundles of small prints. 'Privacy Icons' could be one way to improve the consumer's self-determination on data-driven markets.[74] Yet, one should have no illusions about the efficiency of information models. Even well-informed consumers may take decisions that go against their long-term preferences (so called 'privacy paradox').[75] It is one thing to recognise, at least in principle, the importance of a cautious handling of one's own personal data. But it is another thing to live in accordance with this principle if the consumer is tempted by offerings of contents and services that are based on the collection of its data.

A third reason for market models to fail are transaction costs. The issue of transaction costs may seem remote for transactions over personal data at first glance, since personal data can be transferred without significant costs like all other data. But such a perspective would ignore that transaction costs may also occur after the conclusion of the contract and the performance of the parties' obligations when it comes to the termination of the contract. Transaction costs may occur if the consumer cannot switch from one service to another because he cannot take along his personal data. Such lock-in effects have been described as 'ex post transaction costs'.[76] On a fully functioning market, consumers have the option to switch from one provider to another if they can terminate the contract. This presupposes not only that withdrawal of consent is at no cost but also that data and content portability rules of Article 20 GDPR and Article 16(3), (4) DCSD operate effectively.[77]

74 Efroni et al (n 42).

75 See Alessandro Acquisti and Jens Grossklags, 'Losses, Gains, and Hyperbolic Discounting: An Experimental Approach to Information Security Attitudes and Behavior' [2003] 2nd Annual Workshop on 'Economics and Information Security' 789ff; Patricia Norberg et al, 'The Privacy Paradox: Personal Information Disclosure Intentions versus Behaviors' (2007) 41(1) 2nd Annual Workshop on 'Economics and Information Security' 100ff.

76 Chris Jay Hoofnagle and Jan Whittington, 'Free: Accounting for the Costs of the Internet's Most Popular Price' (2014) 61(3) UCLA Law Review 606, 612ff.

77 Sceptical on the portability rules of Article 16 Metzger et al, 'Data-Related Aspects of the Digital Content Directive' (n 6) 103ff.; Zohar Efroni (n 18) 1–32.

IV. Conclusions

The DCSD's approach to recognise data as counter-performance is innovative and pragmatic at the same time. It is innovative since lawmakers so far shied away to acknowledge that consumers may monetise the economic value of their personal data on the different markets for digital contents and services. The DCSD takes this step. But the approach is also pragmactic. The DCSD does not create a market for personal data. It merely recognises a prevalent social practice and tries to empower the consumers who are already active on these marktes. The safeguards of the GDPR thereby remain untouched. The legal means of the DCSD to achieve these goals are based on contract law. The DCSD increases the intensity of rights of the consumer and duties of the trader. Under the DCSD, the consumer who provides its personal data in exchange for the content or service will have the same rights as in case of a money consideration. Both active and passive consumers may be covered. However, for passive consumers, whose data is collected by the trader, the DCSD emphasises that it is up to the national contract law to decide whether a contract has been concluded.

For the upcoming implementation into the member states' law, the DCSD raises a number of challenges. First, the DCSD has a one-sided focus on the consumer's rights. It does not regulate the rights of the trader and the duties of the consumer. It will be a hot topic for the coming years to decide if and in what circumstances the trader can claim for the promised counter-performance within the limits of data protection law. In this regard, the DCSD creates a great deal of difficult homework for the national legislature. Second, and even more fundamental, the market model recognised by the DCSD will urge the European and national lawmakers to improve the efficiency of the markets for personal data. These markets will not flourish and strengthen the common welfare without competition between different services and offerings, well-informed consumers and low transaction costs.

Regulating the Economic Impact of Data as Counter-Performance: From the Illegality Doctrine to the Unfair Contract Terms Directive

*Philipp Hacker**

I. Introduction

In economic terms, the provision of personal data has long since acquired the status of a functional equivalent for monetary payments. The legal landscape is, step by step, adapting to this new reality, perhaps most visibly in the recently enacted directive on certain aspects concerning contracts for the supply of digital content and digital services (DCDS Directive).[1] According to its Art 3(1), the directive equally covers contracts with a monetary and with a data-based compensation.

However, the devil is, as often, in the details. Other than money, data does not provide a reliable and easily comparable price signal to market participants. Furthermore, its fungibility is encumbered by data protection rules. This leads to two questions concerning the relationship between the economic and the legal value of personal data, which are addressed in this chapter. First, in legal terms, it is unclear whether the provision of data in violation of data protection law may still qualify as counter-performance under general contract law, and whether contracts operating with such illicit transfers fall under the scope of the DCDS Directive. Given recent court and agency rulings which qualify large parts of Facebook's data-gathering practices as non-compliant with data protection law,[2] the practical relevance of this problem can hardly be overstated. Second, even if data is processed lawfully according to data protection law, the indeterminacy of its economic value raises the question of whether consumer markets driv-

---

* Humboldt-University of Berlin.

1 Directive (EU) 2019/770 of the European Parliament and of the Council of 20 May 2019 on certain aspects concerning contracts for the supply of digital content and digital services, [2019] OJ L136/1; see also in greater detail, on the discussion of data as counter-performance and the relationship between data protection and private law, Hacker, *Datenprivatrecht* (Mohr Siebeck forthcoming).

2 See below, Part III.2.a)aa).

en by data transfers do function in a competitive sense. If the question is answered in the negative, a new perspective on the directive on unfair terms in consumer contracts (UCTD) might set limits to the use of data as a counter-performance.

Finally, these problems are compounded by the heterogeneity of privacy preferences, which poses a genuine regulatory problem of its own. As empirical studies have shown, privacy preferences are not normally distributed (with most people preferring a medium level of privacy), but follow a U-shaped curve: most people sit on either extreme end of the distribution, either not caring much for privacy at all or attaching a high importance to it.[3] Any legal solutions for the phenomenon of data as counter-performance should strive to respect both of these diverging preferences and be palatable to both respective groups.

This chapter deals with these problems in four steps. Part II provides a survey of methods for measuring the economic value of personal data and shows that, while that value can be approximated, it can rarely be determined with sufficient precision. Part III discusses to what extent personal data provided in violation of data protection rules may qualify as counter-performance and may fall under the scope of the DCDS Directive. Part IV addresses two types of market failure in the context of data as counter-performance and suggests that this may lead to a – cautious – application of the UCTD even to the price dimension of data. Finally, Part V concludes by advocating for a right to data-free services in the digital economy.

II. Measuring the economic value of personal data

The difficulty to measure the economic value of personal data has become a commonplace. This part of the chapter, however, shows that this uncertainty pertains not only to the evaluations of consumers and other non-experts, but also to the more refined econometric models applied in marketing and academic analyses. There are several methods for undertaking such an evaluation, but all of them provide, at best, a rough estimate of the market value of personal data.

While there is no universally accepted methodology for the estimation of the value of personal data, the methods can be roughly grouped into

3 Alessandro Acquisti, Leslie John and George Loewenstein, 'What is Privacy Worth?' (2009) Working Paper, 26 <http://pages.stern.nyu.edu/~bakos/wise/papers/wise2009-6a1_paper.pdf> accessed 9 September 2019.

two categories: methods based on market valuation and methods based on individuals' valuation.[4] The former category includes four distinct methods:[5] financial results per data record; market prices for data; a comparison of the prices charged for personalised and non-personalised advertisements; and costs of data breaches. Individuals' valuations, in turn, can be measured in two different ways:[6] via economic experiments or surveys measuring value directly (valuation of personal data), and by eliciting individual willingness to pay to protect data (valuation of privacy).

All of these methods have certain advantages and disadvantages; a full picture of the value of personal data can only be painted by combining different methods and stressing the approximate nature of the respective methodologies. One must keep in mind that personal data often acquires value only through the specific combination of different data points in one larger data set; values for data points taken individually therefore need to be treated with caution as they may vary widely depending on the data they are processed together with.[7] Finally, irrespective of the methodology chosen, there are numerous contextual differences between different regions or countries.[8] Therefore, given diverging legislation and privacy attitudes, studies pertaining to the data of US citizens have limited external validity for data concerning EU citizens, for example. The methods described below therefore can only offer educated guesses about the value of personal data.

1. *Market valuation methods*

The first method, financial results per data record, affords the advantage of being straightforward to calculate. The aggregated market capitalisation, the annual revenue or the annual net income of the company is simply divided by the total number of data records in the possession of the company. This method, using annual revenue as the relevant indicator, yielded

4 OECD, 'Exploring the Economics of Personal Data: A Survey of Methodologies for Measuring Monetary Value' (Paris 2013) 18f.

5 Cf OECD (n 4) 19; Philipp Hacker and Bilyana Petkova, 'Reining in the Big Promise of Big Data: Transparency, Inequality, and New Regulatory Frontiers' (2017) 15 Northwestern Journal of Technology & Intellectual Property 1, 23f.

6 Alessandro Acquisti, Curtis Taylor and Liad Wagman, 'The Economics of Privacy' (2016) 54 Journal of Economic Literature 442, 444, 447.

7 Bundesverband der digitalen Wirtschaft, 'Data Economy' (Berlin 2018) 12.

8 OECD (n 4) 19.

an annual value of $12 for the personal data shared by each Facebook user in 2015.[9] Similarly, in 2011, the annual value per data record for the data broker Experian resulted in $19 in terms of capitalisation, $6 in terms of revenue and $1 in terms of net income.[10] For data brokers in the German market, the mean value in terms of revenue for the complete data record of a single consumer amounted to 0.96€ in 2014[11], for the most prominent data broker SCHUFA to 1.91€.[12] However, the difficulty lies in untangling the share of the company performance that is due to the data records from other factors (eg, legislation; press coverage; hiring decisions etc.) that influence financial results.[13] Furthermore, findings fluctuate substantially over the years.[14]

Valuations directly based on market prices for data also provide a straightforward way of measuring their value. They can be divided in prices quoted in legal and illegal markets. Legal markets are operated by professional data brokers; while the conformity of data brokering with EU data protection law may be doubtful in certain cases, the parties generally operate on an assumption of legality. In 2013, the following prices were quoted in these markets: $0.50 for an address, $2 for a date of birth, $8 for a US Social Security number, $3 for a driver's license number, and $35 for a military record.[15] A package including address, date of birth, Social Security number, credit record and military record was estimated to cost $55.[16] For German credit records, companies have to pay between 0.80€ and 7€.[17] There are, however, two drawbacks to the use of data broker pricing. First, as a recent study has shown,[18] market prices for some data are relatively difficult to obtain as data brokers play their cards close to their chest. Second, even when they are obtained, they reflect total prices for data packages which include search costs, fixed costs and other cost factors unrelated

9 Hacker and Petkova (n 5) 23f.
10 OECD (n 4) 21.
11 Klaus Goldhammer and André Wiegand, 'Ökonomischer Wert von Verbraucherdaten für Adress- und Datenhändler' (Berlin 2017) 70.
12 Goldhammer and Wiegand (n 11) 71; net income per data record stands at 0.36€, id 72.
13 OECD (n 4) 24.
14 OECD (n 4) 22, 25.
15 OECD (n 4) 25.
16 OECD (n 4) 25.
17 Goldhammer and Wiegand (n 11) 67f; a simple credit score may be obtained for 0.40–0.99€, see id.
18 Goldhammer and Wiegand (n 11) 6, 69.

to the value of the data itself.[19] These cost factors, however, are generally difficult to differentiate from the amount of the sales price which reflects the mere value of the data. In the case of openly illegal markets, market prices are likely distorted to account for the risk of detection and punishment.[20] Stolen credit card information, for example, currently sells for up to $45 per record, full ID packages for up to $100.[21]

Third, differences between the prices online platforms charge for personalised versus non-personalised advertisements can be used as a proxy to calculate the marginal value of permitting the tracking of personal data. The monthly per user value of personal data collected by Facebook was estimated to amount to roughly $4 in 2017 using this method.[22] However, the exact amount of the price difference is generally non-public information and therefore difficult to ascertain.

The fourth market valuation method uses as a proxy the economic costs of a data breach for data record. However, the cost of the breach need not be identical with the positive value of the data, as it includes potentially expensive repair measures or reputational damage to the firm.[23] Insurance prices against data breach need to reflect these additional factors, too, without necessarily singling them out.

2. *Individuals' valuation methods*

The two methods for measuring individuals' valuations face similar challenges. The elicitation of individual willingness to pay to protect data meets the same objections as the use of the economic costs of data breach: both use a measure of harm as a proxy for the positive value of data.[24] Surveys and experiments, on the other hand, may indeed measure directly the value individuals attribute to their data.

For example, an empirical estimation found consumers to assign only little value to concealing their browser history ($2.28), their contact list ($4.05) or their location ($1.19).[25] Furthermore, another experiment re-

---

19 OECD (n 4) 26f.
20 OECD (n 4) 20.
21 Symantec, 'Internet Security Threat Report', Volume 24 (2019) 56, 58.
22 Hacker and Petkova (n 5) 23f.
23 OECD (n 4) 20, 29.
24 OECD (n 4) 20, 33.
25 Scott J. Savage and Donald M. Waldman, The Value of Online Privacy: Evidence from Smartphone Applications, Technical Report (2014) 20.

vealed that most participants preferred to buy a DVD from a privacy-intrusive company rather than paying 1€ more for the same product offered by a privacy-protective competitor.[26]

However, unless field experiments are used, the external validity of these experiments may be doubtful. Surveys collect opinions that are not necessarily implemented in market settings. Hence, surveys in the US and the EU generally show that people are highly concerned about losing control of their personal data,[27] while they simultaneously fail to act on these preferences.[28] One leading explanation for this privacy paradox is the fact that people fail to appreciate the real value of their data in specific decision-making environments due to different cognitive biases.[29] In addition, lack of information on the consequences of data sharing adds to low valuations of privacy.[30]

One recurring issue, furthermore, consists in the fact that valuations of personal data were shown to be highly sensitive to the context of the valuation,[31] such as the framing of the information,[32] or the environment of the

---

26 Sören Preibusch, Dorothea Kübler and Alastair R Beresford, 'Price versus Privacy: An Experiment into the Competitive Advantage of Collecting Less Personal Information' (2013) 13 Electronic Commerce Research 423, 441, 444–445.

27 European Commission, 'Attitudes on Data Protection and Electronic Identity in the European Union', Special Eurobarometer 359 (June 2011) 74–75 and 148–149; Mary Madden and Lee Rainie, 'Americans' Attitudes About Privacy, Security and Surveillance' (Pew Research Center 2015) 9; Pew Research Center, 'Public Perceptions of Privacy and Security in the Post-Snowden Era' (2014) 3.

28 Patricia A Norberg, Daniel R Horne and David A Horne, 'The privacy paradox: Personal information disclosure intentions versus behaviors' (2007) 41 Journal of Consumer Affairs 100; see also Philipp Hacker, 'Lessons from IP Markets for Data Markets. Moral Rights, Property Rules, and Resale Royalties' (2018) Intellectual Property Quarterly 45, 50–52.

29 See Acquisti, Taylor and Wagman (n 6) 477–478; Yoan Hermstrüwer, *Informationelle Selbstgefährdung* (Mohr Siebeck 2016) 240–249.

30 Peter Blume, 'The Inherent Contradictions in Data Protection Law' (2012) 2 International Data Privacy Law 26, 29; Omri Ben-Shahar and Adam Chilton, 'Simplification of Privacy Disclosures: An Experimental Test' (2016) 45 Journal of Legal Studies S41.

31 Acquisti, Taylor and Wagman (n 6) 446, 478.

32 Alessandro Acquisti, Leslie John and George Loewenstein, 'What is Privacy Worth' (2013) 42 The Journal of Legal Studies 249, 267; Idris Adjerid, Alessandro Acquisti, Laura Brandimarte and George Loewenstein, 'Sleights of Privacy: Framing, Disclosures, and the Limits of Transparency' (2013) Proceedings of the Ninth Symposium on Usable Privacy and Security 1, 2.

decision.[33] Therefore, it is impossible to extrapolate from these studies a 'mean subjective value' of personal data. For example, consumers have been shown to be willing to pay a premium to protect their privacy when privacy is salient.[34] Hence, it would be premature to conclude that consumers, generally, attach only low value to their personal data or privacy even as a matter of revealed preferences. Rather, as mentioned, preferences are distributed on a U-shaped curve.[35]

3. *Key insights*

While the exact contours depend on the precise legal question, market valuation methods generally seem more appropriate for legal assessments than those based on individuals' valuations as the former represent a more objective, rather than an idiosyncratic and subjective, measure of the value of personal data. However, precise information about the market value of personal data is often not available.[36] What emerges clearly from the cited studies, however, is that the value of personal data increases with the degree of user identification.[37] Overall, the market value of data can be approximated, but due to the various drawbacks of the different techniques, these estimates tend to be imprecise and fluctuate over time. Importantly, these techniques and methods are typically not available to consumers, particularly not in concrete online decision-making environments. However, it is equally undeniable that personal data in general does have a

33 Alessandro Acquisti, Laura Brandimarte and Jeff Hancock, 'Online Self-Disclosure and Offline Threat Detection' (2015) WEIS, <weis2015.econinfosec.org/papers/WEIS_2015_acquisti.pdf> accessed 9 September 2019.

34 Janice Y Tsai, Serge Egelman, Lorrie Cranor and Alessandro Acquisti, 'The Effect of Online Privacy Information on Purchasing Behavior: An Experimental Study' (2011) 22 Information Systems Research 254, 263–264 (50–60 % of buyers paying a privacy premium); Nicola Jentzsch et al, 'Study on Monetising Privacy: An Economic Model for Pricing Personal Information' (European Network and Information Security Agency 2012) 36 (30–40 % of buyers paying a privacy premium).

35 See above, text at n 3.

36 Goldhammer and Wiegand (n 11) 6; Bundesverband der digitalen Wirtschaft (n 7) 12.

37 Bundesverband der digitalen Wirtschaft (n 7) 15; other factors are the error rate and the time elapsed since data were collected (id 19).

strictly positive economic value which functions as an equivalent to a monetary counter-performance in countless online transactions.[38]

III. The legal value of personal data as counter-performance

The preceding analysis has shown that personal data has a positive but indeterminate economic value. This raises two interlinked questions. First, given its functional equivalents to monetary transactions, to what extent can the transfer of personal data be considered a counter-performance in the legal sense, too? Second, given its indeterminate nature, what specific limits does law impose on the use of personal data rather than money as a counter-performance?

1. Counter-performance and the Directive on Contracts for the Supply of Digital Content and Digital Services

The second question will be addressed below in Part IV. The first question, in turn, was famously touched upon by the Commission draft of the directive on certain aspects concerning contracts for the supply of digital content.[39] It stated, in its draft Art 3(1), that the directive would apply to the supply of digital content if the consumer pays a price or 'actively provides counter-performance other than money in the form of personal data or any other data'. This half sentence triggered a wide-ranging academic debate about the promises and perils of recognising personal data as a form of counter-performance.[40] Following substantial critique of the use of the

---

38 For a systematisation of the different ways in which personal data is used as counter-performance from an economic perspective, see Philipp Hacker, 'Daten als Gegenleistung. Rechtsgeschäfte im Spannungsfeld von DS-GVO und allgemeinem Vertragsrecht' (2019) Zeitschrift für die gesamte Privatrechtswissenschaft 148, 153ff.

39 European Commission, 'Proposal for a Directive of the European Parliament and of the Council on certain aspects concerning contracts for the supply of digital content' COM(2015) 634 final.

40 See, eg, Carmen Langhanke and Martin Schmidt-Kessel, 'Consumer Data as Consideration' (2015) EuCML 218; Fryderyk Zoll, 'Personal Data as Remuneration in the Proposal for a Directive on Supply of Digital Content' in Reiner Schulze, Dirk Staudenmayer and Sebastian Lohsse (eds), *Contracts for the Supply of Digital Content: Regulatory Challenges and Gaps* (Hart 2017) 179; Axel Metzger, 'Dienst gegen Daten: Ein synallagmatischer Vertrag' (2016) 216 Archiv für die civilistische

term 'counter-performance' by, inter alia, the European Data Protection Supervisor,[41] the Joint Report of the European Parliament proposed to replace the term by the phrase that the digital content must be supplied 'under the condition that personal data is provided by the consumer or collected by the trader or a third party in the interest of the trader.'[42] Similarly, the compromise text of the Council avoided the term 'counter-performance'.[43] The text finally adopted by the European Parliament and the Council (DCDS Directive) now merely states that the directive also applies where 'the consumer provides or undertakes to provide personal data to the trader, except where the personal data provided by the consumer is exclusively processed by the trader for the purpose of supplying the digital content or digital service in accordance with this Directive or for allowing the trader to comply with legal requirements to which the trader is subject, and the trader does not process that data for any other purpose.'[44]

2. *General contract law and data protection law*

Nevertheless, it is now accepted by the majority of scholars who have weighed in on the issue that personal data can generally function as a type of counter-performance.[45] Importantly, both the declaration of consent and the transfer of data itself can assume the function of a counter-performance.[46] The exact details depend on doctrinal aspects of national contract law which are not harmonised under the DCDS Directive, which now

Praxis 817; Axel Metzger, 'Data as Counter-Performance' (2017) 8 JIPITEC 2; Axel Metzger, ''Verträge über digitale Inhalte und Dienstleistungen' (2019) Juristenzeitung 577; Stefan Grundmann and Philipp Hacker, 'Digital Technology as a Challenge to European Contract Law' (2017) 13 ERCL 255, 288ff; Andreas Sattler, 'Personenbezogene Daten als Leistungsgegenstand' (2017) Juristenzeitung 1036; Hacker (n 38) 157ff with further references.

41 European Data Protection Supervisor, 'Opinion 4/2017 on the Proposal for a Directive on certain aspects concerning contracts for the supply of digital content' (14 March 2017) 9f.

42 European Parliament, 'Report on the proposal for a directive of the European Parliament and of the Council on certain aspects concerning contracts for the supply of digital content' A8-0375/2017 (27 November 2017) 53.

43 Council of the European Union, 'Note 9901/17 ADD 1' (1 June 2017) 8.

44 Art 3(1) DCDS Directive.

45 See the references in n 40.

46 See, for German law, BGH (2017) Neue Juristische Wochenschau (NJW) 2119 para 22; BT-Drucksache [Materials of the German Parliament] 17/13951, 72.

avoids the term counter-performance altogether. I have published my own view on these matters concerning German law elsewhere[47] and hence shall not develop this general question here any further. Rather, the following section will focus on one specific and still unresolved aspect of the debate on data as counter-performance: the case of unlawful data processing. It brings to the fore tensions between the economic value of the data and its use as a counter-performance in a legal sense. More specifically, the preceding economic overview has shown that even data which was illegally obtained has a positive and sometimes quite substantial economic value. The most common reason for the illegality of the data source, at least in the EU, however, is likely to be the violation of data protection rules. This raises the question of whether personal data which is transferred in breach of data protection rules can still be considered counter-performance in the legal sense (sub a)), and if it falls within the scope of the DCDS Directive (sub b)).

a) *Partial independence: unlawful data processing and counter-performance*

Indeed, the transfer of personal data from a consumer/user to a supplier of digital content or of a digital service can violate data protection laws in a number of ways. Clearly, in this case, only the data transfer itself (and not the invalid/non-extant consent) may assume the role of counter-performance. However, even that conclusion is doubtful.

aa) The role of data protection law – the Facebook example

As is well-known, to be lawful under the General Data Protection Regulation (GDPR),[48] data processing needs to comply with a number of principles of data protection, listed in Art 5(1) GDPR, including the principles of fair and transparent processing, purpose limitation, data minimisation, and data security. Additionally, the processing must have a legal basis by meeting at least one of the requirements mentioned in Art 6(1) GDPR. For

---

47 Hacker (n 38) 157ff.

48 Regulation (EU) 2016/679 of the European Parliament and of the Council of 27 April 2016 on the protection of natural persons with regard to the processing of personal data and on the free movement of such data, and repealing Directive 95/46/EC [2016] OJ L119/1.

data transfers in the digital economy, this means, in practice, that they must either be legitimised by valid consent (Art 6(1)(a) GDPR), be necessary for the performance of a contract (Art 6(1)(b) GDPR), or pass the balancing test in Art 6(1)(f) GDPR, which is met if the legitimate interests of the controller are not overridden by the interests of the data subject.

To take a concrete and contentious example, the German competition authority has recently concluded that data collection by Facebook via social plug-ins on third-party websites or third-party apps, and data sharing between Facebook and WhatsApp (and other Facebook companies), is illegal, as a matter of data protection law, unless the user validly consents.[49] A number of court rulings have shown, however, that Facebook's consent policy does not stand up to legal scrutiny for violation of the information requirements necessary for valid consent.[50] The German competition authority shares this view and notes that consent is invalid if it forms a necessary precondition for the use of the service offered by Facebook.[51] Taken together, these rulings suggest that large parts of the data transfers from Facebook users to Facebook may violate data protection law. However, Facebook is a paradigmatic case of the supply of digital content and digital services;[52] the (assumed) data protection violations therefore raise the question of the relationship between data protection law and general contract law with renewed urgency.

bb) The illegality doctrine revisited: against the invalidation of contracts

The DCDS Directive confers the authority to decide on the validity of contracts concerning the supply of digital content or services to Member State law.[53] A number of authors have held that the verdict of general contract law should strictly follow the verdict of data protection law:[54] under this view, data shared for processing which is unlawful under data protection

49 Bundeskartellamt, 'Facebook, Exploitative business terms pursuant to Section 19(1) GWB for inadequate data processing', Case B6-22/16, Case Summary (15 February 2019), 10f.

50 See below, Part IV.2.

51 Bundeskartellamt (n 49) 10f.

52 See Recital 24 of the DCDS Directive.

53 Art 3(10), Recital 12 Sentence 1 and End of Recital 24 of the DCDS Directive.

54 Florian Faust, 'Digitale Wirtschaft – Analoges Recht: Braucht das BGB ein Update?' (Gutachten [Legal Opinion] zum 71. Deutschen Juristentag, 2016) 8; Nils Lölfing, *Die App-Ökonomie des Schenkens* (LIT Verlag 2017) 74f; probably also Langhanke and Schmidt-Kessel (n 40) 220f.

law cannot be valid counter-performance under general contract law. Doctrinally, this invalidity follows from the doctrine of illegality.[55] This view is shared, for example, by the Superior Civil Court of Frankfurt am Main.[56]

The following paragraphs challenge this view.[57] They show that, rather than emulating the judgment of data protection law, general contract law should maintain its independence vis-à-vis data protection rules. Four reasons speak in favour of this, at least in cases in which the data subject herself provides the data.[58]

First, applying the illegality doctrine to cases of data protection violation would generally void the contract which links the provision of services to the transfer of personal data.[59] However, upon closer scrutiny of the data protection issues, significant impediments to the implementation of this invalidation arise. This is because data protection law does not qualify as unlawful data sharing practices between two parties as such; rather, the illegality only attaches to specific processing activities concerning this data. Hence, the German competition authority, in its data protection assessment, clearly stated that only some of Facebook's current processing practices are illegal under data protection (third-party tracking and sharing between different companies of the Facebook group).[60] At least some of the remaining data transfers between a user and Facebook are therefore likely justified under data protection law, via either of the above-mentioned requirements of Art 6(1) GDPR.

This points to a general problem: in almost every case, only a fraction of the envisaged processing activities is unlawful. It is entirely unclear, however, how this partial illegality under data protection law should translate into general contract law under the illegality doctrine. Generally, depending on national contract law, it may be possible to only partially invalidate a contract, even as a consequence of illegality.[61] However, typically, the

55 See, eg, § 134 BGB; Hugh Beale (ed), *Chitty on Contracts* (32nd edn, Sweet & Maxwell 2017) ch 16; for US law, see Ian Ayres/Gregory Klass, *Studies in Contract Law* (8th edn, Foundation Press 2012) 556f.

56 OLG Frankfurt a.M. NJW-RR 2018, 887 paras 43f (concerning a provision of the German Data Protection Act preceding the GDPR).

57 See also the discussion in Hacker (n 38) 159ff.

58 The situation is different when two controllers, in trading data, violate the GDPR; in that case the illegality doctrine should apply.

59 For qualifications of this finding, see below, n 61, 66, 67 and 69.

60 Bundeskartellamt (n 49) 1.

61 For an account of partial invalidation of the contract, under German law, see Christian Armbrüster, *Münchener Kommentar zum BGB* (8th edn, C.H. Beck 2019), § 134 BGB paras 122–127; for English law, see Beale (n 55) paras 16–211ff.

promise to provide the service, for example access to a social network, cannot be partially invalidated: either access is granted, or not. Similar problems arise concerning the data-based counter-performance (the data transfer). Often, one cannot say that only those data transfers leading to lawful processing activities may count as counter-performance: usually, the transfer of one piece of personal data is put to multiple uses, some of which may be legal and some illegal (such as sharing with other companies, as in the Facebook case). Clearly, the service provider cannot enforce, against a data subject, obligations[62] to transfer data whose processing would violate data protection law (*dolo agit qui petit quod statim redditurus est*). But this does not imply that, once the transfer has been made, it cannot count as counter-performance. Rather, entirely denying data transfers which include transfers that violate data protection law the status of counter-performance rides roughshod over the complexity of data protection law assessments.

Second, not granting these data transfers the status of counter-performance would add insult to injury for data subjects. After all, data transfers violate data protection law mostly in the case of particularly intrusive types of data processing. However, it seems unjust to deny remedies of contract law that may only apply in the case of the existence of a counter-performance[63] to precisely these data subjects. Furthermore, under German law, for example, contracts without counter-performance privilege the supplier in many ways, for example in the liability standards.[64] In countries following the consideration doctrine, the lack of counter-performance due to illegality leads to a finding that a contract was not even validly formed.[65] Moreover, Recital 48 of the DCDS Directive explicitly states that the contractual remedies provided for in the directive do not apply if the contract is void or voidable under national law. Hence, in this case, users would be left, instead of with contractual remedies, with the typically much weaker provisions of culpa in contrahendo, unjust enrichment and tort law.[66] The unintended consequence of invalidating the contract would be to provide particularly intrusive data controllers with a better position in general con-

62 On the question whether such obligations exist in the first place, or whether data transfer typically should not rather be interpreted as a mere *condition* for the provision of the service, see Hacker (n 38) 167ff.

63 Under German law, this applies to §§ 320–326 BGB, for example.

64 See, eg, §§ 521, 599, 690 BGB.

65 Beale (n 55) paras 4–187.

66 Therefore, under German law, illegality which involves only one party typically leaves the contract intact, see BGH NJW 1985, 2403.

tract law than their law-abiding competitors. Conversely, data subjects who already face unlawful processing would be denied contractual rights; this seems to run counter precisely to the interests of those the GDPR initially intends to protect.[67]

Third, tying the quality of data as counter-performance to its status under data protection law would inject an unwelcome dose of legal uncertainty into general contract law. As is well known, data protection law operates with highly vague terms (eg the principles of data protection, Art 5(1) GDPR) and a broad balancing of interests (eg, Art 6(1)(f) GDPR), the outcome of which is quite unpredictable ex ante.[68] This serves neither the needs of suppliers nor of consumers in the data economy.

Fourth and finally, invoking the illegality doctrine in general contract law is unnecessary because data protection law has its own effective regime to sanction unlawful data processing, both with public *and* private enforcement tools.[69] More specifically, Art 17(1)(d) GDPR gives the data subject a right to erasure if data has been processed unlawfully; and, Art 18(1)(b) GDPR holds that, in the case of unlawful processing, the data subject may demand the restriction of data processing if she does not opt for erasure. This specific, rights-based sanction regime of the GDPR should assume prevalence over the much less fine-grained doctrine of illegality under general contract law.

b) *The scope of the DCDS Directive*

Mutatis mutandis, these arguments also imply that the violation of data protection law should not exclude such contracts from the scope of the DCDS Directive pursuant to its Art 3(1). First, there is nothing in the wording of said Article to suggest otherwise. Rather, the wording does exclude two specific instances of data processing (processing for supplying the digital content or service; processing to comply with legal requirements) without mentioning unlawful processing in the sense of the

67 For the relevance of these interests in setting aside the illegality doctrine under German law, see Armbrüster (n 61) para 119.

68 See Article 29 Working Party, 'Opinion 15/2011 on the definition of consent' WP 187 (13 November 2011), 7f.

69 Under German law, for example, a sufficient sanctioning regime sets aside the illegality doctrine, see Armbrüster (n 61) para 119; for data protection law, see OLG Celle, Judgment of 10 September 2003 – 3 U 137/03, BeckRS 2004, 07985, under B.III.; BGH (2007) NJW 2106 para 32.

GDPR. Recital 25 of the directive does mention a few other processing situations in which the directive should not apply, but also fails to mention unlawful processing.

Second, from systematic perspective, it is noteworthy that Art 3(8) of the DCDS Directive states that the GDPR takes precedence over the provisions of the DCDS Directive with respect to the treatment of personal data. This, however, says nothing about whether the scope of the directive depends on conformity with the GDPR. Rather, Recital 48 of the DCDS Directive clearly states that failure to comply with the GDPR may constitute a lack of conformity of the digital content or service under the DCDS Directive. This logically implies that the scope of the DCDS Directive cannot be excluded by the fact that data protection law is violated.

Third, the purpose of Art 3(1) of the DCDS Directive also speaks in favour of including unlawful data processing within its scope. That scope was formulated deliberately in a broad way to include, beyond monetary payments, data-based transactions precisely to open the remedies foreseen in the directive to users of 'free' digital services.[70] As mentioned above, the exclusion of unlawful data processing would have the unjust effect of denying these remedies precisely to those consumers most negatively affected by data processing activities. If anything, the unlawfulness of data processing should lead to stricter, not less strict, liability of the data controller under the directive.

IV. Limits to data as counter-performance: the Unfair Contract Terms Directive

For the reasons mentioned in the preceding Part, one should look beyond the illegality doctrine to rein in particularly problematic data processing in the context of data as counter-performance. While freedom of contract suggests that consumers should generally be free to trade data for access to services, this freedom is not without limits. This section therefore turns to the directive on unfair terms in consumer contracts (UCTD), where a second legal problem resulting from the indeterminacy of the economic value of personal data surfaces: the efficient functioning of the market mechanism in data-based exchanges.

The need for recourse to the UCTD is limited as long as data processing violates the GDPR, which comes with its own effective mechanism of sanctions. However, some data processing activities may be lawful under

70 See Recital 24 Sentence 3 of the DCDS Directive.

the GDPR, yet still raise concerns with respect to the main market failures the UCTD aims to address.

1. *Market failures in data-based consumer markets*

In fact, in data-based consumer markets, two types of market failures may be identified which are of relevance for the application of the UCTD: inattention concerning privacy policies; and the indeterminacy of the 'price' paid for a service.

The first problem, lack of attention to privacy policies, has long been noted and been identified as one of the main reasons for the existence of the privacy paradox.[71] Recently, an experiment showed that 74% of data subjects completely ignore privacy policies and the remaining 26% look at them for such a brief period of time that it is impossible for them to grasp their content in any meaningful way.[72] Such ignorance is often rational as the expected (cognitive and opportunity) costs of perusing a complex privacy policy outweigh the expected benefits.[73]

This not only implies that consumers often are simply unaware of what is happening to their data; it also creates a competition problem. When consumers ignore privacy policies, competition on the merits of their content is significantly dampened as companies have a much harder time gaining a competitive advantage by offering more favourable privacy conditions: there is not even an informed minority which could steer market demand.[74] This market failure is equivalent to the ignorance of the terms of standard form contracts, which has also been empirically validated.[75] From

71 See, eg, Yoan Hermstrüwer, 'Contracting Around Privacy' (2017) 8 JIPITEC 9, 17; Ben-Shahar and Chilton (n 30).

72 Jonathan Obar and Anne Oeldorf-Hirsch, 'The biggest lie on the Internet' (2018) 21 Information, Communication & Society 1.

73 Hermstrüwer (n 71); Melvin Aron Eisenberg, 'The Limits of Cognition and the Limits of Contract' (1995) 47 Stan. L. Rev. 211, 241–243 (on the parallel problem of standard form contracts).

74 Eisenberg (n 73) 243f.

75 For example, only about one in 1000 data subjects even looks at online end-user license agreements when downloading software, see Yannis Bakos, Florencia Marotta-Wurgler and David R Trossen, 'Does Anyone Read the Fine Print?' (2014) 43 The Journal of Legal Studies 1.

an economic perspective, it is precisely this market failure which justifies court scrutiny of contractual terms via the UCTD.[76]

The discussion of the difficulties in measuring the economic value of personal data, however, points to a second problem which has only recently garnered scholarly attention: data's properties are very different from the ones of money.[77] Not only is money intrinsically scarce, while personal data is being produced in abundance by consumers. More importantly, as mentioned, even economic modelling undertaken in scholarly studies fails to reliably establish the value of personal data. Even more so, consumers are largely unaware of the value their data has for the companies they are sharing it with. This amounts to a structural market problem if that data is the main form of compensation of the company for the services provided, as in many data as counter-performance contexts.[78] Consumers simply do not know what price they are paying for the service. However, in economic theory, price is the central market parameter for steering competitive forces as it makes different offers comparable on a single, easily observable scale.[79] This is the economic reason why price is exempt from scrutiny under Art 4(2) UCTD.

2. *Applicability in parallel to the GDPR*

From an economic perspective, it therefore makes sense to apply the UCTD to privacy policies or, more precisely, to declarations of consent relating to privacy policies: the (rational) ignorance of privacy policies weak-

---

76 Jürgen Basedow, *Münchener Kommentar zum BGB* (8th edn, C.H. Beck 2019), Vor § 305 paras 4–6; Markus Stoffels, 'Schranken der Inhaltskontrolle' (2001) Juristenzeitung 843, 847.

77 See, eg, European Data Protection Supervisor (n 41) 9; Heike Schweitzer, 'Neue Machtlagen in der digitalen Welt? Das Beispiel unentgeltlicher Leistungen', in Torsten Körber and Jürgen Kühling (eds), *Regulierung-Wettbewerb-Innovation* (Nomos 2017) 269, 276.

78 Hans-Peter Schwintowski, 'Preistransparenz als Voraussetzung funktionsfähigen (digitalen) Marktwettbewerbs' (2018) Neue Juristische Online-Zeitschrift 841, 845, 848f.

79 Friedrich A. Hayek, 'The Use of Knowledge in Society' (1945) 35 American Economic Review 519, 525–527; George J. Stigler, *The Theory of Price* (4th edn, Macmillan 1987) 11–16; Hal Varian, *Intermediate Micro-Economics* (8th edn, Norton 2010) 3, 78.

ens competition on the merits of their contents and legitimises court scrutiny if the conditions are unilaterally imposed.[80]

From a legal perspective, there can be little doubt that the UCTD can be applied, in principle, in parallel to the GDPR. Recital 42 of the GDPR explicitly mentions that privacy policies may not contain clauses that are unfair in the sense of the UCTD. Since the GDPR lacks a proper standard for the determination of the unfairness of contract clauses or declarations of consent, this can only mean that a separate and independent assessment of the validity of a declaration of consent must be undertaken under the UCTD even if that declaration fulfils all the criteria of the GDPR.[81]

3. *Transparency obligations*

The first important obligation imposed under the UCTD is the transparency of contractual provisions pursuant to Art 5 UCTD. In fact, this branch of the UCTD has often been invoked by courts even before the entry into force of the GDPR to invalidate consent to privacy policies.[82] Doctrinally, courts have reproduced the data protection criterion of the informed nature of consent by reading it into the transparency obligations under the UCTD.[83] This practice is at least doubtful from an EU perspective as the transparency rules under the GDPR and the UCTD are not entirely identical;[84] to the extent that they match, however, the UCTD indeed reinforces the transparency requirements under the GDPR.

For example, in a much-noted recent case, the Regional Court of Berlin (LG Berlin) invalidated large parts of consumer consent to Facebook's privacy policies due to their alleged infringement of the transparency require-

---

80 See in detail Part IV.4.a).

81 Christiane Wendehorst and Friedrich Graf v. Westphalen, 'Das Verhältnis zwischen Datenschutz-Grundverordnung und AGB-Recht' (2016) NJW 3745, 3749.

82 Natali Helberger, Frederik Zuiderveen Borgesius and Agustin Reyna, 'The Perfect Match? A Closer Look at the Relationship Between EU Consumer Law and Data Protection Law' (2017) 54 Common Market Law Review 1427, 1452f.

83 Hacker (n 38) 184f; BGH, Judgment of 14 March 2017, Case VI ZR 721/15 = (2017) NJW 2119, paras 23–26.

84 See the analysis in Damian Clifford, Inge Graef and Peggy Valcke, 'Pre-Formulated Declarations of Data Subject Consent – Citizen-Consumer Empowerment and the Alignment of Data, Consumer and Competition Law Protections' German Law Journal 2019, forthcoming, CiTiP Working Paper 33/2017, 13–15 <https://papers.ssrn.com/sol3/papers.cfm?abstract_id=3126706> accessed 9 September 2019.

ments under the (German transposition of the) UCTD.[85] Again, the court read the more specific requirements imposed by (pre-GDPR) data protection law into the rather unspecific transparency rules under Art 5 UCTD.[86] Most notably, the invalidation concerned the transfer of data to the US and their processing there; consent to use the profile name and profile picture for commercial, sponsored and similar content; and the general, prospective consent to Facebook's privacy policy, including future updates.

While unprecise disclosure of the exact scope and circumstances of processing must be sanctioned *de lege lata*, such rulings make less sense from a policy perspective. Given rampant inattention to privacy policies, making these policies ever more precise (and hence complex) will not necessarily lead to more informed decision making on the part of consumers. The only significant benefit is that exact and scrupulous disclosure can be a source of information for privacy analysts and watchdogs who may then inform the public, in more accessible formats, about data sharing practices.[87] Even if consumers, through these sources or otherwise, do become more informed about the exact data processing practices under a certain contract, though, the second problem identified above remains: the indeterminacy of the value of data. This is where the unfairness assessment of the UCTD may come into play.

4. *The unfairness assessment*

The unfairness assessment is enshrined in Art 3(1) UCTD, which stipulates that a 'contractual term which has not been individually negotiated shall be regarded as unfair if, contrary to the requirement of good faith, it causes a significant imbalance in the parties' rights and obligations arising under the contract, to the detriment of the consumer'. However, before it can be discussed whether some contracts using data as counter-performance may create a significant contractual imbalance contrary to good faith (under c)), it must be shown that the UCTD even applies to the data dimension of

85 LG Berlin, Judgment of 16 January 2018, Case 16 O 341/15, BeckRS 2018, 1060 = (2018) MultiMedia und Recht 328; appeal pending.

86 LG Berlin (n 85) paras 65–68.

87 One example is Paul Bischhoff, 'Comparing the privacy policy of internet giants side-by-side' (20 March 2017) <https://www.comparitech.com/blog/vpn-privacy/we-compared-the-privacy-policies-of-internet-giants-side-by-side/> accessed 9 September 2019.

the contract (under a)), and an appropriate yardstick for the assessment of unfairness must be found (under b)).

a) *The applicability of the UCTD to the main subject matter of the contract*

According to Art 4(2) UCTD, the '[a]ssessment of the unfair nature of the terms shall relate neither to the definition of the main subject matter of the contract nor to the adequacy of the price and remuneration, on the one hand, as against the services or goods supplies in exchange, on the other [...]'. This provision exempts two different contractual categories from the unfairness assessment (but not from the transparency requirement). First, the main subject matter of the contract *itself* is beyond scrutiny. The CJEU ruled, in *Kásler*, that the main subject matter comprises the contractual terms 'that lay down the essential obligations of the contract and, as such, characterise it', but not ancillary clauses.[88] Hence, Art 4(2) UCTD applies to the characteristic performance and counter-performance, for example the obligation to deliver and confer ownership of certain goods, the obligation to provide certain services, or to pay a price. Second, the *relationship* between performance and counter-performance, ie, the adequacy of the quality/price ratio,[89] is not subject to the UCTD unfairness assessment (if the trader provides a specific service or good for the specific price component[90]).

aa) Data as a price

Taken literally, Art 4(2) UCTD therefore exempts consent to data processing and data transfer clauses from the unfairness assessment insofar as they constitute counter-performance and hence characterise the contract. Indeed, whenever there is no significant monetary payment accompanying the data transfer, such clauses precisely function as an economic equivalent of a monetary price. On the face of it, the exemption then extends to both

---

88 CJEU, Case C-26/13 *Kásler* [2014] ECLI:EU:C:2014:282, paras 49–50.
89 See Recital 19 of the UCTD.
90 CJEU, Case C-26/13 *Kásler* [2014] ECLI:EU:C:2014:282, para 58; Case C-143/13 *Matei* [2015] ECLI:EU:C:2015:127, para 70; Beale (n 55) paras 38–234.

the clauses themselves (the main subject matter) and their relationship to the obligation of performance (adequate ratio).[91]

However, the arguments justifying these exemptions arguably do not apply when data constitutes the counter-performance. First, the main reason for exempting the adequacy of the price from court scrutiny is that there is a strong assumption, as discussed, that markets tend to find the right price more efficiently than courts could do.[92] While this is fairly uncontroversial as a general claim, it hinges on the premise that the market functions efficiently. With respect to pricing, this implies, as Hayek has stressed, that the price signal needs to be undistorted and clear.[93] However, as Part II of this chapter showed, this assumption fails when personal data functions as the price component. There is no clear signal that can be easily observed by consumers and that could therefore efficiently steer the forces of market supply and demand.[94]

Second, the reason for exempting the main subject matter of the contract from UCTD scrutiny is that it is believed that, other than ancillary clauses, these decisive parameters of the exchange will generally garner the attention of consumers,[95] this being a further prerequisite for functioning price competition. However, as mentioned, this assumption also fails because consumers patently disregard privacy policies and therefore ignore, rather than focus on, the price they pay in contracts where data functions as counter-performance.

Therefore, it is submitted that the reasoning for exempting the price dimension does not apply to these contracts. According to the CJEU, however, the interpretation of EU law requires, beyond a focus on the word-

---

91 In this vein Damian Clifford, Inge Graef and Peggy Valcke, 'Pre-Formulated Declarations of Data Subject Consent – Citizen-Consumer Empowerment and the Alignment of Data, Consumer and Competition Law Protections' German Law Journal 2019, forthcoming, CiTiP Working Paper 33/2017, 23 <https://papers.ssrn.com/sol3/papers.cfm?abstract_id=3126706> accessed 9 September 2019.

92 Wolfgang Wurmnest, *Münchener Kommentar zum BGB* (8th edn, C.H. Beck 2019), § 307 BGB para 1; see above, n. 79.

93 Hayek (n 79).

94 Cf also Heike Schweitzer and Martin Peitz, 'Datenmärkte in der digitalisierten Wirtschaft: Funktionsdefizite und Regelungsbedarf', ZEW Discussion Paper No. 17–043 (2017) 44 <http://ftp.zew.de/pub/zew-docs/dp/dp17043.pdf> accessed 9 September 2019.

95 Paolisa Nebbia, *Unfair Contract Terms in European Law* (Hart 2007) 115, 130f; Wurmnest (n 92) para 13; Stoffels (n 76) 847; cf also Christoph Brömmelmeyer, 'Belohnungen für gesundheitsbewusstes Verhalten in der Lebens- und Berufsunfähigkeitsversicherung? Rechtliche Rahmenbedingungen für Vitalitäts-Tarife' (2017) r + s 225, 231.

ing, a consideration of the context and objectives of the rules at play.[96] From a functional, teleological perspective, the wording of Art 4(2) UCTD must hence be interpreted restrictively: data provided as counter-performance, or clauses permitting such processing, should not be included within the meaning of 'price and remuneration' or 'the main subject matter of the contract'. As a result, the unfairness assessment should extend to clauses stipulating such data transfer. Doctrinally speaking, this means that the declaration of consent relating to such transfers may be scrutinised under the UCTD even if, economically speaking, this consent or the data transfer consented to function as the equivalent of a monetary price.

bb) Broad service obligations

Beyond consent, there is a second way in which data processing may be legitimised in contracts with data as counter-performance. According to Art 6(1)(b) GDPR, processing is lawful if it is necessary for the performance of a contract. Hence, controllers could be tempted to include broad service obligations in their contracts to legitimise subsequent data processing.[97] For example, the provider of a social network could oblige itself vis-à-vis its customers to provide personalised advertising, and to facilitate personalised advertising by other companies. If that provision was valid, all processing activities for personalised advertising could be lawful under Art 6(1)(b) GDPR.[98]

However, precisely for this reason, it is important to complement the GDPR assessment of such broad service obligations with a UCTD assessment. Such clauses should not be considered exempt under Art 4(2) UCTD, either. First, they are often ancillary clauses and therefore do not pertain to the main subject of the contract. While the latter comprises the provision of access to a social network, for example, obligations to provide personalised advertising lie beyond the characteristic obligation of the trader. Second, this matches the fact that the legitimising effect of such a clause, under Art 6(1)(b) GDPR, will generally escape the attention of even rather sophisticated consumers. Therefore, again, competitive forces are likely to fail to attach to this particular nexus of contract and data protec-

96 See, eg, CJEU, Joined Cases C-14/06 and C-295/06 *Parliament/Commission* [2008] ECLI:EU:C:2008:176, para 67.

97 Wendehorst and Graf v. Westphalen (n 81) 3746f.

98 For a suggestion to interpret Art 6(1)(b) GDPR restrictively in this case, see Wendehorst and Graf v. Westphalen (n 81) 3747.

tion law. Hence, the unfairness assessment should apply to these clauses, too.

Importantly, even if the CJEU did decide otherwise, this would not preclude Member States from introducing legislation subjecting the discussed clauses to an unfairness assessment, as the UCTD only provides for minimum harmonisation.[99]

b) *The unfairness yardstick*

Once the unfairness assessment is found to apply, a yardstick must be determined to operationalise this assessment, which requires the finding of a significant contractual imbalance contrary to good faith. This is particularly important in the present context as the CJEU cautioned that one reason for the exemption of the quality/price ratio in Art 4(2) UCTD is the fact that no legal scale or guide for a review of these clauses exists.[100]

aa) Data protection law

The German Federal Court of Justice (BGH) has repeatedly held, before the enactment of the GDPR, that data protection law constitutes the one and only yardstick against which the unfairness of declarations of consent can be measured under the (German transposition of the) UCTD.[101] This would imply that one would need to prove a violation of data protection law to find unfairness under the UCTD. Under the GDPR, however, the relegation of the UCTD to such an ancillary position, merely mirroring data protection law, is incompatible with the explicit requirement, in Recital 42 GDPR, to scrutinise declarations of consent for unfair terms pursuant to the UCTD. If the UCTD only duplicated the GDPR assessment, the reference to it would have been superfluous. The scale against which to measure data transfer clauses is therefore larger than data protection law alone.

---

99 CJEU, Case C-484/08 *Ausbanc* [2010] ECLI:EU:C:2010:309, paras 43f.

100 CJEU, Case C-26/13 *Kásler* [2014] ECLI:EU:C:2014:282, para 55.

101 BGH, Judgment of 16 July 2008, Case VIII ZR 348/06 = (2008) NJW 3055 para 15, 19; BGH, Judgment of 11 November 2009, Case VIII ZR 12/08 = (2010) NJW 864 para 16.

bb) Data protection principles

Still within the realm of data protection law, however, the data protection principles enshrined in Art 5 (1) GDPR as well as the principle of data protection by design and default, Art 25 GDPR, do provide some guidance.[102] As true legal obligations,[103] they constitute the 'backbone of data protection law'.[104] The BGH has held, for the German Data Protection Act preceding the GDPR, that the legislator has opted for a general protection of personal data, and used this orientation to invalidate clauses about unrestricted sharing of credit scores.[105] The same can be said about the principles contained in the GDPR. Therefore, if the principles are violated, this will generally indicate a significant imbalance contrary to good faith.[106]

The interesting question, again, is whether the UCTD can be more restrictive than data protection law on its own. It seems reasonable to assume that, when a clause permitting a certain data processing activity runs counter to a data protection principle, this may provide an indication of a significant contractual imbalance even if that principle is, after due weighting with opposing interests, not explicitly violated. Just like with default rules, what is permitted in individual negotiations under data protection principles may arguably be unlawful when clad in standard forms – precisely because of the market failures described above. In other words, the use of standard terms may tip the balance toward the unlawfulness of the clause. This would mean that, for constellations that constitute borderline cases under the GDPR in terms of the violation of data protection principles, the protection of the data subject is strengthened via the UCTD: the negative implication (even though not necessarily violation) of a data protection principle may count toward the unfairness of the clause legitimising a certain data processing activity.

---

102 Cf, on the latter, Wendehorst and Graf v. Westphalen (n 81) 3749.

103 See Art 83(4)(a) and (5)(a) GDPR.

104 Orla Lynskey, *The Foundations of EU Data Protection Law* (OUP 2015) 35.

105 BGH, Judgment of 9 September 1985, Case III ZR 213/83 = NJW 1986, 46, sub 5.a).

106 Cf also Wurmnest (n 92) para 71; the same holds true for Art 6(1) GDPR, cf, on the pre-GDRP provisions, BGH (n 105); OLG Nürnberg, Judgment of 27 May 1997, Case 3 U 3837/96 = (1997) NJW-RR 1556, sub 4; OLG Düsseldorf, Judgment of 31 October 1996 – Case 6 U 206/95 = (1997) NJW-RR 374, sub II.5.; LG Berlin, Judgment of May 29, 2002, Case 26 O 4/02, BeckRS 2002, 11506, sub I.3.c)aa).

cc) Beyond data protection law

Finally, beyond data protection law, the CJEU has generally ruled that the unfairness assessment may be operationalised by the simulation of a contractual bargaining process. Under this test, a specific clause is deemed unfair[107] if, in a hypothetical bargaining situation in which the consumer deals with the trader, the parties would not have agreed on this clause.[108] While it is often difficult to find the precise result of that hypothetical bargaining process with scientific rigor, it does provide a procedural plausibility test for the unfairness assessment that can be applied to data sharing practices as well.

c) Selected cases

These general considerations shall now be applied to two selected cases: data collection via social plug-ins, and the legitimisation of personalised advertising via broad service obligations.

aa) Data collection via social plug-ins and third-party tracking

The German competition authority has required valid consent for data collection through social plug-ins.[109] Such data collection clearly forms part of the data transfer that constitutes the counter-performance for a number of social networks, such as Facebook. Under the assumption that such consent was validly granted under the GDPR, could that pre-formulated consent, however, be unfair in the sense just expounded?

Generally speaking, the indeterminacy of the value of personal data implies that consumers will face significant difficulties in assessing whether what they provide approximately matches what they gain in terms of value

---

107 More specifically: contrary to the requirement of good faith; cf also Hans-W Micklitz, 'Unfair Terms in Consumer Contracts' in Hans-W Micklitz, Peter Rott and Klaus Tonner (eds), *European Consumer Law* (2nd edn, Intersentia 2014) 125, 152.

108 CJEU, Case C-415/11 *Aziz* [2013] ECLI:EU:C:2013:164, para 69; Joined Cases C-537/12 and C-116/13 *Banco Popular Español* [2013] ECLI:EU:C:2013:759, para 66; Joined Cases C-96/16 and C-94/17 *Banco Santander* [2018] ECLI:EU:C:2018:643, para 63.

109 See above n 49.

or utility. This problem is particularly virulent in the case of data collection via social plug-ins, because consumers are often unaware of the fact that they are being tracked through them even if they do not click on them.[110] On the other hand, it is precisely this wide reach of tracking technology via social plug-ins that conveys the personal data gathered with them a particularly high value.[111]

While the pricing mechanism of the market is likely negatively affected by the use of data instead of money as counter-performance, this does not necessarily imply that a significant contractual imbalance has been created. Rather, in a market economy, courts should be reluctant to proclaim that the price paid for a certain product was objectively too high and hence unbalanced, as the debates surrounding a *iustum pretium* show.[112] Therefore, the judgment of unfairness because of excessive data collection needs to be reserved to extreme cases. Doctrinally, where applicable, it could also fall under the unconscionability doctrine or similar provisions guarding against contracts *contra bonos mores*.[113] This is for national law to determine.[114]

Concerning the line to be drawn for what one might call a 'data-based *laesio enormis*', one proposal would be to distinguish on the basis of the service provided. If the trader offers a functionally significantly complex product, such as access to a social network, even third-party tracking, for example through social plug-ins, should not – in isolation – lead to the finding of a significant imbalance. It cannot be said with sufficient confidence that, in this case, the hypothetical bargaining test would have failed. After all, the consumer receives a complex product in return.

---

110 Cf Case C-40/17 *Fashion ID* [2019] ECLI:EU:C:2018:1039, Opinion of AG Bobek, paras 17, 138.

111 Cf Bundesverband der digitalen Wirtschaft (n 7) 15.

112 See, eg, Reinhard Zimmermann, *The Law of Obligations* (Juta & Co. 1990) 255–270.

113 Thus, under German law, the following distinction should rather be made under the *contra bonos mores* clause of § 138(1) BGB, see Hacker (n 38) 188, 193f; on English law, see Patrick S. Atiyah, 'Contract and Fair Exchange' (1985) 35 The University of Toronto Law Journal 1; on French, US and German law, see James Gordley, 'Equality in Exchange' (1981) 69 Calif. L. Rev. 1587.

114 If a national rule controlling the main subject matter or the adequacy of the quality/price ratio is stricter than the unfairness assessment proposed here, the former would not be precluded by way of primacy of the latter as the UCTD clearly does not regulate these issues exhaustively. If there is no such national rule, the UCTD transposition must be applied in the sense described here.

If, however, the trader merely offers a functionally very limited product – for example an app to activate the flashlight on a smart phone or a background picture app randomising pictures for a screen saver – clauses stipulating wide-ranging third-party tracking should, in general, be held to induce a significant imbalance. In this case, data collection runs counter to the data minimisation principle of Art 5(1)(c) GDPR, but is not matched by the provision of a functionally significant product. While the exact value of personal data is often unclear, courts could even resort to expert testimony to approximate the value of data collected, with the methods mentioned in Part II, in order to compare it with the approximate value of the service provided.[115] If the difference in value is unbearable or if, in case the value cannot be approximated, the dimension of data collection and sharing seems utterly inadequate when compared with the limited functionality of the product offered, it can be concluded that the hypothetical bargaining test would have been failed and that the clause is, therefore, unfair.

While such a 'price control' via the UCTD, or other legal instruments, must remain an exception in a market economy, the unfairness assessment does provide a mechanism to address certain types of clearly excessive data collection and sharing practices in the presence of the market failures discussed above. It should, however, only be invoked if one can be sufficiently confident that the hypothetical bargaining test would have been failed.

bb) Broad service obligations: personalised advertisements

Similarly, courts should not jump to the conclusion that broad service obligations are generically unfair even if they provide leeway for further data processing. Rather, they should only be taken to create a significant imbalance if three criteria are fulfilled.[116] First, the obligation should lack a clear functional nexus with the characteristic obligation of the trader. For example, an obligation to provide personalised advertisements is functionally independent of the obligation to provide access to a social network. Second, the obligation should not bring significant marginal utility to the consumer vis-à-vis standard market practices. In the case of an obligation to personalise advertisements, the customer does not gain anything from such an obligation because advertisements are typically personalised al-

115 To determine the value of this service, one may look at applications that provide a similar service against monetary payment.

116 See also Hacker (n 38) 191.

ready. Third, it must enable further data processing via an invocation of the clause under Art 6(1)(b) GDPR. Again, it can be stipulated that, had the consumer known that the object of the clause was not to provide a better service, but to facilitate additional data processing while the consumer does not gain any significant advantage, she would not have assented to it in a hypothetical bargaining situation.

Interpreted in this way, particularly with the first criterion mentioned, the unfairness assessment of the UCPD mirrors the limits to declarations of consent enshrined in the bundling provision of Art 7(4) GDPR; this is critical, however, because Art 7(4) GDPR does not apply to data processing on the basis of Art 6(1)(b) GDPR. In this sense, the UCTD complements the GDPR by filling a gap in the data protection framework.

d) Consequences

As a result of the violation of the UCTD, the declaration of consent, or the respective contractual clause, is invalid, Art 6(1) UCTD, and cannot constitute a legal basis for processing. However, the outcome of the unfairness assessment will also influence the balancing exercise of Art 6(1)(f) GDPR and, at least potentially, the fair processing principle under Art 5(1)(a) GDPR. While these points deserve further exploration, the upshot seems to be that, in the end, the UCTD and the GDPR will typically go hand in hand in cases of substantive unfairness. However, under the approach proposed here, the direction of inference is reversed: while courts typically argue that a clause violates data protection law and, as a result, also the UCTD,[117] the reasoning works in the inverse sense in the cases contemplated here. Methodologically, this affords the advantage that the hypothetical bargaining test of the UCTD, which provides a rather concrete yardstick, can be applied.

V. Conclusion and outlook: further limits for data as counter-performance?

The beginning of this chapter has shown that personal data diverges in significant respects from money when it is used as counter-performance. Most importantly, while its economic value is strictly positive, that value is highly indeterminate and context-dependent. Consumers involved in data-

117 See references in n 83 and n 86.

for-service trade-offs are therefore arguably not well-positioned to meaningfully evaluate the economic value of their data or to compare different offers made in the 'currency' of personal data. This is why data protection law and general contract law assume a specific importance in these data-based exchanges.

This chapter makes two claims with respect to the interconnection of these legal fields. First, even when the provision of data violates data protection law, that finding should, as a general rule, not bar that data from qualifying as counter-performance under general contract law. Furthermore, such contracts should also fall under the scope of the DCDS Directive to enable consumers to claim the full array of remedies included therein. Second, the indeterminacy of data's economic value is at odds with the pricing mechanism of the market economy. In addition, rational ignorance of privacy policies drives a market failure concerning conditions contained therein. Hence, the UCTD, which is generally not applicable to the price dimension of the contract, should apply when personal data constitutes the main counter-performance.

Functionally interpreted, the UCTD may thus remedy some of the most rampant imbalances in contracts in which data constitute counter-performance. However, courts should in general be cautious to invoke unfairness when it comes to the pricing dimension of a contract: unfairness should only affect a limited number of particularly obvious imbalances. While it does afford some protection to data subjects, the UCTD, or other legal instruments enforcing equality of exchange, do not, therefore, substantially improve the conditions for the sovereign use of data by data subjects in the digital economy.

Transparency of data processing activities is also of limited help to this end, given the – often rational – ignorance of data subjects concerning the exact terms and conditions of processing. What is lacking is a simple format for data subjects to choose between paying for their products through personal data or via monetary payments. Some companies do already offer such differential pricing options that depend, inter alia, on the range of third-party tracking.[118] It would therefore be worthwhile, particularly in the context of the revision of the ePrivacy Regulation, to discuss the introduction of a right to a 'data-free' option of concluding a contract in the

118 See, eg, the tariffs provided by the Washington Post under <https://www.washingtonpost.com/gdpr-consent/> accessed 9 September 2019.

digital economy.[119] This would imply that traders are under an obligation, as a matter of principle, to provide consumers at least the option to pay for the product with their money instead of their data – potentially with two buttons, one for 'paying with money' and one for 'paying with data'.[120] Under the data-free option, data processing activities should be limited to what is strictly necessary for the functioning of the product; Art 6(1)(f) GDPR could generally not be invoked. The estimates for the value of personal data given in Part II suggest that monetary prices need not be prohibitively high. While it can be expected that many consumers would still opt for payment with their data,[121] such a right to a data-free option would respect the privacy preferences of consumers on the other side of the U-shaped distribution: those who value privacy and data protection highly.[122] Only such a real choice, one might argue, befits the pronounced position accorded to data protection and privacy in EU primary law, both under Art 7 and 8 of the Charter of Fundamental Rights and under Art 16 TFEU.

119 See Maximilian Becker, 'Ein Recht auf datenerhebungsfreie Produkte' (2017) Juristenzeitung 170, 175ff; Hacker and Petkova (n 5) 20ff; see also Chris J Hoofnagle and Jan Wittington, 'Free: Accounting for the Costs of the Internet's Most Popular Price' (2014) 61 UCLA Law Review 606, 661f.

120 Cf Arbeitsgruppe 'Digitaler Neustart' der Konferenz der Justizministerinnen und Justizminister der Länder, 'Bericht vom 15. Mai 2017', 2017, 215f.

121 See references in n 25f.

122 See above, text at n 3.

Management as Ownership of Data

Sjef van Erp[*]

I. Introduction

It is often stated that the law is confronted with the consequences of, what are being called, disruptive technologies. But is it really the technology that we are talking about when we use the word 'disruptive' or do we mean the impact of data, data processing, data analysis, data profiling and data transactions, to put it short: the data economy? The technologies referred to are (1) Distributed Ledger Technology, (2) smart contracts, (3) the Internet of Things and (4) Artificial Intelligence. Two other essential elements, not being a technology but closely related and crucial to the functioning of these technologies, are (5) the use of sensors, which collect data about the 'real' world, and (6) the rapidly building up of 'Big Data'. Why are these technologies seen as disruptive? The word 'disruptive' by itself has a negative connotation and seems to imply that nothing good may come out of it. It is typically terminology used by lawyers, who fear that inherited legal systems and well-established legal practices (including the role of legal actors such as advocates and notaries) are at serious risk. The concern is of a mixed nature. Lawyers are worried that the new technologies will upset existing balances of interests, for example in the area of consumer protection. At the same time their concerns are closer to home, as they worry about their own role as such and possible loss of earning capacity if it becomes really true that new technologies might take over (at least some aspects of) their role. Already now it is sometimes being said that Artificial Intelligence is better equipped for contract management than a human being and it is also every so often posited that perhaps various tasks of notaries could be done more efficient and quicker by allowing the use of smart contracts to, e.g., draft a last will.[1]

---

* Professor of Civil Law and European Private Law, University of Maastricht.

1 Cf J Linarelli, 'Advanced Artificial Intelligence and Contract' forthcoming, Uniform Law Review (Special Issues on Transnational Commercial Law and the Technology/Digital Economy, available at SSRN: <https://ssrn.com/abstract=3341307> or <http://dx.doi.org/10.2139/ssrn.3341307> accessed 9 September 2019. An essential aspect of smart contracts is that a 'Trusted Third Party', more particularly a

However the word 'disruptive' is not used by those involved in the actual development of IT. For them this is innovative technology, which brings us as a society further. That lawyers have problems with that technology is seen as a problem for lawyers, and the law. IT is developed from a purely technical viewpoint, almost following the expression: 'If it would have been illegal, it would not have been technically possible' and 'the law is simply an impediment, which needs a work-around'. This is the view of those who are convinced that, indeed, (computer) code is law.[2]

The new technologies can be briefly described in the following way. Distributed Ledger Technology (DLT) is software, which makes it possible to create 'blocks' (also called 'coins' or 'tokens') which contain data that, once the block is created, cannot be changed anymore. The tokens can be of three kinds: (1) payment tokens, (2) utility tokens and (3) asset or security tokens.[3] Payment tokens have the characteristics of currencies, examples are Bitcoin (based on the Bitcoin protocol) and Ether (based on the Ethereum protocol). Utility tokens aim at providing access to a service or application, an example is a token which allows access to personal computing power, which otherwise would have been idle.[4] Asset or security tokens represent 'real' assets. This could be a debt of the issuer, but these to-

---

(Common Law) notary public, will no longer be needed in the fully automated environment which it creates. See N Szabo, 'Smart Contracts: Building Blocks for Digital Markets' (This is a partial rewrite of the article which appeared in Extropy #16), to be found on the Internet: <https://kcl.rl.talis.com/items/BB89B8A9-A075-83DA-B874-A05115BC9B80.html> accessed 9 September 2019.

2 Cf L Lessig, *Code version 2.0* (Basic Books 2006), to be found in digital format at <http://codev2.cc/> accessed 9 September 2019.

3 See T Weingärtner, 'Tokenization of physical assets and the impact of IoT and AI' 5–6, to be found on the website of the EU Blockchain Observatory and Forum (<https://www.eublockchainforum.eu/> accessed 9 September 2019) and Swiss Financial Market Supervisory Authority FINMA, 'Guidelines for enquiries regarding the regulatory framework for initial coin offerings (ICOs)' (published 16 February 2018) 3, available at: <https://www.finma.ch/en/news/2018/02/20180216-mm-ico-wegleitung/> accessed 9 September 2019. An ICO is aimed at obtaining funds by entering into individual contracts with lenders, without making use of the capital markets. If the latter would be the case, the upstart IT company would need to fulfil the stringent requirements as laid down in national, European and international financial rules. In the case of ICO's not a prospectus is issued, but a 'white paper' that describes the aim and goal of the company, its work processes, business opportunities as well as the rights and duties of those providing money. The lenders do not receive a share in the traditional sense of the word, but a 'token' that represents their status as if a shareholder.

4 An example is the Golem network (<https://golem.network/home/> accessed 9 September 2019). Its aim is described as follows: 'Golem is a decentralized market-

kens may also represent physical assets, such as immovable property, and could be used as security. Sometimes tokens are hybrid: an asset token could at the same time be a payment token. Not only is the 'block' immutable, it can also only be traded once by the entity having a right to it, in other words 'double spending' is impossible. A Bitcoin, referring to the for the general public most well-known of these blocks, can only be used for payment once by the entity holding a right to that particular Bitcoin. This is done by having the transaction checked by all computers ('nodes') involved in the network. Such a checking is possible, because every node has a full overview of who has which block under its control and of the various transactions. That is why a parallel is drawn with old-fashioned hand-written ledgers, which also contained a full overview of transactions, but, however, only existed as a single copy. The difference with the old ledgers is, not only of course that the ledger is digital, but also that any computer in the network has a copy. So any node can check whether a Bitcoin has already been used by the entity-transferor or not. If anyone can become involved in the network it is qualified as 'public', if the number of nodes is limited it is qualified as 'private'. Networks can also be qualified as 'permissionless' or 'permissioned', depending on whether everybody is entitled to check or only specific nodes may validate a transaction. Once a transaction took place – by using a smart contract, i.e. a self-executing computer programme – the outcome of the transaction is also stored in a block, which is cryptographically connected with the block that is the object of the transaction, thus creating the chain of blocks.

Connected with Distributed Ledger Technology are smart contracts. The idea behind smart contracts was developed by Nick Szabo.[5] Smart contracts are self-executing programmes, which are stored in a blockchain environment and the outcome of which is also stored in a block. Frequently, these contracts need input of variables about the outside 'real' world. Such – viewed from the smart contract and the connected block chain – external source is called an 'oracle'. These oracles can be human beings

place for computing power. It enables CPUs and GPUs to connect in a peer-to-peer network, enabling both application owners and individual users ("requestors") to rent resources from other users' ("providers") machines. These resources can be used to complete tasks requiring any amount of computation time and capacity. Nowadays, centralized cloud providers are in control of these services, these platforms are constrained by closed networks, proprietary payment systems, and hard-coded provisioning operations. Golem proposes an open-source, decentralized and user-controlled alternative.'

5 N Szabo (n 1).

(judges, notaries, land registrars), but also computer systems. Practical examples can already be found in the insurance industry. The insurance company AXA offers insurance against flight delays. The whole process is done by entering certain information on a special website ('Fizzy'), after which Flightstats checks whether the flight is delayed. If so, the computer system Fizzy will pay the agreed compensation, without human intervention.[6] The Austrian developer of decentralised insurance Etherisc assists insurance companies in offering, for example, crop insurance. Payment of compensation follows upon input based on the amount of rain fallen.[7]

Described as such, these are technologies, nothing more and nothing less. Any qualification could apply, both positive and negative, because every technology has its upsides and downsides. Atomic energy can be used to save lives in a hospital environment, it can provide electricity, but it can also kill people. It all depends upon how technology is applied, and this also concerns Distributed Ledger Technology and smart contracts. The disruptive aspect is both the possibility and the likelihood that we can go even further than we already have done with the creation of a digital ('virtual', but just as real as the 'real') world, thus provoking the existence of two worlds next to one another which constantly interact and intersect. At the heart of this digital world are data. According to the definition of the International Organization for Standardization (ISO): 'Reinterpretable representation of information in a formalized manner suitable for communication, interpretation, or processing.'[8] Data can be information as such (raw data), but it can also be aimed at the process of creating further data (software). The digital world is becoming more and more a reflection of the real world, at the same time it also goes further. It not only connects with the real world by being attached to a carrier (which could be a physical object, but also an animal or even a human being (think of a person's DNA or an implanted chip), but it also may and does provide information about that real world which we otherwise would not know. In other words: our world is becoming hybrid.

The prime example of this phenomenon that we more and more live in a hybrid world is the Internet of Things. More and more physical things only function in combination with software. Examples are self-driving

6 For Fizzy see <https://fizzy.axa/en-gb/> accessed 9 September 2019 ('Your flight is cancelled or is 2h late? Get your money without claiming.').

7 Regarding the services offered by Etherisc see <https://www.etherisc.com/> accessed 9 September 2019.

8 International Organization for Standardization (ISO) definition of data (ISO/IEC 2382-1, revised by ISO/IEC 2382:2015 – Information technology – Vocabulary).

cars, where software is gradually becoming a co-driver. But also a different type of interaction between physical things and software is possible. The central heating system in our homes and the solar panels on our roofs can through apps be connected to the Internet, allowing us from a distance to be informed about what is happening and to communicate with these systems (e.g. turn the central heating system on or off, or change the temperature settings by using an app). It is being said that the Internet of Things now can make a house 'smart', and even that it starts 'thinking', as based on the input of sensors the software will react to changes in the real world and without human interference may react to that change. Sensors play a critical role here, as we are ever more surrounded by them. Everywhere there are public and private camera systems observing us, our gas and electricity meters are now 'smart' so that our gas and electricity companies do not have to send someone to visit our home and check the meter. Apps on our mobile phone (such as provided by Google) trace and track us constantly.[9] The outcome is an already immense and still growing amount of data: Big Data, which is a pool from which the digital reality may be constructed even without the aid of human intervention, made possible by advanced analytic software (machine learning, deep learning and even Artificial Intelligence). What can be concluded, therefore, is that it is not the technology which is disruptive, but the data which this technology enables to discover and create. Data and not the technology should be at the heart of the debate. At the time when the steam engine was invented, steam was seen as disruptive. However, it was not the steam engine as such, but the use that was made of it, resulting in, what we now call, the first Industrial Revolution that disrupted the existing agricultural society. According to the World Economic Forum we are now in the fourth Industrial Revolution, having passed the stage of mass production, computerisation and digitalisation, where we will have to learn how to live in a hybrid world. Will this mean that we will also have to accept a hybrid, i.e. 'real' and 'data', legal system? Does the fact that we are faced with a world of data impose upon us the necessity for a critical and fundamental rethinking and re-evaluating of our traditional law? In the following paragraphs I will try to formulate an answer from the perspective of property law, focussing on the question whether our notion of ownership can survive the data economy.

9 For an overview of sensors in the Dutch city of Eindhoven see the pilot by the Netherlands Cadastre and Mapping Agency, aimed at creating a registry of sensors: <https://www.sensorpilot.nl/> and for Amsterdam see: <https://slimmeapparaten.amsterdam.nl/> both accessed 9 September 2019.

Do we still need the notion of 'ownership' to describe the entitlement of a subject vis-à-vis a relevant and considerable group of other subjects regarding data, or would it be sufficient, perhaps even: unavoidable, to accept that data are without an owner in the traditional sense of the legal term?[10] If data are 'ownerless', can they still be accessed, controlled, ported and erased? Perhaps the best description might then be that we manage 'our' data and that data ownership is data management.

II. A hybrid private law

Arguing that traditional private law is in a 'crisis' will not help us much further. In the past contract law was in a crisis (the 'death' of contract law, but contract law is still developing well) and some may argue that ownership is in a crisis. What we see is a revisiting of an age-old notion in light of new developments. This is not a crisis, but we have to rethink existing law in light of the particular nature, growing amount and enormous impact of data. Furthermore, it is not traditional private law that might be in a crisis, but lawyers are. The existing law no longer gives them the full support they need to solve problems and this loss of certainty makes them feel uneasy and creates an atmosphere of antagonism towards the data economy. In that atmosphere of rejection we see, on the one hand, a clear focus on the status and role of the subject in a digital world. The fear is growing that subjects are losing their personhood and are no longer being valued as the person who they are, but are being reduced to what data tell about them. It is dreaded that subjects become objects of data mining, research

10 The academic debate is intensifying. Among many other publications I refer to A Boerding, N Culik, Chr Doepke, Th Hoeren and T Juelicher, 'Data Ownership—A Property Rights Approach from a European Perspective' [2018] Journal of Civil Law Studies, available at: <https://digitalcommons.law.lsu.edu/jcls/vol11/iss2/5> accessed 9 September 2019; V Janeček, 'Ownership of personal data in the Internet of Things' [2018] Computer Law & Security Review 1039ff and JD Michels and Chr Millard, 'Mind the Gap: The Status of Digital Files Under Property Law', available at SSRN: <https://ssrn.com/abstract=3387400> accessed 9 September 2019; M Lehmann, 'Who Owns Bitcoin? Private Law Facing the Blockchain', forthcoming, Minnesota Journal of Law, Science &Technology, available at SSRN: <https://ssrn.com/abstract=3402678> accessed 9 September 2019. See also the illuminating study about the various questions on data ownership in the area of precision farming, published by the European Parliament: M Kritikos, 'Precision agriculture in Europe: Legal, social and ethical considerations' (European Union 2017), 16ff and 39ff.

and targeting. There is, of course, some truth here. When Google, Facebook and others collect data about us, the final analysis of these data is aimed at targeting us with specific other data, for example inviting us to buy certain goods or services or to support certain (political) views. We are targeted to buy goods or services, because, at the end of the day, we are still legal subjects which have a patrimony. This patrimony consists of assets which we can spend, but the existence of a patrimony also makes it possible to hold us liable. It creates the impression as if we are only legal subjects when it comes to spending our patrimony. Because following this view data are almost seen as a threat to personhood and therefore close to a denial of fundamental human rights, the acceptance of data as being part of precisely that same person's patrimony (and therefore can be considered a tradable asset, as if it were a commodity) is nearly intolerable. This explains why privacy lawyers consider the suggestion that data can be 'owned' as unacceptable. But not only privacy lawyers have that view. Also private lawyers share that approach, but for very different reasons. For private lawyers it is the very nature of data as a legal object that is highly problematic. Data exist as bits and bytes on carriers and need other data (software) to be made understandable. These carriers can be physical (USB sticks, hard disk drives, servers), they can be animals (tags, implanted chips) and even human beings (medical devices, such as a pacemaker, and also implanted chips). Could and should we separate the legal status of data from the carrier? Does not ownership of a physical carrier or animal imply ownership of everything on or in it? Is not the pacemaker or chip part of your body and is not, for that reason alone, ownership a non-issue? Furthermore, data are not only intangible, they are also non-rivalrous (they can be copied), fluid and can be moved effortlessly from one carrier to another, while crossing borders. Traditional private lawyers will also argue that property rights in data – if at all accepted – can only be found in the law of intellectual property: copyright and rights related to copyright ('neighbouring rights' of, e.g., performers) and industrial property rights (trademarks, logos, patents and designs), to which can be added the law protecting trade secrets.

The difficulty with both approaches – the privacy approach and the traditional private law approach – is that the IT developments described above have resulted in the existence of an already vast amount of data and which is still growing at an exponential rate. These data are continuously processed, analysed and transferred. The resulting digital economy has simply become a fact of life. The law is already lagging behind and arguing that data are outside the realm of private law will only result in leaving the legal developments to global market forces and to what some call 'might is right': whoever controls the data on its servers decides who has which right (if any). In my view it is, for that reason, more than understandable that the European legislator has accepted that data can be used as a counter performance. I refer to Directive (EU) 2019/770 of the European Parliament and of the Council of 20 May 2019 on certain aspects concerning contracts for the supply of digital content and digital services, stating in article 2(7) that "price' means money or a digital representation of value that is due in exchange for the supply of digital content or a digital service'.[11]

The collection, processing, analysis and use of data is here to stay and so is the data economy. What we should analyse is whether the existing legal system can incorporate in itself data as a new legal object. Such critical rethinking, delineating where traditional private law no longer provides sufficient and adequate answers and where data private law begins, must be aimed at taking the existing rules with their inherent and inherited balances of interests as a starting point. Wherever existing law can solve problems regarding the data economy, albeit perhaps with some adaptation, this would promote the stable, balanced and fair development of both the law and the digital economy. If the existing law is not able to solve a particular problem, we should start developing new approaches, but as much as possible built upon the pillars which form the foundation of our present legal system. Comparative analysis in the area of property law has, for example, shown that property law systems, irrespective of their further historical development, are built upon certain values (such as long term stability and legal certainty), policy choices (e.g. promoting the protection of commerce), leading principles (an example is the numerus clausus of property rights) and ground rules (for instance the *nemo plus/nemo dat* rule). As a working hypothesis, to avoid that the debate goes in all directions and does not result in a pragmatic agreement on practically useful results, we should start from these building blocks. Furthermore we should work to-

---

11 OJ 22.5.2019, L 136/1. In its consideration (24) the tension between the privacy approach and the more pragmatic and functional approach of the directive becomes very clear. The consideration reads in part: 'Digital content or digital services are often supplied also where the consumer does not pay a price but provides personal data to the trader. Such business models are used in different forms in a considerable part of the market. While fully recognising that the protection of personal data is a fundamental right and that therefore personal data cannot be considered as a commodity, this Directive should ensure that consumers are, in the context of such business models, entitled to contractual remedies. This Directive should, therefore, apply to contracts where the trader supplies, or undertakes to supply, digital content or a digital service to the consumer, and the consumer provides, or undertakes to provide, personal data.'.

wards cross-border solutions. Data are by definition fluid and any attempt to promote (or perhaps even impose) national solutions will create tensions in an environment where data escape from the traditional control of states invoking their sovereign rights. We should remember how IT developers look at the law and at legal solutions they find unworkable: the law will then, indeed, be nothing else but an obstacle that needs a work-around. Therefore stating that German law might be a good model, as it has the strictest rules on when someone can 'own' something, or the English approach that we perhaps should wait for the development of case-law or the approach that before we can act at a practical level we need theoretical underpinnings all seem to me unrealistic. Technology follows its own path and lawyers must, first of all, understand that path before they start arguing from preconceived ideas about how that path should be. I can, therefore, understand Lehmann when he writes: 'Law and technology must neither ignore or fight each other. They should live in a symbiosis, with each leaving to the other its own field of competence.'[12] We need to look for a pragmatic solution, avoiding dogmatic trenches, while respecting different legal cultures.

Given the area we are discussing any solution must be sufficiently dynamic to cope with a constantly changing IT environment. Data is such a disruptive new legal object that it requires its own legal analysis and the development of a hybrid private law: next to traditional private law a data private law. Until now the debate has focussed on whether data can be 'owned'. It has led to a fierce debate about the legal qualification of data in light of its nature, but particularly in light of an ideological debate about the ambit of fundamental human rights vis-à-vis market oriented private law, and against the background of the author's legal tradition from which the question is perceived. A public lawyer is inclined to argue that ownership of data is an unacceptable notion, because it denies the vital importance of relevant fundamental human rights. Article 8 of the EU Charter of Fundamental Rights states that everyone 'has the right to the protection of personal data ,concerning him or her' and that such data 'must be processed fairly for specified purposes and on the basis of the consent of the person concerned or some other legitimate basis laid down by law', to which is added that everyone 'has the right of access to data which has been collected concerning him or her, and the right to have it rectified'.

12 M Lehmann, 'Who Owns Bitcoin? Private Law Facing the Blockchain', forthcoming, Minnesota Journal of Law, Science &Technology, available at SSRN: <https://ssrn.com/abstract=3402678> accessed 9 September 2019, 19.

However, what about protection of property? Also this is a fundamental human right, according to article 17 of the EU Charter, stating that everyone 'has the right to own, use, dispose of and bequeath his or her lawfully acquired possessions' and that no one 'may be deprived of his or her possessions, except in the public interest and in the cases and under the conditions provided for by law, subject to fair compensation being paid in good time for their loss', to which is added that the 'use of property may be regulated by law in so far as is necessary for the general interest'. Protecting privacy through public law means, such as in particular the EU General Data Protection Regulation, is an expression of the right to be protected regarding your personal data. But this does not exclude, from the viewpoint of the EU Charter, that these data at the same time could be 'owned'. This would justify why, whenever personal data are being used with consent or when it concerns non-personal data, these may be traded in and become part of the digital economy. It must additionally be realised that without some (private law) entitlement to these data such transactions would not have an object. The essential question here is whether that entitlement should be qualified as a right governed by public law (comparable to a public law license), with its own public law rules, or governed by private law. If we follow the human rights analysis, entitlement to personal data should be qualified as being of a public law nature and non-personal data of a private law nature, assuming that personal and non-personal data can be separated clearly and that no co-generation will happen. The latter could prove to be a grave mistake and would complicate matters even more.

Consent to use personal data would then also be governed by public law and its impact on private law would be uncertain. If consent is withdrawn, does this mean that any contracts regarding personal data are without an object and, consequently, invalid? Almost like the withdrawing of a public law license after it has been legally transferred. But the debate does not end here. Whenever the entitlement is qualified as being of a private law nature, it is questioned whether the source of such entitlement is contract law or property law. But if it is contract law, we must assume that we conclude a contract about something. Data do not come into existence because we can show an end-user license agreement. Data is pre-existent to contracts, we are concluding contracts about data, not creating them as such by contract, although by contract we can shape the types of data which the agreement is about. So the really fundamental question is how to qualify the entitlement to data from the perspective of property law.

III. Data property law: management as ownership

Property law is characterised by three leading principles: numerus clausus, transparency and hierarchy. Numerus clausus refers to the limited number and content of property rights. We only accept certain by the law explicitly prescribed rights as being effective against everyone else, or at least against a considerable and relevant group of third parties; these rights can only have a certain, well-described content. Transparency implies that property entitlements, given their strong character, must be made known to relevant third parties. This requires, first of all, that the object of the property right is certain (specificity requirement) and that information is provided about the legal status of the object (publicity). It also requires a balancing act between the necessary transparency from a property law viewpoint and protection of privacy from the perspective of public law and the protection of fundamental human rights. Publicity may result from possession of objects, but also frequently from registration of objects and rights. Another leading principle of property law is hierarchy. Because property rights can be invoked against third parties, a hierarchy exists to establish which right, in case of conflicts between several property rights, comes first. These principles bring with them that, in order to analyse which property rights (in particular what type of primary, i.e. maximum, right) can exist regarding data, we must first look at the numerus clausus principle, then at transparency and hierarchy.

Let us, therefore, begin with the numerus clausus principle. What was not realised until the Digital Revolution was that at the heart of the numerus clausus principle are not only property rights as such, but also the possible objects of these rights. There is also a numerus clausus of legal objects. From a comparative viewpoint two examples can be given here. The German Civil Code (BGB) defines in its § 903 ownership as follows: 'The owner of a thing may, to the extent that a statute or third-party rights do not conflict with this, deal with the thing at his discretion and exclude others from every influence.' § 90 BGB then defines a 'thing' as follows: 'Only corporeal objects are things as defined by law'.[13] In other words, the object is part of the definition of ownership and qualifies the content and ambit of that right. If we want to find different exclusive rights which also confer upon its holder (the maximum of) rights, privileges, powers and immunities, to use Hohfeldian terminology, we need to take a different object as

13 For an English translation of the German Civil Code see <https://www.gesetze-im-internet.de/englisch_bgb/englisch_bgb.pdf> accessed 9 September 2019.

our starting point.[14] Monetary claims, for example, cannot be 'owned', but you can be 'entitled' to these and consequently, according to § 398 BGB, such claims can be transferred and (§ 1273) used as security for a loan, not unlike physical objects. The Common Law tradition shows a comparable approach. The maximum right regarding land and buildings is, according to s 1(1)(a) of the Law of Property Act 1925, the estate in fee simple absolute in possession ('freehold'). Regarding movables and claims, however, the maximum right is 'title', the strongest right to possession.[15] In all legal systems the creative expressions of the human mind are, because of their non-physical and unique nature, protected in the law of intellectual property. These objects receive their own specific treatment.

By their very nature data are non-physical and, consequently, must be excluded from traditional definitions of ownership which have physical objects as their qualifier. Data sometimes fall in the category of intellectual property, but frequently do not. Copyright may exist regarding software, but most data (such as raw data) are not protected by any form of intellectual property rights. If you cannot own data, are our traditional notions of possession perhaps open to accepting that you can 'possess' data? This will prove to be difficult if a legal system does not accept ownership of intangibles or rights. Besides that, also from a comparative viewpoint it must be remarked that possession is not a universally clear a-priori concept. In German law a distinction is made between possession for yourself (*Eigenbesitz*) and possession for someone else (*Fremdbesitz*), which distinction is not to be found in French law that distinguishes between possession as holding a thing for yourself (*possession*) and holding it for someone else (*détention*). Perhaps we should give up looking for the possibility to qualify any primary right regarding data as ownership (or, for that matter, possession) and accept that data are, from a more traditional legal viewpoint, ownerless. It sounds somewhat radical and perhaps even contradictory in light of my arguments against a strict public law approach and in favour of a private, market based approach. Does this mean that data are there for anybody to use? This certainly does not have to be so and we can find an example how to deal with this in the Québec law of trusts, which is now also influencing

14 WN Hohfeld, 'Some fundamental legal conceptions as applied in judicial reasoning' [1913] Yale Law Journal 16ff and 'Fundamental legal conceptions as applied in judicial reasoning II' [1917] Yale Law Journal 710ff.

15 Cf A Rahmatian, 'A comparison of German moveable property law and English personal property law' [2008] Journal of Comparative Law 197ff.

the developments in Europe, because it became the model for the law of trust in the Czech Republic.[16]

A Common Law (express) trust is a tripartite engagement between a settlor, who creates the trust, a trustee who becomes the 'owner' of the trust property and a beneficiary who takes the economic advantages of the property managed by the trustee. Once the trust has been created, the settlor is no longer involved, only the trustee and the beneficiary. The position of the trustee is governed by the Common Law in a strict sense, the position of the beneficiary is ruled by Equity. From a Civil Law viewpoint the outcome is that the Common Law tradition accepts two degrees of ownership (ownership then defined as the maximum of rights, privileges, powers and immunities a person can have over an object), depending upon the interest of the parties involved. The trustee is legal owner, the beneficiary is economic owner. After the French Revolution the Civil Law tradition rejects degrees of ownership, only recognises unitary ownership (one owner, who has all rights etc. over an object) and, directly connected with this, applies a strict numerus clausus of property rights to avoid that by creating new secondary (i.e. less than ownership) rights the unitary concept of ownership would be undermined. Before the French Revolution also the Civil Law tradition accepted differing degrees of ownership: the *dominium directum* of the feudal lord and the *dominium utile* of those actually living on the land. Given the direct connection with the feudal system, continental property law systems are almost built to avoid the re-creation of such split ownership, as no one wants a return to a society in which you might be obliged to give something to someone else only because you lived, worked and profited from the land to which that other person had *dominium directum*. Positive land burdens are no longer allowed. As a consequence civil lawyers feel a deep resistance against accepting degrees of ownership. The resistance also seems to come from the need to distinguish itself from the Common Law tradition (a feeling which is very strong in a jurisdiction such as Québec, which is integrated in a Canadian and US economy that has the Common Law as its prime legal framework) and a deep rooted fear to return to pre-French Revolutionary property law with feudal characteristics and a semi-closed list of property rights. Given regional and global

16 See A Popovici, 'Trust in Quebec and Czech Law: Autonomous Patrimonies?' [2016] European Review of Private Law 929ff. Cf for a brief overview of developments in Eastern European countries: I Gvelesiani, 'The development of "trust-like" mechanisms in today's Bulgaria, the Czech Republic and Romania' in I Dodovski et al (eds), *The Europe of Tomorrow: Creative, Digital, Integrated* (University American College Skopje 2014) 333ff.

economic integration, and accepting that data easily flow across borders, I think that the latter (i.e. need for distinction) argument against accepting degrees of ownership should be set aside immediately. Economic integration will put pressure on legal systems to grow closer in areas important for international trade. Some adaptation and convergence will be necessary and unavoidable. We see this in the mixed jurisdiction of Québec, where accepting some form of trust law became inevitable. The first-mentioned (i.e. legal-historical) argument against accepting differing degrees of ownership is also untenable. It is very well possible to re-introduce various types of ownership without re-creating the feudal system. Again, Québec trust law is a good example, although it went even further than only this. It introduced management as ownership, where no one is owner in the classical French legal sense of the word. Ownership is a fluid notion, able to adapt itself to changing circumstances and show a revolutionary evolution.[17]

Let me discuss the Québec trust in more detail, to clarify my argument. The Québec trust is a 'fund' without legal personality and is qualified as a *patrimoine d'affectation autonome*.[18] There is a settlor, trustee (manager) and beneficiary, but no one 'owns'. This is expressed in article 1278 of the Québec Civil Code, which reads: 'Le fiduciaire a la maîtrise et l'administration exclusive du patrimoine fiduciaire et les titres relatifs aux biens qui le composent sont établis à son nom; il exerce tous les droits afférents au patrimoine et peut prendre toute mesure propre à en assurer l'affectation. Il agit à titre d'administrateur du bien d'autrui chargé de la pleine administration.' In other words: the trustee is managing a fund, which does not have legal personality, and which he represents as manager (not as owner) for the benefit of beneficiaries, who are also not the owner. These ideas go

17 S van Erp, 'Fluidity of ownership and the tragedy of hierarchy. A sign of a revolutionary evolution?' [2015] European Property Law Journal 56ff.

18 Cf for an introduction in the Québec trust: R Becker, *Die fiducie von Québec und der Trust. Ein Vergleich mit verschiedenen Modellen fiduziarischer Rechtsfiguren im Civil Law* (Mohr Siebeck 2007). See also AJ McClean, 'The Quebec Trust: Role Rich and Principle Poor? Fourth Wainwright Lecture' [1984] McGill Law Journal 312ff; JEC. Brierley, 'Regards sur le droit des biens dans le nouveau Code civil du Québec' [1995] Revue Internationale de Droit Comparé 33ff; LD Smith, 'Trust and Patrimony' [2008] Revue Générale de Droit 379ff; Y Emerich, 'Les fondements conceptuels de la fiducie française face au trust de la common law: entre droit des contrats et droit des biens' [2009] Revue Internationale de Droit Comparé 49ff.

back to the French author Lepaulle.[19] In essence the approach taken comes down to accepting that not all property needs a person entitled to unitary ownership, as long as it is clear who has the power to manage such property and for whose benefit such management should take place.

Thinking along these lines and taken into consideration the nature of data it might, therefore, not be an unworkable idea to abandon any attempt at arguing against or in favour of data 'ownership' in the traditional sense of the legal term – where already much confusion exists from a comparative law perspective – and search for a more dynamic and pragmatic approach based on finding the relevant characteristics of entitlements to data. When ownership of data is being discussed, we should take into account the nature of the object concerned, as it this object that qualifies the right. What we mean is: access, control (exclusion), portability and erasure, in other words: management. Managing data can be done at various levels. When it comes to personal data we assume that the data subject is very well able to manage those data, although we have set up a fairly extensive public law framework to regulate such management by providing rules on processing and control in the EU Data Protection Regulation. But even regarding personal data we have to accept that others may also be in control by persons whom we, remarkably enough, call 'controller'. In the words of article 4(7) of the GDPR: '"controller" means the natural or legal person, public authority, agency or other body which, alone or jointly with others, determines the purposes and means of the processing of personal data; where the purposes and means of such processing are determined by Union or Member State law, the controller or the specific criteria for its nomination may be provided for by Union or Member State law'. The GDPR also distinguishes the role of 'processor', defined in article 4(8) GDPR as 'a natural or legal person, public authority, agency or other body which processes personal data on behalf of the controller'. So even with regard to data outside the scope of the framework for the free flow of non-personal data, EU law makes a distinctions between various types of man-

19 See for an overview of Lepaulle's ideas A Popovici and LD Smith, 'Lepaulle appropriated' in R Valsan (ed), *Trusts and Patrimonies* (Edinburgh University Press 2015) 13ff, where they offer a translation of the first chapter of Lepaulle's treatise from 1932 entitled 'Traité théorique et pratique des trusts en droit interne, en droit fiscal et en droit international'. See also P Lepaulle, 'Civil law substitutes for trusts' [1927] Yale Law Journal 1126ff; and P Lepaulle, 'Trusts and the Civil Law' [1933] Journal of Comparative Legislation and International Law 18ff.

agers with various rights.[20] In that setting and from that perspective, data is 'ownerless', but that does not mean that no one is managing and that we cannot speak of management as ownership.

IV. Concluding remarks

The debate about data ownership has not, so far, brought us very far. The private law debate is characterised by strong dogmatic discussions, based on 19th century legal concepts. We must accept that next to the real world as we know it, we now also live in a digital world and that these two worlds mix, thus creating a hybrid reality. What does this mean for our traditional views on the three basic pillars of property law: subjects, objects and legal relations between these subjects regarding objects? I leave aside the debate whether next to natural and legal persons we should accept e(lectronic)-personality, thus accepting that artificial intelligent software (acting, e.g., through robots) might be seen as a legal subject. My focus is on the question which assets the law should include in its numerus clausus of legal objects. Or, to put it differently, which assets belong to a person's patrimony, can data be such an asset and which entitlements can a legal subject have regarding data? A patrimony is a person's reflection in the world outside that person. Whether a person can have different types of patrimony is crucial to accepting differing degrees of ownership, as 'ownership' (more generally: property rights) are qualified by the object of that right. For a common lawyer this is obvious: the trustee is owner at Common Law, the beneficiary is owner in Equity and the trustee must, therefore, keep the trust property separate from his other assets as these are not limited by Equity. For a civil lawyer this is far more difficult to accept. However, if a legal subject owns property partly for himself and partly for someone else, this cannot but cause differing degrees of ownership with it. Owning for someone else brings with it more limited rights, privileges, powers and immunities than owning for yourself. We can try to hide this, but arguing that the trustee is still owner in the classical Civil Law sense of the word and that his position is merely limited by contractual and/or legal obligations is looking for dogmatically correct answers, not answers which would be more workable in practice. This become particularly clear

20 Regulation (EU) 2018/1807 of the European Parliament and of the Council of 14 November 2018 on a framework for the free flow of non-personal data in the European Union, OJ L303/59, 28.11.2018.

if in the Civil Law these contractual and/or legal obligations are given third party effect to protect the beneficiary. We are then very close to accepting that ownership as management is not the same as ownership plain and simple. The debate about again accepting degrees of ownership in the Civil Law should not be ideological, aimed at preserving dogmatic purity or a denial of economic reality, but functional and pragmatic. Otherwise we will never be able to adequately protect those who we consider to be entitled to access, control, port and erase data.

In the old real world we already accepted that certain intangibles and creations of the human mind – at least from a functional viewpoint and looking at characteristics and not abstract notions – could be treated almost in the same way as physical objects but taking into account their different nature. A monetary claim is not the same as a parcel of land, neither is a novel. Data are not the same as physical objects, monetary claims or creations of the human mind. Data are connected to the physical world, as they need a carrier, but they cannot be identified with that carrier. Therefore arguing that the owner of the carrier is owner of the data implies a fundamental mix-up of two objects, one of which is a qualifier for the definition of ownership (the physical carrier) and the other one is neither a physical object, nor qualifies as an object of any intellectual property right. Data are further connected with the physical world through the Internet of Things: physical objects which either need software to function or produce data which is then processed and analysed. But again the physical thing must be distinguished from the data, because these are very different legal objects.

Data are so fundamentally different from any object which we recognised so far as belonging to the numerus clausus of legal objects that we also need to reconsider deeply which rights may exist regarding such data. We need to accept that, upon in-depth functional analysis, we already accept various degrees of ownership, depending on the object concerned: physical, intangible, human creativity. As to data the degree of ownership we should try to understand is management, as the expression of access, control, portability and erasure. Conceptually we can find support for such an approach in the analysis of the Québec trust with its ownerless property, although the trust property is not without management as ownership.

Data Extra Commercium

Václav Janeček[*] / *Gianclaudio Malgieri*[**]

I. Introduction

Law permits trade in data, so it seems that data are *res in commercio*.[1] In this chapter, we argue that commerce in some data is, and should be, prohibited by the law (*data extra commercium*) because some data embody values and interests that would be detrimentally affected by trade. We devise the term *data extra commercium* to disambiguate data from other objects of trade and from the concept of *res extra commercium*. Unlike in the case of traditional goods (*res*), inalienability of data cannot be ascertained *ex-ante* because the question of whether or not a particular dataset represents values and interests that can be compromised by commerce is not a question about a static property of the dataset. The fluid nature of data implies that their alienability can be limited even *ex-post*. For example, if a data subject withdraws her consent in relation to processing of personal data (Article 7(3) GDPR) or if an algorithm derives some personal information from the dataset, the properties of those datasets, and consequently their legal status, change dynamically.

This phenomenon of dynamic (in)alienability of data means that we cannot normally assert that data are *res in commercio* or *res extra commercium*. At best, we can assert that their alienability is 'dynamically limited'. The Roman law concept of *res extra commercium*, although inspiring in relation to trade in data, cannot account for the fluid nature of data and the infosphere, as is argued in Section II which also explains the Roman law concept. The dynamic understanding of data (in)alienability helps to ex-

---

* University of Oxford, St Edmund Hall and the Faculty of Law; <vaclav.janecek@law.ox.ac.uk>.

** Free University of Brussels (VUB), Law, Science, Technology & Society (LSTS) Research Group; <Gianclaudio.Malgieri@vub.be>.

1 See, eg, A De Franceschi, 'European Contract Law and the Digital Single Market: Current Issues and New Perspectives' in A De Franceschi (ed), *European Contract Law and the Digital Single Market: The Implications of the Digital Revolution* (Intersentia 2016) 5: 'In the digital world, data are in fact an important *res intra commercium*, namely tradeable good'.

plain why the law sometimes treats data as *extra commercium* and thereby protects certain values and interests. We give examples of these legal rules in Section III. Yet it also invites practical difficulties that neither the existing law nor the literature addresses. For instance, it is difficult to ascertain when data qualify objectively as *data extra commercium* for the purposes of legal sanctions such as nullity or partial ineffectiveness of contracts, and for the purposes of remedies such as restitution or damages. We propose a two-stage test to help overcome these difficulties in the context of civil litigation (Section IV) and in the context of automated and autonomous trading systems (Section V), where the concept of *data extra commercium* is likely to have important practical significance.

Overall, our main original claims are that data are subject to a *dynamically limited alienability rule* and that responsibility for the consequences of inalienability of data can be determined using the two-stage test that we propose. We argue that *data extra commercium* is a useful dynamic concept that helps protect certain values and interests in the infosphere and that can be employed in traditional European contract law.

For reasons set out below, we restrict this chapter to questions of when and how we should protect some data. In contrast, we do not look at how we should protect parties if their contract is negatively affected by data protection tools (ie what remedies should be available to them). For reasons also set out below, we focus primarily on trade regarding personal data and other sensitive data.

II. From res extra commercium to data extra commercium

The civil (Roman) law protected multiple types of thing (*res*) by excluding them from commerce (*extra commercium*). The commercial inalienability of these things was entrenched in values and interests that *res extra commercium* embodied. Accordingly, Roman law prohibited trade in free humans (*liberi homines*),[2] things of divine interest (*res divini iuris*),[3] and things of

2 Dig.18.1.4–6pr., Dig.18.1.34.2, Dig.18.1.70; Inst.III.23.5. But see Cod.4.43.2, allowing parents in extreme poverty to sell their child immediately upon birth.

3 These included temples, shrines, sacred groves (*res sacrae*), tombs, burial-grounds, funerary urns (*res religiosae*), or things under the protection of a deity or of deities, such as the walls or gates of cities (*res sanctae*). See Inst.II.1.7–10; G.II.5–6; Inst.III.23.5; Dig.11.7.8.1; Dig.18.1.4; Dig.18.1.22–23; Dig.18.1.62.1. See also JB Moyle, *The Contract of Sale in the Civil Law* (Clarendon Press 1892) 19; JAC Thomas, 'The Sale of *Res Extra Commercium*' (1976) CLP 136, 137; R Evans-Jones

secular public interest (*res publicae*).[4] These categories evoke some strong parallels with the recent prohibitions regarding human trafficking,[5] trade in human organs,[6] trade in some religious and cultural artefacts,[7] unlicensed commerce in publicly dangerous or invaluable things,[8] or traffic in publicly important things which are either considered common to everyone or that belong to no-one.[9]

A purported sale of any of these three categories of thing was first deemed void[10] as legally impossible, except where the purchaser, without fault on his part, was unaware of their real nature.[11] The tendency to protect the buyer is understandable as 'it can be difficult to distinguish a free

---

and G MacCormack, 'The Sale of res extra commercium in Roman Law' (1995) ZRG Rom Abt 330, 342.

4 Thomas (n 3) fn 6 gives examples of 'buildings the sale of which for demolition might produce speculative profits [... or the sale of] noxious poisons' (referring to Dig.18.1.52; Dig.18.1.35.2; Dig.39.2.48). Elsewhere, Thomas notices that although it is clear that traffic in public property which is destined for public use is forbidden, 'no text deals with *res publicae* in isolation' from other types of things extra commerce (ibid 138). This makes the category relatively hard to distinguish from things of divine interest.

5 eg the Protocol to Prevent, Suppress and Punish Trafficking in Persons, Especially Women and Children of 2000, supplementing the United Nations Convention against Transnational Organized Crime.

6 eg the Council of Europe Convention against Trafficking in Human Organs (CETS No 216) of 25 March 2015.

7 eg UNESCO Convention on the Means of Prohibiting and Preventing the Illicit Import, Export and Transfer of Ownership of Cultural Property of 1970. See also W Kowalski, 'Trust and *res extra commercium*. In search of legal instruments to strengthen the protection of cultural heritage' in M Habdas and A Wudarski (eds), *Ius est ars boni et aequi* (Peter Lang 2010) 227 and 233 (highlighting public interest in cultural objects); K Kuprecht, 'The concept of "cultural affiliation" in NAGPRA: its potential and limits in the global protection of indigenous cultural property rights' (2012) IJCP 33, 34, 36–37, 42, 51 (commenting on the Native American Graves Protection and Repatriation Act 1990 (United States)).

8 eg the Single Convention on Narcotic Drugs of 1961 (United Nations); the Convention on International Trade in Endangered Species of Wild Fauna and Flora (CITES) of 1973; the Arms Trade Treaty of 2013 (United Nations).

9 eg the Treaty on Principles Governing the Activities of States in the Exploration and Use of Outer Space 1967 (United Nations). See also ZA Paliouras, 'The non-appropriation principle: the Grundnorm of international space law' (2014) LJIR 37, 41.

10 Dig.18.1.34.1: '[...] earum nulla venditio est'.

11 Dig.19.1.4. See also Moyle (n 3) 19; Thomas (n 3) 138–39.

man from a slave'.[12] It is also understandable to consider the buyer's fault, because 'even the greenest provincial on his first visit to the mother city could [not] honestly believe that he could take effective possession [...] of, say, the Temple of Venus or the *Porta Capena* or, turning to *res publicae*, of the Theatre of Pompey or the *Via Sacra*'.[13]

Eventually, the various rules have been compiled into a specific provision of Justinian's *Institutes* (Inst.III.23.5), according to which a person who, in full awareness of the facts, bought a thing in which trade is forbidden, bought in vain and his contract was void. Yet if the purchase was based on the seller's fraud, deception or (even innocent) misrepresentation,[14] the law granted the buyer a remedy in damages for mischiefs such as eviction, confiscation and misapprehension induced by the seller. To the extent that these remedies were conditioned on a breach of contract, the jurists were pressured not to deem the contract void, but this required an exception to be made to the general rule that fraud renders a contract void *ab initio*.[15]

Recent EU laws and other legal rules also protect certain types of valuable assets by excluding them from commerce. We focus on data. The laws regarding data and digital content seem to exclude (although somewhat ambiguously) some data types from commerce, as we will show in Section III. Thus, it looks as if, effectively, some types of *data*—due to characteristics of the information they embody—cannot be the subject of a sale contract (*extra commercium*) similarly to how Roman law prohibited trade in certain types of thing. Yet as we have seen in the introduction, trade in data (unlike trade in material objects) poses some very challenging questions. In particular, it seems that we need to think dynamically about the values and interests that the data represent, and it is unclear what implications this may have for validity of contracts and availability of contractual remedies in relation to *data extra commercium*. Let us start investigating these issues in relation to personal data.

The parallels between *res extra commercium* and our proposed concept of *data extra commercium* look particularly strong in the case of free humans

---

12 Dig.18.1.5: 'Quia difficile dinosci potest liber homo a servo.' See also E Metzger, 'Remarks on David Daube's Lectures on Sale, with Special Attention to the *liber homo* and *res extra commercium*' in E Metzger (ed), *David Daube: A Centenary Celebration* (Traditio Iuris Romani 2010).

13 Thomas (n 3) 139.

14 Innocent deception incurred milder redress (cf Thomas (n 3) 138 and Dig.18.1.45; Dig.19.1.13pr.–4).

15 Evans-Jones and MacCormack (n 3) 350.

and personal data. Illicit trade in free humans (unlike trade in things of divine or public interest) was allegedly an increasingly common source of practical trouble in Roman times,[16] which seems parallel to recent illicit handling of personal data by tech-giants such as Facebook.[17] Also, in Roman times, free individuals were not 'things' in legal sense just as data are not considered to be 'things' in many jurisdictions.[18] Finally, the distinction between a slave and a free individual is epistemically obscure, just as there is no clear line between non-personal and personal data.[19] Both a slave and a free individual are humans, although they embodied different values in Roman law. Both non-personal and personal data are data, although they encapsulate different types of valuable information.

Given that the distinction between a free individual and a slave is no longer legally significant, we could instead seek to draw an analogy with trade in human organs. Although organs are different from 'data'—and, generally, from intangible goods—what is particularly interesting is that legal protection of human organs has been widely compared with legal protection of personal data.[20] This is perhaps due to the central role of personal data in constructing personal identity and to the inherently 'personal' nature of both organs and data (as components of moral and physical integrity of the human being).[21] Accordingly, if the human body and its

---

16 ibid 331.

17 eg LG Berlin judgment of 16 January 2018, 16 O 341/15 <https://perma.cc/D75S-ETC3> accessed 5 August 2019.

18 cf, eg, § 90 BGB (Germany): 'Sachen im Sinne des Gesetzes sind nur körperliche Gegenstände' (things in legal sense are only physical objects). See also in the Italian Civil Code Art 810 jointly with Art 814. See also A Boerding et al, 'Data Ownership—A Property Rights Approach from a European Perspective' (2018) 11 J Civ L Stud 323, 336–38.

19 See S Stalla-Bourdillon and A Knight, 'Anonymous Data v. Personal Data-False Debate: An EU Perspective on Anonymization, Pseudonymization and Personal Data' (2016) 34 Wis Int'l LJ 284; C Wendehorst, 'Of Elephants in the Room and Paper Tigers: How to Reconcile Data Protection and the Data Economy' in S Lohsse, R Schulze and D Staudenmayer (eds), *Trading Data in the Digital Economy: Legal Concepts and Tools* (Hart Publishing, Nomos 2017) 332; V Janeček, 'Ownership of personal data in the Internet of Things' (2018) CLSRev 1039, 1042–44.

20 See S Rodotà, 'Trasformazioni del corpo' (2006) 37 Politica del diritto 3; G Finocchiaro, 'Corpo digitale e informazioni nella sanità elettronica' (2017) 16 Salute e Società 32; G Malgieri, 'R.I.P.: Rest in Privacy or Rest in (Quasi-)Property? Personal Data Protection of Deceased Data Subjects between Theoretical Scenarios and National Solutions' in R Leenes et al (eds), *Data Protection and Privacy: The Internet of Bodies* (Hart Publishing 2018).

21 See Rodotà (n 20).

components are capable of being considered *res extra commercium*, one might be tempted to conclude that personal data—ie data that already relate to an identifiable human just like organs pertain to an individual—are likewise inalienable in the European digital market.

Indeed, the rationales for excluding trade in human organs can partly translate to commerce in personal data—as we will see in the next two sections of this chapter—but arguments about (non)tradability of data must take a very different form. This is so because the logic of the infosphere does not follow the logic of the real world. Non-personal data can become personal, and vice versa. The difficulty with all (not just personal) data is that one must always first 'compute' the information that data embody (digital content) in order to find out their legal status. Data (as an object of digital transactions) can therefore never be excluded from commerce *ex-ante*, because they can be *ex-post* linked with values and interests that would be compromised by sale. Think, for example, of biomedical Big Data analytics which encounter precisely these issues.

The dynamic nature of data is unparalleled in the physical world. The closest we could perhaps get is the example of 3D-printed organs.[22] Unlike organs extracted from a human, organs printed on a 3D printer are a tradable commodity. In the physical world, it is relatively easy to understand why the law prohibits trade in human organs but not trade in 3D-printed organs. The rationale for this protection seems to be based on moral and ethical considerations, grounded on human dignity (in terms of moral and physical integrity).[23] For the same reasons, one could argue that it would be illicit to trade 3D-printed organs that have already been successfully implanted in a human body. However, while this looks like a dynamic change in the nature of those 3D-printed organs, it is important to highlight that this is a one-off change. In contrast, the nature of data may change repeatedly.

A further complication is that data subjects may *ex-post* withdraw their consent with processing of personal data for a specific purpose. Again, in the physical world it would be hard to imagine that the producer of 3D-

---

22 eg D Radenkovic, A Solouk and A Seifalian, 'Personalized development of human organs using 3D printing technology' (2016) 87 Medical hypotheses 30; European Commission, *Human Organ Replacement – Targeted scenario N°8* (European Union Publications Office 2018).

23 See, eg, the Preamble of the Convention on Human Rights and Biomedicine of 1997 (ETS No 164): 'Convinced of the need to respect the human being both as an individual and as a member of the human species and recognising the importance of ensuring the dignity of the human being'.

printed organs will terminate the contract and withdraw the organ from the human body. In the infosphere, however, a data subject (as the producer of personal data) can demand her data back, which causes some headaches for the contracts involving those data and attendant remedies.[24] We will get to these issues in Sections III, IV, and V.

For now, it suffices to highlight that these dynamic *ex-post* changes in the nature of data are a new phenomenon that might lead to exclusion of data from trade. This issue seems to have slipped the attention of law-makers as well as many scholars, although it presents a distinct problem for the data economy. As, for instance, Basedow argues, '[i]t should be clarified to what extent personal data are *res extra commercium* and what this means for contracts covering such data'.[25] The uncertainty over when the law excludes data from commerce is further magnified by the fact that there is no clear set of reasons for treating certain things as *res extra commercium* such as is the Roman law triad of reasons (free human's liberty, a divine interest, a public interest). Further, the implicit danger that contracts involving data would be invalidated *ex-post* looms wherever (personal) data are provided instead of a monetary price for the provision of digital content and in other cases of hidden data commodification.

Hence, it seems worth attempting to map the concept of *data extra commercium* onto the Roman law moral and public policy reasons (or a similar set of reasons) so as to clarify the constraints on trading data which are implicitly baked in our laws and provide a higher degree of certainty for the data economy. Due to the number of parallels and the reasons given, we will use personal data as a vehicle for our argument, although we aspire to make more general claims about limits on trade in data.

In this regard, many readers will find it helpful to refer to Margaret Radin's work in which she challenges the idea of 'paternalism' as a basis for market inalienability.[26] By criticising Calabresi and Melamed,[27] Radin argues that the real justification of trade limitations (eg on children or hu-

---

24 See S Grundmann and A Hacker, 'The Digital Dimension as a Challenge to European Contract Law—The Architecture' in S Grundmann (ed), *European Contract Law in the Digital Age* (Intersentia 2018) 42–44; and G Spindler, 'Contracts for the Supply of Digital Content—The Proposal of the Commission for a Directive on Contracts for the Supply of Digital Content' in ibid 285, 292, 306–07.

25 J Basedow, 'The EU digital single market strategy and insurance law' (2018) JBL 455, 462 (discussing the contractual implications (termination, restitution, retroactiveness) of a consent withdrawal or a claim for erasure of personal data).

26 M Radin, 'Market Inalienability' (1987) 100 Harv L Rev 1849, 1885.

27 G Calabresi and AD Melamed, 'Property Rules, Liability Rules and Inalienability: One View of the Cathedral' (1972) 85 Harv L Rev 1089.

man bodies) should not be based on traditional liberalism or economics but on a conception of personhood and human flourishing. *Human flourishing*, a key concept in virtue ethics,[28] means the development and fulfilment of one's own personality, based both on positive freedom (life, health, thought) and negative freedom and autonomy. Allowing individuals to trade their body parts or entire bodies, for instance, would impair the foundation of individuals' freedom, because it would be detrimental to personhood itself. Accordingly, inalienability should not be justified through paternalism but, on the contrary, through human freedom.

Radin was one of the first to discuss personal information in the context of inalienability of human beings.[29] Indeed, she affirms that personal information ('attributes', 'characteristics') is what makes personhood unique and, thus, it cannot be separated from persons themselves.[30] Following this line of argumentation, we can infer that if humans are inalienable, their personal data should be inalienable, since only objects separate from the self are suitable for alienation. For example, the French national advisory committee for ethics, when interpreting Article 16-10 of the French Code Civil, considered the technology of genetic fingerprints ('empreintes génétiques') as 'res extra commercium',[31] because fingerprints are inseparably liked with an individual.

In other words, we think Radin's work identifies a strong rationale for what we call *data extra commercium*: inalienability of personal information justified through arguments concerned with human flourishing. Interest-

---

28 See MC Nussbaum, 'Capabilities and Human Rights' (1997) 66 Ford L Rev 273, 297.

29 Radin (n 26) 1932: 'There is certainly the danger that women's attributes, such as height, eye color, race, intelligence, and athletic ability, will be monetized. Surrogates with "better" qualities will command higher prices in virtue of those qualities.'; ibid 1925: 'When the baby becomes a commodity, all of its personal attributes—sex, eye color, predicted I.Q., predicted height, and the like—become commodified as well. This is to conceive of potentially all personal attributes in market rhetoric, not merely those of sexuality' (footnote omitted).

30 ibid 1885: 'Universal market rhetoric transforms our world of concrete persons, whose uniqueness and individuality is expressed in specific personal attributes, into a world of disembodied, fungible, attribute-less entities possessing a wealth of alienable, severable "objects." This rhetoric reduces the conception of a person to an abstract, fungible unit with no individuating characteristics' (footnote omitted).

31 E Kindt, *Privacy and Data Protection Issues of Biometric Applications: A Comparative Legal Analysis* (Springer 2013) 210. See also F El Atmani, 'Données sensibles: la notion de consentement de la personne concernée' (1996) 86 Lamy Droit de l'Informatique 1, 4.

ingly, privacy scholars have recently affirmed that the right to *human flourishing* might be the general justification (or even the 'raison d'être') for the right to privacy as protected under Article 8 of the European Convention on Human Rights.[32] Overall, it seems that inalienability of personal data could be justified on a moral basis, just like Roman law advanced moral reasons when prohibiting trade in free humans, because the morally-laden values and information that personal data embody would be compromised by sale.

III. When the law limits trade in data?

The law is, however, not bound to follow such abstract moral arguments. It may build on them to provide a principled legal ground for excluding data from commerce, but it could also disregard those rationales. Accordingly, the aim of this section is to explore whether, and under what conditions, there are already some forms of *data extra commercium* in EU law and/or in national legislation.

Before we begin, we stress that several leading commentators consider data to be *intra commercium* by default.[33] Indeed, Article 2(11) of the Directive on Consumer Rights seems to protect the commercial use of data in sales law by explicitly addressing production and supply of digital content.[34] The Regulation on free flow of non-personal data[35] and the Digital Content and Digital Services Directive[36] support the same conclusion, as they consider data as tradable goods. The Regulation, for instance, explicitly declares the objective of 'removing obstacles to trade' (recital 7). The

---

32 B Van der Sloot, 'Privacy as Human Flourishing: Could a Shift towards Virtue Ethics Strengthen Privacy Protection in the Age of Big Data?' (2014) 5 JIPITEC 230.

33 eg De Franceschi (n 1) 5; H Zech, 'Data as a Tradeable Commodity—Implications for Contract Law' (2017) SSRN Scholarly Paper (Rochester, NY: Social Science Research Network), <https://papers.ssrn.com/abstract=3063153> accessed 5 August 2019.

34 Directive 2011/83/EU of the European Parliament and of the Council of 25 October 2011 on consumer rights [2011] OJ L304/64.

35 Regulation (EU) 2018/1807 of the European Parliament and of the Council of 14 November 2018 on a Framework for the Free Flow of Non-Personal Data in the European Union [2018] OJ L303/59.

36 Directive (EU) 2019/770 of the European Parliament and of the Council of 20 May 2019 on certain aspects concerning contracts for the supply of digital content and digital services [2019] OJ L136/1.

Digital Content and Digital Services Directive, then, defines 'digital content' as 'data which are produced and supplied in digital forms'[37] and allows for data (even personal data) as an alternative payment for the supply of digital content and services.[38] Although the proposal for this directive has been severely criticised from the perspective of personal data protection,[39] the debate about data (in)alienability is still underdeveloped.[40] Below, we advance this debate.

1. *Inalienability of personal data?*

The Digital Content and Digital Services Directive goes as far as to assert that 'the protection of personal data is a fundamental right and that therefore personal data cannot be considered as a commodity'.[41] Although this may indicate a clear political aspiration of EU leaders to exclude personal data from commerce, we think that black-letter law is not as clear. Consider, for example, how the EU Charter of Fundamental Rights addresses personal integrity and personal data protection. While Article 3(2) affirms that body parts cannot be 'a source of financial gain' and thus sends a clear message as regards trade in human organs, Article 8 merely declares that everyone has the right to the protection of personal data concerning her. It does not prohibit financial gain from one's own personal data, which suggests that the Charter does not take any position in relation to (in)alienability of personal data.

As regards personal data in general and their being in the nature of inalienable goods, we should take into account EU secondary law, in particular the GDPR, and national data protection legislation. We need also to acknowledge that among personal data, there are some special categories of

37 ibid Art 2(1).

38 ibid Art 3(1).

39 See, eg, European Data Protection Supervisor, 'Opinion 4/17 on the Proposal for a Directive on certain aspects concerning contracts for the supply of digital content (EDPS 2017)'; R Robert and L Smit, 'The Proposal for a Directive on Digital Content: A Complex Relationship with Data Protection Law' (2018) 19 ERA Forum 159.

40 See more in G Malgieri and B Custers, 'Pricing Privacy—the Right to Know the Value of Your Personal Data' (2018) 34 CLSRev 289; G Malgieri, '"User-Provided Personal Content" in the EU: Digital Currency between Data Protection and Intellectual Property' (2018) 32 International Review of Law, Computers & Technology 118.

41 Recital 24 of the Digital Content and Digital Services Directive (n 36).

personal data (hereinafter *sensitive data*, ie racial or ethnic origin, political, religious or philosophical beliefs, or trade union membership, genetic data, biometric data for the purpose of uniquely identifying a natural person, health data or sex life or sexual orientation data) whose processing is limited to even more restricted cases (Article 9 GDPR, see more below).

The GDPR does not explicitly address inalienability of personal data or their nature as *res extra commercium*. Nor does it use the terms 'trade' or 'sale' when referring to personal data. However, the centrality of the data subject as a holder of inalienable data protection rights (rights to access, object to processing, revoke the consent, erasure, portability) seems to be the first relevant element to be considered. It is true that personal data can be processed on the basis, among others, of consent and contract and that these are two elements that could also justify tradability of personal data. Nevertheless, consent should be free and revocable (Article 7 GDPR).

Revocability of consent is thus an apparent index of the not-fully-tradable nature of personal data.[42] In addition, Article 7(4) states that, '[w]hen assessing whether consent is freely given, utmost account shall be taken of whether, inter alia, the performance of a contract, including the provision of a service, is conditional on consent to the processing of personal data that is not necessary for the performance of that contract'. In other words, when consent to data processing is given merely as a counter-performance in exchange for ('is conditional on') the provision a service, one may doubt the freedom with which consent is given.

The wording of Article 7(4) GDPR has triggered a vivid debate about its proper interpretation. On the one hand, commentators largely recognise the nature of data as a de facto 'price', 'consideration' or 'counter-performance' in the digital market.[43] On the other hand, Article 29 Data Protection Working Party (Art 29 WP) has explicitly affirmed that personal data can never be a 'counter-performance', thus strengthening the argument that personal data should not always be considered alienable.[44] However,

---

42 See, in particular, recital 42 of the GDPR: 'Consent should not be regarded as freely given if the data subject has no genuine or free choice or is unable to refuse or withdraw consent without detriment'.

43 See, eg, Malgieri and Custers (n 40) 285, 292, 306 and 307. See also A Metzger et al, 'Data-Related Aspects of the Digital Content Directive' (2019) 9 JIPITEC 90.

44 See Art 29 WP, *Guidelines on consent under Regulation 2016/679* (2018, WP 259 rev.01) 8: 'the GDPR ensures that the processing of personal data for which consent is sought cannot become directly or indirectly the counter-performance of a contract'. See also the European Data Protection Supervisor's opinion (n 39); Robert and Smit (n 39).

Art 29 WP seems to accept that personal data may be monetised if specific conditions are respected, ie if the controller offers data subjects *genuine choice* 'between a service that includes consenting to the use of personal data for additional purposes on the one hand, and an equivalent service offered by the same controller that does not involve consenting to data use for additional purposes on the other hand'.[45] Further, Art 29 WP remarks that 'both services need to be genuinely equivalent'.[46] One might wonder whether a premium service upon payment and a free service upon accepting additional purposes of data processing could ever be 'genuinely equivalent' alternatives. Still, if there is—at least in principle—the possibility of accepting a service delivered by the controller without consenting to the additional data use in question, then the consent could be considered genuinely free.

These considerations seem to suggest that, in principle, the data subject should not be asked to disclose her personal data in exchange for money or as an alternative to money, but if her will (expressed through consent) is genuinely free (consent is not conditional, Article 7(4) GDPR), it is possible that personal data are 'monetised'. Of course, the consent can be always revoked (Article 7(3) GDPR).

Accordingly, we submit that the flow of personal data is based on a limited alienability rule: personal data can be 'traded' in exchange for a monetised service only if specific conditions are met.[47]

Interestingly, at least two European Member States' legislation implementing the GDPR—that of the UK and of Denmark—mention the wording 'sale of personal data'. The UK Data Protection Act 2018 (similarly to the UK Data Protection Act 1998) prohibits the 'sale of data' as part of the crime of 'unlawful obtaining of personal data'.[48] In particular, it is prohibited to sell data (or offer to sell data) that have been obtained without the consent of the data controller. However, these provisions criminalise only business-to-business (or more accurately, 'controller-to-controller') data trading. What is protected here is the consent of the data controller to commercialise personal data that were lawfully obtained and processed.

The UK Data Protection Act 2018 would seem to imply that any 'sale of personal data' is permitted and lawful, provided that the first data controller consents. But that would be a misunderstanding of what the law de-

45 Art 29 WP (n 44) 9.
46 ibid 9.
47 cf A Porat and SD Sugarman, 'Limited Inalienability Rules' (2019) 107 Geo L J 701.
48 UK Data Protection Act 2018, s 170.

mands. According to the GDPR, the exchange of personal data from one data controller to another data controller must respect the data protection principles. Namely, it must have a legal basis according to Article 6 GDPR such as is the data subject's consent or is the necessity of processing (more on this principle in Section III.2.B) below) and the data subject should be informed about any recipient of the personal data (Articles 13(1)(e) and 14(1)(e) GDPR). If and only if all the GDPR safeguards are respected, the exchange of personal data between two data controllers is permitted, even if that exchange is monetised. In other words, we think we can already affirm at this point that personal data are based on a limited alienability rule.

The same argument must apply to other national legal systems in the EU, including the Danish law. The Danish Data Protection Act states that 'data controllers who *sell lists of groups of persons* for direct marketing purposes or who print addresses or distributes messages to such groups on behalf of a third party may only process: (1) data concerning name, address, position, occupation, e-mail address, telephone and fax number; (2) data contained in trade registers which according to law or provisions laid down by law are intended for public information; and (3) other data if the data subject has given explicit consent'.[49] This confirms the possibility of trading personal data, but again only where the data protection principles set out above are met.

In order to understand tradability of personal data, it is instructive to look outside the EU, for instance to the Silicon Valley in California. Presumably, European businesses would want to trade data with innovative entities incorporated there. Californian laws seem to recognise personal data as *res intra commercium*. In the California Consumer Privacy Act 2018 (CCPA), for instance, the concept of 'sale of personal data' is largely accepted as the basic rule in the relationships between different data controllers.[50] In addition, such 'sale' of data is recognised as the basic rule, while the individuals have only the right to be notified that their data will

49 Fremsat den 25. oktober 2017 af justitsministeren (Søren Pape Poulsen) Forslag til Lov om supplerende bestemmelser til forordning om beskyttelse af fysiske personer i forbindelse med behandling af personoplysninger og om fri udveksling af sådanne oplysninger (databeskyttelsesloven), Part 3, § 13(5) (emphasis added, for translation see <https://perma.cc/7TBD-YW7W> accessed 5 August 2019).

50 Section 1798.140t(1) clarifies what the concept of 'sale' in relation to trade in a consumer's personal information. Just as in the UK and Danish Data Protection Laws, in Californian Law the 'sale' of personal data is mentioned only as a business-to-business practice.

be sold and the right to opt out from any sale of data relating to them.[51] The rights of notification and opt-out seem similar to the requirements of information disclosure and legal bases in the GDPR (Articles 14 and 6) as described above. Thus, alienability of personal data is arguably also limited in California.

Interestingly, the CCPA seems even to declare an absolute inalienability rule. Section 2 acknowledges that 'the right to privacy is among the "inalienable" rights of all people'. However, the same section further clarifies the content of such inalienable right: 'Fundamental to this right of privacy is the ability of individuals to control the use, including the sale, of their personal information'. In other words, the (inalienable) right to privacy includes basically the right of individuals to limit the trade of data related to them. Overall, we thus submit that one can identify a limited alienability rule for personal data even in the US.[52]

A similar declaration of inalienability is in the Quebec Civil Code, where Article 3 affirms: 'every person is the holder of personality rights, such as the right to [...] privacy. These rights are *inalienable*'.[53] Even in this case, inalienability does not refer to market inalienability of personal data as *res extra commercium*, but to the 'right to privacy' as a right that cannot be removed from individuals.

In sum, the analysis of personal data as *res extra commercium* is problematic: their nature as an (in)alienable commodity might appear ambiguous in many legal frameworks. However, regardless of definitions and pronouncements in legal documents, if we focus just on the possibility of processing personal data on a monetisation basis (either the data controller asks the data subject for personal data in exchange for money or for a valuable service, or the data controller exchanges personal data with a third recipient, eg a business, in exchange for money), we conclude that there is a limited alienability rule. In the following sections we will summarise the 'limits' for trading personal data in EU law.

---

51 California Consumer Protection Privacy Act 1798.120.

52 See, on the concept of limited inalienability and limited property rules, Porat and Sugarman (n 47).

53 Civil Code of Québec, Chapter CCQ-1991 (emphasis added).

2. *Trading personal data under the GDPR: conditions and uncertainty*

In order to understand the conditions under which the GDPR allows 'trade' in personal data we should first clarify what 'trading data' means and then differentiate amongst relevant scenarios. We accept here that trading data means *obtaining personal data in exchange for money or for other valuable assets* (digital services, other valuable information, etc). Two different scenarios should be addressed here. Primary data trade where the data controller obtains personal data from the data subject, and secondary data trade where the data controller exchanges personal data with a third recipient (eg a business that can thus become a second data controller).

In both primary and secondary data trade, the trader(s) need to consider two variables:

1. the nature of data (Are they personal or non-personal data? If they are personal data, are they sensitive or non-sensitive data? See Section III.2.a)); and
2. the legal basis for trading data (These variables shall be considered not as merely static, but as dynamic. See Section III.2.b)).

a) *The first variable for limited alienability of data: the dynamic and uncertain nature of data*

As regards the nature of data, Article 4(1) GDPR clarifies that 'personal data' means any information relating to an identified or identifiable natural person. More interestingly, recital 26 explains that when determining whether a natural person is identifiable 'account should be taken of all the means *reasonably* likely to be used, such as singling out, either by the controller or by another person to identify the natural person directly or indirectly'. To ascertain whether some means are reasonably likely to be used to identify the natural person 'account should be taken of all objective factors, such as the costs of and the amount of time required for identification, taking into consideration the available technology at the time of the processing and technological developments' (recital 26). If, considering reasonable efforts (time, cost, available technology), it is not possible to link the information to a natural person, the information shall be considered anonymous.[54]

As discussed in Section II, it appears clear that the nature of data is relative. Several variables such as reasonable costs, time, or available technology significantly affect our realistic capacity to *single out* individuals.[55] The CJEU in *Breyer v. Germany* has recently clarified that data are anonymous not just if it is *technically unfeasible* to identify the natural person to whom they are related, but also if it is *legally unfeasible*.[56] In particular, if there are no legal channels for obtaining (eg from a third data controller) the 'identifiers' that would turn those 'anonymous' data into 'personal' data, personal data shall be considered anonymous.[57] Owing to a broad interpretation of the CJEU's statement, it is sometimes thought that pseudonymous data (personal data separated from identifiers)[58] could also be considered as anonymous data for a third party that cannot (technically or legally) access the identifiers.[59]

It is noteworthy that the nature of data is also variable across time. For example, advancements in technology could make it easier to reidentify some originally anonymous data; or a party processing anonymous data could *ex-post* obtain the identifiers in a lawful way. It thus should be accepted as given that the nature of data is not only 'uncertain' for traders at the moment of the trade (eg when it is not clear whether some data are really anonymous or relatable to an identifiable person), but also dynami-

---

54 L Bolognini and C Bistolfi, 'Pseudonymization and Impacts of Big (Personal/Anonymous) Data Processing in the Transition from the Directive 95/46/EC to the New EU General Data Protection Regulation' (2017) 33 CLSRev 171.

55 F Borgesius, 'Singling out People without Knowing Their Names—Behavioural Targeting, Pseudonymous Data, and the New Data Protection Regulation' (2016) 32 CLSRev 256, 260.

56 Case C-582/14, *Patrick Breyer* v. *Bundesrepublik Deutschland*, EU:C:2016:779, paras 46 and 47.

57 ibid para 47.

58 See Art 4(5): '"pseudonymisation" means the processing of personal data in such a manner that the personal data can no longer be attributed to a specific data subject without the use of additional information, provided that such additional information is kept separately and is subject to technical and organisational measures to ensure that the personal data are not attributed to an identified or identifiable natural person'.

59 See Information Commissioner's Office, *Anonymisation: managing data protection risk code of practice* (Wilmslow 2012) 13; M Mourby at al, 'Are "Pseudonymised" Data Always Personal Data? Implications of the GDPR for Administrative Data Research in the UK' (2018) 34 CLSRev 222, 225.

cally uncertain in the future (anonymous data might become personal data).

Once it has been verified that traded data are personal data under the GDPR, another test should be performed to find out whether that data are of a *sensitive* nature. This extra categorisation exercise is necessary in the context of trading data because Article 9(1) provides for stricter rules for processing sensitive data. Accordingly, sensitive data are based on a 'more limited' alienability rule than personal data generally.

For the reasons given above, the border between sensitive and non-sensitive data is uncertain, relative and dynamic.[60] In particular, it has been affirmed that in the age of Big Data, machine learning and data mining it becomes increasingly easier to infer sensitive information from (apparently) non-sensitive data.[61] All personal data have a certain degree of intrinsic sensitiveness and an inversely proportional (computational) distance from sensitive information.[62] How this distance can be covered depends on advancements in technology (eg our health conditions can be statistically predicted even from our daily location data) but also on the collection of further data. Accordingly, data traders should not only consider the uncertain and dynamic nature of data, but also the uncertainty and dynamism of the sub-category of sensitive data, which have implications for the legal bases for trading data.

b) The second variable: legal bases for primary data trade

Insofar as data qualify as personal data or even sensitive data, data traders need a legal basis for the commercial exchange of such data. Legal bases

60 See, eg, the problematic issue of sensitivity and dynamism of 'genetic data': D Hallinan, M Friedewald and P de Hert, 'Genetic Data and the Data Protection Regulation: Anonymity, Multiple Subjects, Sensitivity and a Prohibitionary Logic Regarding Genetic Data?' (2013) 29 CLSRev 317; G Malgieri and G Comandé, 'Sensitive-by-Distance: Quasi-Health Data in the Algorithmic Era' (2017) 26 Information & Communications Technology Law 229.

61 G Comandé and G Schneider, 'Regulatory Challenges of Data Mining Practices: The Case of the Never-Ending Lifecycles of "Health Data"' (2018) 25 European Journal of Health Law 284. See also E Vayena and U Gasser, 'Strictly Biomedical? Sketching the Ethics of the Big Data Ecosystem in Biomedicine' in B Mittelstadt and L Floridi (eds), *The Ethics of Biomedical Big Data* (Springer 2016) 20–24.

62 Malgieri and Comandé (n 60) 230 and 240. See also Art 29 WP, *Annex to the Letter from the ART 29 WP to the European Commission, DG CONNECT on mHealth* (5 February 2015) 5.

for processing of personal data are listed in Article 6 GDPR. For sensitive data there is an additional (and a more demanding) list of conditions in Article 9 GDPR.[63]

Let us consider personal data first. We will focus on consent, a contract and a legitimate interest as the potential bases for trading data lawfully (Article 6(1)(a), (b), (f) GDPR).[64] As mentioned above, consent can serve as a legal basis for collecting data for monetisation purposes.[65] However, according to Article 7, this consent must be unambiguous, fully informed (about, inter alia, the commercial purpose of the data processing), revocable and free (not conditional on the provision of services *with no other genuinely equivalent alternatives*). Accordingly, businesses who 'trade' personal data must ascertain that consent has been provided unambiguously, that it was informed, free and that it remains valid. The consent remains valid if it has not been revoked by the data subject.

Another legal basis for monetising personal data could then theoretically be a contract, but commentators have dismissed this possibility.[66] Even Art 29 WP has clarified that the provision of Article 6(1)(b) GDPR (stating that processing is lawful if it is 'necessary for the performance of a contract to which the data subject is party') 'must be interpreted strictly and does not cover situations where the processing is not genuinely *necessary* for the performance of a contract, but rather unilaterally imposed on the data subject by the controller'.[67] Art 29 WP thus effectively excluded the use of contract as a legal basis for processing data for monetisation purposes including marketing purposes.[68] We agree with Art 29 WP's view.

---

63 See also EG González and P de Hert, 'Understanding the legal provisions that allow processing and profiling of personal data—an analysis of GDPR provisions and principles' (2019) 20 ERA Forum 1.

64 We do not discuss the possibility to 'monetise' data on the basis of a legal obligation to which the controller is subject (Art 6(1)(c)), vital interests of the data subject (Art 6(1)(d)) or a performance of a task carried out in the public interest (Art 6(1)(e)), because these bases do not fit the private commercial nature of data trade which we want to address.

65 See Art 29 WP, *Opinion 06/2014 on the notion of legitimate interests of the data controller under Article 7 of Directive 95/46/EC* (2014, WP 217) 18. See also F Borgesius, 'Personal Data Processing for Behavioural Targeting: Which Legal Basis?' (2015) 5 International Data Privacy 163, 176.

66 C Kuner, *European Data Protection Law: Corporate Compliance and Regulation* (2nd edn, OUP 2007) 234–35; Borgesius (n 65) 170.

67 Art 29 WP (n 65) 16 (emphasis in original).

68 See ibid 17: '[contract] is not a suitable legal ground for building a profile of the user's tastes and lifestyle choices based on his click-stream on a website and the items purchased. This is because the data controller has not been contracted to

The last variant is a legitimate interest as a basis for lawful processing of personal data. Pursuant to Article 6(1)(f) GDPR, this could be where 'processing is necessary for the purposes of the legitimate interests pursued by the controller or by a third party except where such interests are overridden by the interests or fundamental rights and freedoms of the data subject'. This legal basis thus requires us to take account of several tests, including (1) the necessity test; (2) the legitimacy test; and (3) the balancing test considering the counter-interests of the data subject.[69]

The use of 'legitimate interest' as a legal basis for monetisation purposes is problematic,[70] especially as regards the necessity test (1). Art 29 WP has indeed clarified that data controllers should 'consider whether there are other less invasive means to reach the identified purpose of the processing and serve the legitimate interest of the data controller'.[71] In data trade the identified purpose might be an economic profit from personal data, but such a purpose would probably be considered insufficiently specific to meet the necessity test.[72] In addition, one could always argue that the desired economic profit could be achieved through less invasive means (eg the content providers might provide 'premium' services upon a payment).

The legitimacy test (2) allows for more freedom and can be interpreted expansively.[73] Still, the interest must always be lawful, sufficiently clear, and represent a real and present interest.[74] Finally, the balancing test (3)[75] should have regard to the controller's legitimate interest, impact on the data subjects (eg intrusiveness of profiling), provisional balance, and to addi-

---

carry out profiling, but rather to deliver particular goods and services, for example. Even if these processing activities are specifically mentioned in the small print of the contract, this fact alone does not make them "necessary" for the performance of the contract'.

69 eg G Zanfir-Fortuna, *Deciphering 'Legitimate Interests': Report based on more than 40 cases from practice* (Nymity—Future of Privacy Report 2018) 5–7.

70 Borgesius (n 65) 170.

71 Art 29 WP (n 65) 55.

72 See Art 29 WP, *Opinion 3/2013 on purpose limitation* (2013, WP 203) 16: 'For these reasons, a purpose that is vague or general, such as for instance "improving users' experience", "marketing purposes", "IT-security purposes" or "future research" will—without more detail—usually not meet the criteria of being "specific".'

73 See Art 29 WP (n 65) 24.

74 ibid 25.

75 See, in particular, I Kamara and P de Hert, 'Understanding the Balancing Act Behind the Legitimate Interest of the Controller Ground: A Pragmatic Approach' in E Selinger, J Polonetsky and O Tene (eds), *Cambridge Handbook of Consumer Privacy* (CUP 2018).

tional safeguards applied by the controller to prevent any undue impact on the data subjects (transparency, ease of exercising the right to object, etc).[76]

All these considerations make it extremely difficult to use the category of legitimate interest as a legal basis for trading personal data. It will be necessary to evaluate on a case-by-case basis whether a specific data transaction involves intrusive profiling, unclear information about purposes or commercial implications, etc. And although even '[t]he processing of personal data for direct marketing purposes may be regarded as carried out for a legitimate interest', as is confirmed in recital 47 of the GDPR, the data subject has the right to object at any time to such processing (Articles 21(2) and 21(3)). Accordingly, the legal basis for data transactions could be invalidated *ex-post*, which seems to be very similar to the right to revoke consent in case of processing based on consent.

In addition, if the traded data are not only personal, but also sensitive data (Article 9(1) GDPR), they can never be processed merely for legitimate interest purposes, since under Article 9 there is no reference to legitimate interest as a legal basis for processing. In that case, just two legal bases might in principle be adequate for processing of sensitive data for monetisation purposes: (1) when the data subject has given 'explicit consent for one or more specified purposes' (Article 9(2)(a)), given that the consent is free, informed and revocable (Article 7); or (2) when processing relates to '[sensitive] data which are manifestly made public by the data subject' (Article 9(2)(e)). In this second case, however, we observe that if personal data are already made public, this might lower their commercial value for data traders since they would not need to 'buy' these data (they just would need a technology to collect them). Still, even in this second case, it is worth remembering that for processing sensitive data, controllers need a legal basis under both Articles 9 and 6 (since sensitive data also count for personal data).[77] Therefore, in the case of processing sensitive data which were manifestly made public by the subject, the data controller should either seek the consent of the subject under Article 6(1)(a) or prove that there is necessity for a legitimate interest under Article 6(1)(f). The route of a legitimate interest then poses the multiple hurdles, namely the

76 Art 29 WP (n 65) 33.

77 See ibid 15 fn 31: 'Publicly available data are still personal data subject to data protection requirements, including compliance with Article 7 [of the Data Protection Directive, now Art 6 of the GDPR], irrespective whether or not they are sensitive data'.

legitimacy test, the necessity test, and especially the balancing test when trading sensitive data for merely commercial reasons.[78]

Overall, we submit that this second variable is also uncertain and dynamic. In cases of consent, even when the data traders pass the freedom of consent test, consent could be revoked in the future.[79] In cases of legitimate interests, even when the data controllers pass the three tests (necessity, legitimacy and balancing tests), the data subject could easily object to data processing and thereby delegitimise it. As regards secondary data trade, ie a commercial exchange of data between two data controllers such as a service provider and an advertising company, the same conditions apply. In addition, it might be necessary to obtain a separate consent for exchanging data with a third party: Art 29 WP has clarified that in order to respect the principle of 'granularity', the data controller that processes data for her own purposes must ask for a separate consent to communicate the data to a third party (eg an advertising company).[80]

c) Dynamically limited alienability rule for personal data under the GDPR

Given the evidence in the legal sources and literature set out above, we conclude that personal data are not based on an inalienability rule and are, therefore, not *res extra commercium*. Nonetheless, we also conclude that strict conditions apply to the commercial flow of personal data, and so we can talk about a *dynamically limited alienability rule* in relation to personal data.

---

78 See ibid 35 which affirms that when processing data for purely consumer profiling reasons, 'the inference of sensitive data (health data) [...] contributes to tipping the balance in favour of the data subject's interests and rights'. Similarly, ibid 59 (discussing an example of an on-line pharmacy performing extensive profiling). Generally, ibid 38–39 (arguing that processing sensitive data (or even data that could reveal sensitive data) contributes to set the balance test in favour of the data subject because 'the more sensitive the information involved, the more consequences there may be for the data subject').

79 In this case the processing of data before withdrawal is not unlawful (Art 7(3) GDPR), but no new processing of such data is allowed. At the same time, if there are no more legal bases, such data should be erased (see European Data Protection Board, *Opinion 3/2019 concerning the Questions and Answers on the interplay between the Clinical Trials Regulation (CTR) and the General Data Protection regulation (GDPR) (Art 70.1.b)* 7).

80 Art 29 WP (n 44) 10.

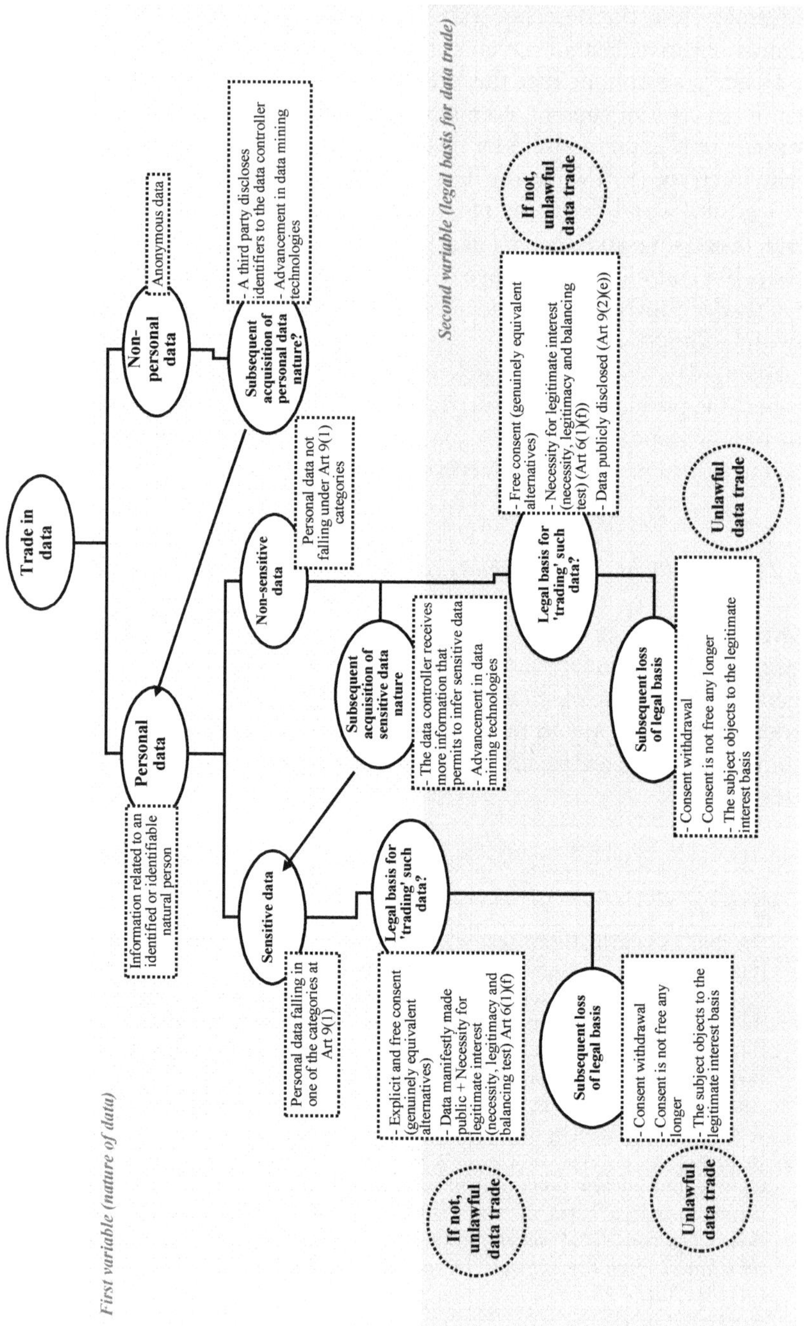

Figure 1: Dynamically Limited Alienability Rule derived from the GDPR and explaining conditions under which personal data can be traded.

Figure 1 (see above) visualises how this complex rule might look. Accordingly, the GDPR arguably forbids trade in data when:

1. data are personal data from the outset or become personal data subsequently AND there is:
    a. no free consent of the data subject under Articles 6(1)(a) and 7 GDPR or
    b. no necessity for a legitimate interest under the conditions of Article 6(1)(f) GDPR for processing those data;

OR

2. personal data are also sensitive data according to Article 9(1) GDPR from the outset or become sensitive data subsequently, AND:
    a. there is no free consent of the data subject under Article 9(2)(a) and Article 7 GDPR or
    b. those data are not manifestly made public by the data subject or, even if made public, there is no necessity for a 'legitimate interest' under the conditions of Article 6(1)(f) GDPR for processing those data;

OR

3. the legal basis is subsequently lost, ie
    a. consent is revoked or loses its required qualities (Article 7 GDPR) or
    b. in case of legitimate interest basis, the data subject objects to the processing of personal data (Article 21 GDPR).

IV. The two-stage data extra commercium test

While Roman law provided a clear and principled test that helped indicate when contracting parties should be held responsible for illicit transactions in *res extra commercium*, and consequently when the parties' commercial interests are to be protected by legal remedies,[81] current law does not feature any similar test in relation to data. The Digital Content and Digital Services Directive provides consumers with some contractual remedies and deals with some aspects of onward data transfers to third parties,[82] but it is

81 See Inst.III.23.5 and Section II of this chapter.

82 See the Digital Content and Digital Services Directive (n 36), eg recitals 24, 67 and Art 16.

does not address these issues in a complex and principled way that would be useful also for business-to-business contracts. This section fills this gap and proposes a test that is specifically designed for transactions in *data extra commercium*. We suggest that this test be thought of as a reasonable proxy on the basis of which national contract laws can be interpreted in accord with the EU law limits on trade in personal data.

We already know that the Roman law *res extra commercium* test was not designed for the dynamic nature of the digital infosphere and that it cannot be applied in full to trade in data. This does not mean, however, that we should dismiss the common core of European contract law and its Roman law origins. It is possible to make connections with the doctrine of *res extra commercium* via the underlying principles of the Roman law test in its historical variations. It is safe to assume that the test was underpinned by the following set of abstract principles that are based on the authority of reason: (1) if a contracting party is not responsible for the forbidden trade (eg an innocent buyer), it would not be unjust to provide that party with a remedy for the spoiled commercial transaction; (2) if the other party is responsible for the mischief (eg a fraudulent seller), the law could grant the innocent party a remedy against the defaulter; (3) or else, the contract is void and the law only protects the non-correlative interests vested in the object of trade. The parties are responsible for the void transaction if they knew, or should have known, that the object was *extra commercium*. Let us translate these principles into the context of data.

The dynamic nature of data implies that all contracting parties can, in full awareness of the fact, foresee that the relevant data may eventually be excluded from commerce on the basis of the reasons outlined in Section II and as demonstrated for trade in personal data in Section III. It could thus be argued that all parties should have known this (potential) status of the data and, accordingly, be responsible for the void or ineffective contract and its consequences. This line of thought would result in legal protection of *data extra commercium* only. No party would be entitled to a remedy.

The difficulty is that such a strategy does not take into account the legitimate interests and reasonable expectations of the parties. For example, it seems unreasonable to expect that a data subject will be able successfully to claim her interests (and withdraw her consent) in relation to fully anonymised data or to personal data that are collected and processed in the public interest.[83] Similarly, it would be unreasonable to assume that data

83 cf Art 6(1) GDPR that gives a list of various acceptable grounds for lawful processing of personal data.

regarding levels of humidity around the globe would be eventually analysed as personal data. In theory, it is possible, but seems as unlikely as the authors of this chapter being tenured next year. You would (hopefully) struggle to say we are responsible for not being tenured next year. By the same token, it is unreasonable to assume that parties can have limitless responsibility for *data extra commercium*. Given the dynamic nature of data, it is also unreasonable to assume that the parties' limited responsibility is fixed at the time of the conclusion of a contract or another key event in the digital trade. According to this line of thought, the parties' limited responsibility should be dynamic, too.

In response to these issues, we propose to translate the corrective element of reasonableness[84] into the following two-stage test. Stage 1: A party is responsible for trade in *data extra commercium* if and when, given the current state of knowledge and technology that is normally available to a person in a similar position, it is reasonably likely that the relevant data reveal personal (or other restricted) information. Stage 2: If those conditions are met, the party cannot succeed in arguing that they are not responsible for infringing the values and interests in which trade is (or should be) legally prohibited, unless they have a special justifying reason (eg the data subject's free consent with processing of personal data or a compelling legitimate interest of the controller) that serves as a defence to their liability for consequences caused by transactions concerning *data extra commercium*.

Stage 1 of the test protects reasonable expectations and legitimate interests in that the basic rule is that data are in commerce and the validity and enforceability of the contract should remain untouched, provided that there is no reasonably likely interpretation which would reveal that the relevant data embody values and interests that would be compromised by sale (see Section II). Of course, the parties cannot prove negative facts, which is why the Stage 1 test must take a positive form as set out in the preceding paragraph. This positive test helps indicate whether the parties knew, or should have known, that data are excluded from commerce. The 'current state of knowledge' requirement allows us to have regard to the (so far speedy) developments in the field of data science. The requirement of technology that is 'normally available' to a person in a similar position is designed so as to indicate objectively whether and when the relevant party could have discovered that the data qualify as *extra commercium*, and there-

84 Note that we do not regard reasonableness as a distinctly legal standard. See, eg, Gardner, 'The Many Faces of the Reasonable Person' (2015) 131 LQR 563.

fore whether and when that party has responsibility for trade in that data. This requirement is also justified by recital 26 of the GDPR.[85]

Stage 2 further limits the parties' responsibility in that it provides the parties with relevant excuses to responsibility and, consequently, defences to liability. A party that becomes responsible at Stage 1 should prove that they have a relevant excuse that allows them to trade data that would otherwise be *extra commercium*. This could be a free consent by the data subject, or a compelling legitimate interest of the data controller winning the three tests (the legitimacy, necessity and balancing tests) under Article 6(1)(f) GDPR (and in case of sensitive data either explicit consent or data made public by the subject and legitimate interests winning the tests under Article 6(1)(f), or any other exemption provided by the law at the time when the party faces Stage 2. In this sense, Stage 2 reasonably limits responsibility for *data extra commercium* but does not deny it.[86]

If we now reconnect the two-stage test with its Roman law roots, we can see why the reasonable basic position of the law should be to protect only *data extra commercium* and the valuable information they embody. We can also see why it would often be the case that those who are in control of powerful analytic algorithms would be more likely to be responsible for *data extra commercium* than those to whom such tools are not available (typically consumers and data subjects). The question of specific legal sanctions and remedies is an important matter which we do not have space to open here. The key point is that the test could potentially be deployed in any type of data transactions and could be seen as a test that enforces requirements that are reasonable, principled and in this sense non-arbitrary.

V. The unique benefits of the data extra commercium test

The two-stage test helps allocate responsibility for trade in *data extra commercium*, and thus also for the consequences of purporting such trade, in relation to both problematic scenarios set out in the introduction and Section II, ie in relation to *ex-post* analytic exclusion of data from commerce and *ex-post* withdrawal of consent. The same applies to the specific conditions of trade in personal data as discussed in Section III. These are un-

85 See Section III.2.A).

86 A detailed analysis of defences and denials in relation to civil liability can be found in J Goudkamp, *Tort Law Defences* (Hart Publishing 2013) and A Dyson, J Goudkamp and F Wilmot-Smith (eds), *Defences in Contract* (Hart Publishing 2017).

doubtedly unique and significant benefits that already justify why we should adopt the two-stage test in our thinking about data transactions in European contract law.

Here we want to highlight two practical benefits of the two-stage test. The first benefit relates to enforcement of the limited alienability rule in technologically advanced data trading and data processing systems (in the infosphere),[87] where human end users are virtually out of the loop. Think, for instance, of 'smart' environments and the Internet of Things. In order to deliver their functions, smart devices and their data processing algorithms often automatedly, and sometimes even autonomously, connect to other devices in order to transfer or process data. This can happen without the end user having any knowledge about such activity and the character of the data traded. Still, legal obligations can arise even in such autonomous environments and, likewise, the reasons for excluding some data from commerce apply there too.[88]

How then, if the human end users—who are traditionally considered the relevant contracting agents—are out of the loop, can we enforce the limited alienability rule? Consider, for instance, how difficult it would be to apply principles relating to defects of consent (mistake, fraud, threat or undue influence) and misrepresentation in scenarios where the human user is out of the loop. Similarly, consider how difficult it would be to establish that the dynamic change of the nature of data amounts to an unforeseeable

87 See L Floridi, 'Technology's In-Betweeness' (2013) 26 Philosophy and Technology 111; L Floridi, *The Fourth Revolution: How the infosphere is reshaping human reality* (OUP 2014) ch 2.

88 Notice the lack of literature addressing this fundamental shift and the inadequacy of existing contract law to address some of the implication of the 'out of the loop' phenomenon. Rare exceptions are M Loos, 'Machine-to-Machine Contracting in the Age of the Internet of Things' in R Schulze, D Staudenmayer and S Lohsse (eds), *Contracts for the Supply of Digital Content: Regulatory Challenges and Gaps* (Nomos 2017) 74–79 and G Sartor, 'Contracts in the Infosphere' in S Grundmann (ed), *European Contract Law in the Digital Age* (Intersentia 2018) 263–64, 271, 276. See also J Drexl, 'On the Future EU Legal Framework for the Digital Economy: A Competition-based Response to the "Ownership and Access" Debate' in S Lohsse, R Schulze and D Staudenmayer (eds), *Trading Data in the Digital Economy: Legal Concepts and Tools* (Hart Publishing/Nomos 2017) 232–34; R Janal, 'Fishing for an Agreement: Data Access and the Notion of Contract' in S Lohsse, R Schulze and D Staudenmayer (eds), *Trading Data in the Digital Economy: Legal Concepts and Tools* (Hart Publishing/Nomos 2017) 271–72 (both addressing the fact that a buyer of a smart device is out of the loop in relation to data transactions).

change of circumstances.[89] These issues demonstrate the obstacles relating to enforcement of the limited alienability rule when it comes to automated trading of data between autonomous agents. The existing European contract law tools are simply not designed for the infosphere where our traditional notions of time, space, and identity of objects start breaking down.

This is where the two-stage test is likely to help. The law is well positioned to provide a legal (not technological) tool to open black-boxed algorithmic trading systems, and thereby to protect the values and interests that certain types of data embody. The two-stage test could steer these challenges at the technological level by incentivising development and implementation of suitable algorithms that would be designed to protect *data extra commercium*. Such protection by design could result in various auditing algorithmic protocols (regulation by code)[90] that would flag up potential issues in the black box. Stage 1 of the test explains why it would be reasonable for stakeholders to use such auditing technologies and responsibly to develop the necessary technical standards.[91]

The second implication relates to Stage 2 in that it demands development of adequate legal and technical standards for *ex-post* authorisation of processing of autonomously derived or inferred data. From a traditional European contract law perspective, trade in these derived or inferred data would be permitted if they were derived or inferred from *data in commercio*. The traditional contract law approach—we may call it a pre-Big Data or pre-infosphere paradigm—looks at data as a mere accidental form of goods, rather than as primary objects of transactions.[92] If the primary good is excluded from commerce, data are too; if not, data are *in commercio*. We already know, however, that the relationship between data and the infor-

89 cf G Spark, *Vitiation of Contracts: International Contractual Principles and English Law* (CUP 2013); J Smits, *Contract Law: A Comparative Introduction* (Edward Elgar Publishing 2014) ch 9; N Jansen and R Zimmermann (eds), *Commentaries on European Contract Law* (OUP 2018) chs 4, 6 and 15.

90 See L Lessig, *Code version 2.0* (BasicBooks 2006) 83–153; M Hildebrandt, 'Law as Information in the Era of Data-Driven Agency' (2016) 79 MLR 1; C Yeung, 'Regulation by Blockchain: The Emerging Battle for Supremacy between the Code *of* Law and Code *as* Law' (2019) 82 MLR 207.

91 See Art 25 GDPR; JP Quemard et al, *Guidance and gaps analysis for European standardisation* (European Union Agency for Network and Information Security (ENISA) 2018).

92 Even the paradigm adopted in the Digital Content and Digital Services Directive (n 36) sees data as a mere carrier of some content which we want to trade. The traditional view can also be found in C-128/11, *UsedSoft* v. *Oracle*, EU:C:2012:407, paras 41, 61.

mation they embody is not this straightforward and that, once the human user is out of the loop, we could lose sight of trading data that should be dynamically excluded from commerce. In other words, even derived and inferred data might eventually infringe upon non-tradable values and interests as set out in Section II.

Again, this is where the two-stage test might help. Unlike existing European law which addresses issues of *ex-post* withdrawal of consent and, relatedly, the legal implications of this *ex-post* exclusion of data from the relevant transactions (including the some implications for onward transfers of such *data extra commercium* to third parties), the two-stage test incentivises development of reasonable legal and technical standards that would allow for *ex-post* authorisation of data and, accordingly, *ex-post* inclusion of derived or inferred data in commerce. This second benefit is, again, characteristically significant for enforcement of the limited alienability rule in the era of Big Data and the infosphere and demands us to adopt some new contract law rules for allocating responsibility for *data extra commercium*. What shape these rules will take in national legal systems, or whether there will be pan-European standard terms or implied terms for business-to-business and business-to-consumer contracts, are questions ripe for further consideration that exceeds this chapter.[93] Overall, the two-stage test could incentivise more efficient legal and technical standards for detecting and protecting *data extra commercium* even in fully automated and autonomous trading systems.

VI. Conclusions

No matter how tempting the intellectual parallel may be, data are not *res extra commercium* and we should seek to avoid thinking about them in these terms. This does not mean, however, that data are *res in commercio*. That would also be a misunderstanding. The nature of data is more complicated than that and we cannot simply apply traditional concepts and contract law doctrines to them.

---

93 For instance, Graf von Westphalen talks about 'default rules' for B2B contract regarding Big Data but in essence is talking about supply of digital content only (F Graf von Westphalen, 'Contracts with Big Data: The End of the Traditional Contract Concept?' in S Lohsse, R Schulze and D Staudenmayer (eds), *Trading Data in the Digital Economy: Legal Concepts and Tools* (Hart Publishing/Nomos 2017) 245 and 249). Similarly, Drexl (n 88) 233.

In this chapter, we argued that transactions in data can be limited and that data are subject to what we call a *dynamically limited alienability rule*. In Section III, we demonstrated how this rule would apply in the context of the laws regarding trade in personal data. We also visualised the rule in Figure 1, so that our readers might easily refer to it in their own work or legal practice.

Further, we argued that the dynamically limited alienability rule can be explained on a principled basis (Section II) and, therefore, applied more generally to trade in any data. In this regard, Section IV pioneered a general two-stage test that should help legal practitioners, judges and law-makers to navigate in considering when trade in data is illicit and who (if anyone) shall be held responsible for this mischief.

Finally, we showed how the two-stage test and the limited alienability rule may help link EU data protection laws with contract law rules and principles, and help enforce legal principles of *data extra commercium* in fully automated and autonomous data trading systems.

We thus proposed that *data extra commercium* be thought of as a dynamic concept for future European contract law or national laws implementing the Digital Content and Digital Services Directive. After all, in a world of speedy technological advancements and changes in business practices and models, it seems a more efficient, and sustainable, regulatory strategy to link contractual sanctions and remedies with the object that is traded—ie data—rather than with the specific types of contractual transaction. Besides, a standard requirement of commercial law is that the object of a transaction is lawful, and it would be difficult to conceive of the law permitting otherwise. For this reason, we coined the term *data extra commercium* and the two-stage test to help enforce the limited alienability rule pertaining to all data transactions. As such, *data extra commercium* may even serve as an elementary tool of data protection.[94]

Acknowledgments and authorship

Thanks are due to the organisers of the 5th Münster Colloquia on EU Law and the Digital Economy, the TILTing Perspectives 2019, and the Oxford EU Law Discussion Group for inviting us to present this paper, and to the participants in these events for their valuable feedback. Thanks are also due to Jürgen Basedow, Kristin Boosfeld, and Leah Grolman for their com-

94 cf M Hildebrandt, 'Primitives of Legal Protection in the Era of Data-Driven Platforms' (2018) 2 Geo L Tech Rev 252, 267.

ments. The usual disclaimer applies. Both authors contributed to this paper equally.

Performance of Contract and Withdrawal from the Contract with respect to Data Protection – Contract Law at a Crossroads?

Right to Withdraw Consent to Data Processing – The Effect on the Contract

Martin Schmidt-Kessel[*]

I. Introduction

A general discussion on data markets and especially on a digital internal market cannot neglect contracting over privacy. From an international perspective, the discourse on this particular issue can be divided into at least two – usually separate – approaches, namely the US-American[1] and the European. For the most part, the latter was triggered by the European Commission's initial proposal for a Directive on certain aspects concerning contracts for the supply of digital content.[2] Moreover, it is now influenced by the several rules referring to contracting over privacy contained in the recent EU Digital Content Directive 2019/770 ('DCD') and by the questions added to the topic by the General Data Protection Regulation 2016/679 (GDPR), in force in the European Union since 25 May 2018. In referring to EU data protection law and the GDPR in particular, it becomes clear that contract law in relation to privacy is heavily influenced – if not determined – by the effects of data protection law.

The freedom of the data subject to consent to data processing is a core element of data protection within the European Union as it empowers the controller to process legally the personal data of that subject. However, such consent by the data subject is limited only to a certain extent and in particular underlies the data subject's right to withdraw consent at any

* Professor of German and European Consumer Law, Private Law and Comparative Law, University of Bayreuth.

1 This, in particular, includes the contributions to the Chicago conference on 'Contracting over Privacy' organised by Omri Ben-Shahar and Lior Strahilevitz in October 2015, see i.a. Omri Ben-Shahar and Lior Strahilevitz, 'Contracting over Privacy: Introduction' (2016) 45 Journal of Legal Studies 1; Omri Ben-Shahar and Adam Chilton, 'Simplification of Privacy Disclosures: An Experimental Test' (2016) 45 Journal of Legal Studies 41; Oren Bar-Gill and Ben-Shahar, 'Optimal Defaults in Consumer Markets' (2016) 45 Journal of Legal Studies 137.

2 COM(2015) 634 final. For an earlier approach, see Carman Langhanke and Martin Schmidt-Kessel, 'Consumer Data as Consideration' (2015) 6 EuCML 218.

time, Art 7(3) GDPR. This precarious nature of consent (and the legal position obtained by the controller by means of such consent) leads to the more general question on how contracting over privacy could produce binding contracts. In other words, how far do rules on data protection affect the binding effect of a contract? This question, central to this paper, consists of two main parts: (i) how far data protection law produces situations of illegality (due to serving as *ordre public interne*)? (ii) how far do (legal) impediments brought about by data protection to the performance of a valid contract limit the binding effect of the contract?

In dealing with these questions one has to first reflect in general on the relationship between a contract and the standards of lawful processing under data protection law (II.). Although the result is that contract and consent to data processing have to be understood as being different and separated notions, such clear distinction does not exclude overlaps between the two regimes and disciplines. Here, rules on illegality of contracts when deviating from data protection law are the first junction (III.). Even if conflicting data protection law and its effects do not affect the validity of the contract, contract law rules on impossibility of performance may continue to apply, thereby giving rise to the second junction between the two disciplines (IV.). Where the data subject's right to withdraw consent to data processing is concerned, the question arises as to the extent to which the parties to a contract may – directly or indirectly – deviate from the rules on consent and how far these rules establish mandatory law also for the contract itself (V.). This relationship between contract and data protection can then serve as a basis to examine the consequences and effects on the contract of the withdrawal of consent by the data subject (VI.).

II. Contract and standards of lawful processing

The topic of this contribution lies at the heart of the relationship between contracts and the processing of personal data. Accordingly, it is important to emphasize at the outset the differences in legal framework: whereas the GDPR has a general perception of this relationship, EU contract law and the laws of the Member States have only just started to develop such perception or, more generally, a kind of *Datenschuldrecht*, a legal discipline on data related obligations.

1. *Separation of contract from standards of processing*

As a starting point, the GDPR considers the legality of processing on the one hand and contract and the contractual relationship on the other as being different and separate institutions.[3] Arguments for this separation may be derived not only from the several references to contract (Arts 6(1)(b) and 9(2)(h) GDPR in particular) but also from several rules on consent. For example, Art 7(2) GDPR clarifies that consent shall be clearly distinguishable from the other matters, thereby establishing a particular standard of transparency for the consent in the context of the conclusion of a contract.[4] Moreover, the rule in Art 7(4) GDPR on bundling of consent with other contractual obligations demonstrates that the GDPR understands consent as being something 'under' the contract, which might even become the object of a promise so becoming the object of a contractual obligation.[5] The fact that contract law for minors largely remains unaffected in spite of rules on consent given by minors (Art 8(3) GDPR) hints further at a separation between contract and lawfulness of processing.

2. *(Re-)connecting contract and lawfulness of processing*

Having separated contract and consent – and thereby data processing and contract – from each other on a conceptual level, the GDPR deliberately reconnects contract and the lawfulness of processing by referring to the

3 Dirk Heckmann and Paschke, 'Art 7' in Eugen Ehmann and Martin Selmayr (eds), *Datenschutzgrundverordnung* (C.H. Beck 2018) para 30; Carman Langhanke, *Daten als Leistung* (Mohr Siebeck 2018) 148–151; Axel Metzger, 'Dienst gegen Daten: Ein synallagmatischer Vertrag' (2016) 216 AcP 216 817, 831; Martin Schmidt-Kessel, 'Consent for the Processing of Personal Data and its Relationship to Contract' in Alberto De Franceschi and Reiner Schulze (eds), *Digital Revolution – New Challenges for Law* (C.H. Beck 2019) no. 13-17; Louisa Specht, 'Daten als Gegenleistung – Verlangt die Digitalisierung nach einem neuen Vertragstypus?' (2017) 15-16 JZ 763, 765.

4 *Schmidt-Kessel* (n 3) para 14; cf *Specht* (n 3) 766.

5 *Schmidt-Kessel* (n 3) para 16; Thomas Riehm, 'Freie Widerrufbarkeit der Einwilligung und Struktur der Obligation' in Tereza Pertot (ed.), Rechte an Daten (Mohr Siebeck 2020) 176, 186 et seq.

contract as a potential basis for lawful processing. Such references appear in Arts 6(1)(b) and 9(2)(h) GDPR and for profiling in Art 22(2)(a) GDPR.[6]

Art 6(1)(b) GDPR reflects the first junction between contract and the lawfulness of processing; it may be called the *general contract privilege* of data protection law: data processing shall be lawful if it is necessary for the performance of a contract to which the data subject is party. The provision focuses on controllers' duties and obligations under such a contract in particular, whereas it is not yet entirely clear whether the contractual duties of the data subject would also authorize the controller to process the respective personal data.[7] This general contract privilege does not apply to the special categories of personal data falling under Art 9 GDPR. Instead, Art 9(2)(h) GDPR provides a much more restricted legal basis in relation to the performance of contracts for medical treatment and preventive medicine in particular. Moreover, Art 22(2)(a) GDPR establishes an additional particular contract privilege in instances where automated individual decision-making (including profiling) is necessary in order to enter into or perform of a contract between the data subject and the controller. In all these cases the contract privilege aims to enable performance of the contract and to set aside possible impediments from data protection law to the performance.

3. *The scope of Art 6(1)(b) GDPR*

At present, the scope of Art 6(1)(b) GDPR is not sufficiently settled; in particular the provision does not provide for a conclusive concept for data-related duties and obligations of the data subject.[8] Moreover, it can be seriously doubted whether the provision applies to duties and obligations to provide for (rights to use) personal data for data-based business and earning models.

While it is understood that the general contract privilege applies to the duties and obligations of the controller (cf Recital 40 GDPR) it is not entirely clear whether the general contract privilege also applies to duties and obligations of the data subject. The qualification 'necessary for the perfor-

---

6 Whether Member States are allowed under the GDPR to also (re-)connect contract and consent by making the valid contract a prerequisite to the validity of consent, is still an open question, cf *Schmidt-Kessel* (n 3) paras 30–39.

7 See below, subsection 3.

8 cf for a rather German perspective Sebastian Schulz, 'Art 6' in Peter Gola (ed.), *Datenschutz-Grundverordnung* (2nd edn, C.H. Beck 2018) paras 28–40.

mance of a contract' mainly formulates the purpose of the rule, namely to enable contract performance and avoid impediments to the performance of the contract by data protection law. This purpose – as the wording of the provision – is not restricted to duties and obligations of the controller or other parties, but would also cover duties and obligations of the data subject.

On the other hand, the regulatory system within the GDPR (in particular, the rules on consent and legitimate interest) raises an argument in the opposite direction and asks for reluctance: including duties and obligations of the data subject to provide a legal basis for data processing under Art 6(1)(b) GDPR would undermine the pressure for other legal bases in particular for consent (and for legitimate interests, Art 6(1)(f) GDPR).[9] Moreover, Recital 40GDPR may be read in the sense of Art 6(1)(b) GDPR only covering duties and obligations of the controller. A final argument might be drawn from the second part of Art 6(1)(b) GDPR dealing with pre-contractual situations which obviously only covers activities by the controller 'at the request of the data subject prior to entering into the contract'. Whereas the precise calibration of the general contract privilege remains an open question (ultimately to be decided by the ECJ), there appears to be a tendency – based on arguments of the structure, wording and the wider purpose of the provisions – towards a restrictive approach to Art 6(1)(b) GDPR. The general contract privilege, therefore, tends to cover only duties and obligations of the controller, which should not to be impeded by data protection law.

A second approach to restrict the scope of application of Art 6(1)(b) GDPR argues that the provision is restricted to accessory processing only.[10]

---

9 Christiane Wendehorst and Friedrich Graf von Westphalen, 'Das Verhältnis zwischen Datenschutz-Grundverordnung und AGB-Recht' (2016) 52 NJW 3745, 3747.

10 *Langhanke/Schmidt-Kessel* (n 2) 220; Andreas Sattler, 'Personenbezug als Hindernis des Datenhandels' in *Pertot* (n 5) 49, 69–70; Schantz, 'Art 6' in Spiros Simitis, Gerrit Hornung and Indra Spiecker (eds), *Datenschutzrecht* (Nomos 2019) para 33; Martin Schmidt-Kessel and Anna Grimm, 'Unentgeltlich oder entgeltlich? – Der vertragliche Austausch von digitalen Inhalten gegen personenbezogene Daten' [2017] ZfPW 84, 90. Similarly Dimitrios Linardatos, 'Daten als Gegenleistung im Vertrag mit Blick auf die Richtlinie über digitale Inhalte' in Louisa Specht-Riemenschneider, Nikola Werry and Susanna Werry (eds), *Datenrecht in der Digitalisierung* (Erich Schmidt 2019) para 45, Friedrich Graf von Westphalen and Christiane Wendehorst, 'Hergabe personenbezogener Daten für digitale Inhalte – Gegenleistung, bereitzustellendes Material oder Zwangsbeitrag zum Datenbinnenmarkt?' [2016] BB 2179, 2184; *Wendehorst/Graf von Westphalen* (n 9) 3747.

According to this view, the provision does not apply where data are the core object of the data subject's performance. The main argument is again the purpose of the provision, which would not cover the commercialization of personal data but is restricted to enable other performance, for which (ancillary) data processing is necessary. Again, such a restriction of Art 6(1)(b) GDPR is not mirrored by the wording of the provision. Such a restricted scope would however be in line with the origins of the general contract privilege, which emerged before data-based business models became a significant issue.

The advocates of this restriction have so far left open the application to the controller's core obligations: does Art 6(1)(b) GDPR cover contractual promises by the controller to the data subject to process its personal data being at the core of the contractual relationship? A practical example would be the profile, established for the use of a dating service app, preparing automated propositions for possible matches. The amendment of the general contract privilege by the particular one for profiling in Art 22(2)(a) GDPR shows the general systematic direction: the controller's core obligations provide for a justification for processing under Arts 6(1)(b), 22(2)(a) GDPR at least insofar as the much more restrictive requirements under Art 9 GDPR do not apply.

III. Illegality of contracts deviating from the GDPR?

Deviations from the GDPR may be sanctioned in several cases with high administrative fines or even criminal sanctions, though the latter are at the discretion of the Member States. Therefore, the various national and European rules on the illegality of contracts, contractual promises, contract terms, and on performance of contractual obligations provide for a second important category of junctions between contract law and the GDPR. From this perspective, it could be seen as surprising that the GDPR also adheres to the general principles of freedom of contract and party autonomy (1). In contrast, illegality of contract or contract clauses is the exception under the GDPR (2). On the other hand, illegality and voidness of contract terms are a well-known instrument under the GDPR (3), the scope of which is not fully clear at present.

1. GDPR adheres to freedom of contract

The autonomy of the data subject is a central principle underpinning European data protection law. First and foremost, the autonomy is mirrored by the importance of consent as a legal basis for data processing (i.a. Arts 6(1)(a), 7, 8 GDPR). Moreover, the right to object to data processing based on the legitimate interest of the controller (Art 6(1)(f) GDPR) established by Art 21 GDPR flanks this general approach. Information duties and information access rights aim to enable the data subject to autonomously control the data processing.

Beyond these direct references to the autonomy of the data subject, several provisions of the GDPR refer to contracts among private parties including the data subject. These references not only concern the aforementioned contract privileges in Arts 6(1)(b), 9(2)(h), 22(2)(a) GDPR but also cover *inter alia* the (weak) bundling prohibition (Art 7(4) GDPR), the relationship to contract law rules on the protection of minors (Art 8(3) GDPR), the scope of information duties (Art 13(2)(e) GDPR), the right to data portability (Art 20(1) GDPR) and transfers of personal data to third countries (Arts 46(2)(c) and (d), (3)(a), 49(1)(b) and (c) GDPR). Through these cross-references European data protection law incorporates the national standards of contract law (including party autonomy and freedom of contract) into the system of data protection.

Moreover, Recital 42 GDPR clarifies the applicability of the Unfair Contract Terms Directive 93/13/EEC not only to the respective contracts with consumers but also to the terms of the consent by the data subject.[11] This Directive also takes freedom of contract as a starting point and on this basis prohibits particular contract terms. The cross-reference to the Directive in Recital 42 GDPR demonstrates the fundamental nature of the principle of freedom of contract for data protection law, which remain in a significant contrast to the general prohibitions principle of the GDPR.

---

11 Jan Henrik Klement, 'Art 7' in *Simitis/Hornung/Spiecker* (n 10) paras 80–81. For more details see *Vanessa Mak*, 'Contract and Consumer Law' in Vanessa Mak, Eric Tjong Tjin and Anna Berlee (eds), *Research Handbook in Data Science and Law* (Edward Elgar 2018) 17, 30.

2. *Illegality and voidness as the exception*

As a consequence of the application of the general principle of freedom of contract to data protection law, illegality of contract and illegality of contract terms form the exception under the GDPR. Aside from Recital (42) GDPR and its reference to the Unfair Contract Terms Directive 93/13/EEC, the weak bundling prohibition (Art 7(4) GDPR) is the only case which come closes to declaring the invalidity of a juridical act, yet probably does not always lead to invalidity of consent.[12] Where the contract otherwise deviates from the prerequisites of the GDPR, the consequence is not illegality of the contract but rather other negative consequences, though the contract remains valid: This is particularly the case where a contract between controller and processor does meet the legal requirements under Art 28(3) GDPR with the consequence that the processor will be qualified as a (joint) controller, while the contract between the two remains valid.

Beyond the Unfair Contract Terms Directive 93/13/EEC and – possibly – Art 7(4) GDPR illegality may serve as an important tool to prevent restrictions of the data subject's autonomy and freedom of contract between data subject and controller. Such a consequence should be derived from national principles and provisions functionally equivalent to Arts II.–7:301 and II.–7:302 DCFR for prohibited deviations from core provisions of the GDPR.[13] Important examples thereof are the voidness for illegality of those agreements and terms excluding or restricting withdrawal of consent (Art 7(3) GDPR) or the objection to processing (Art 21(1) GDPR).[14] Moreover, Arts 7(3), 21(1) GDPR have to be understood to also prohibit obligations to refrain from withdrawing or objecting.[15] Sometimes the consent of the data subject is even seen as a prerequisite for the contract giving rise to obligations,[16] or freedom of consent is used as an argument against the

---

12 cf *Langhanke* (n 3) 136f.; *Linardatos* (n 10) para 49. See also the Italian Cass. 2.7.2018 – no. 17278 (with case note by Tereza Pertot, 'Die Auslegung des datenschutzrechtlichen Koppelungsverbots – Lockerung durch den Corte di Cassazione' (2019) 2 GPR 54) and the Austrian OGH 31.8.2018 – 6 Ob 140/18 h (with case note by *Sebastian Schwamberger*, 'Reichweite des datenschutzrechtlichen Koppelungsverbots nach alter und neuer Rechtslage' (2019) 2 GPR 57).

13 *Heckmann/Paschke* (n 3) para 30; Alisa Rank-Haedler, 'Daten als Leistungsgegenstand: Vertragsrechtliche Typisierung' in *Specht-Riemenschneider/Werry/Werry* (n 10) para. 14.

14 See below, section VI.

15 See below, section VI.

16 See, in particular, *Linardatos* (n 10) para 41.

possibility of a valid contractual obligation to consent to data processing[17]. Others hold the bargaining on the ways of data processing or the duties of the controller to be precluded by the GDPR overriding national contract law.[18]

IV. Impediments to performance affecting binding effect

Affecting the binding effect of contracts, which are in conflict with data protection law, is not necessarily restricted to illegality. A contract may also be affected by legal impediments to performance. In particular, the unlawfulness of data processing may lead to a legal impediment to performance.[19] Such unlawfulness may bar both duties and obligations of the data subject and duties and obligations of the other party:[20] In either case, it would at least bar the enforcement of performance in kind.

Additionally, a relevant impediment would affect counter obligations under the contract. Under most contract laws of the EU Member States, such legal impediment would not lead to an *ipso iure* termination of the contract. However, there is a strong traditional trait to such a solution. In particular, such cases represent the historical *raison d'être* of the classical *condictio causa data causa non secuta*, which is also mirrored in some older provisions such as § 326(1) BGB and the Hague Convention on the sale of goods. Moreover, many classical *force majeure* clauses lead to an *ipso iure* termination, which would, however, usually not apply to the cases at hand on initial impediments to performance caused by conflicts with data protection law.

Termination of the contract due to a legal impediment to performance is usually rather framed as a remedy triggered by declaration (or in older provisions by court order on the application of the aggrieved party). Such a solution is much more flexible for calibrating the consequences of termination to, *inter alia*, the values in exchange, the amounts earned (in particular by the controller) and the degrees of amortization. Keeping in mind that the value of data-related performances is presently very difficult to de-

17 *Giovanni De Cristofaro*, 'Die datenschutzrechtliche Einwilligung als Gegenstand des Leistungsversprechens' in *Pertot* (n 5) 151, 165–166.

18 cf Guiseppe Versaci, 'Personal Data and Contract Law: Challenges and Concerns about the Economic Exploitation of the Right to Data Protection' (2018) 4 ERCL 374, 388.

19 *Schmidt-Kessel/Grimm* (n 10) 103.

20 cf *Metzger* (n 3) 855 (denied for withdrawal of consent).

termine, such a more flexible right to terminate should be preferred over the erratic solutions of *ipso iure* avoidance.

V. *Right to withdraw from consent as a part of the ordre public interne*

The data subject may withdraw his consent at any time (Art 7(3) GDPR). The wording of the provision does not give clear guidance whether the right to withdraw is mandatory and thus belongs to the *ordre public interne* of the *acquis*. Art 8(2) of the EU Charter of Fundamental Rights ('CFR') indeed mentions consent but not the right to withdraw consent. Likewise, Art 21 GDPR does not expressly state whether the right to object is mandatory or not. Some authors have argued, therefore, that under a binding contract withdrawal may be restricted by good faith and fair dealing[21] or by the binding effect of the contract[22]. However, the better reasons support the opinion that the right to withdraw and the right to object are impliedly established as mandatory rights of the data subject.[23] Moreover, Art 8 CFR supports this mandatory nature on the level of primary law at least for the right to withdraw consent.[24] Recital 39 DCD now seems to confirm this.

The main reasons for this view may be drawn first from the principle of party autonomy, which governs the GDPR and the CFR. As opposed to freedom of contract, which by definition must be a bilateral (or multilateral) freedom, the freedom of the data subject to consent (or not to consent) to data processing by the controller is a unilateral concept aiming to protect only the interests of the data subject. Therefore, as opposed to the basic principles of contract law, the capacity to become legally bound by consent is not an element of the freedom to consent. The consent is, therefore,

---

21 See Benedikt Buchner, *Informationelle Selbstbestimmung im Privatrecht* (Mohr Siebeck 2006) 270 et seq.

22 *Linardatos* (n 10) paras 56–59. Cf Andreas Sattler, 'Personenbezogene Daten als Leistungsgegenstand' [2017] JZ 1036, 1042–1042.

23 Alberto De Franceschi, *La circulazione die dati personali tra privacy e contratto* (Edizioni Scientifiche Italiane 2017) 73, 120; Peter Schantz and Heinrich Wolff, *Das neue Datenschutzrecht* (C.H. Beck 201) para 532; *Schmidt-Kessel/Grimm* (n 10) 91; *Versaci* (n 18) 391; *Graf von Westphalen/Wendehorst* (n 10) 2183ff. More radically *De Cristofaro* (n 17) 166 argues against the validity of consent-related obligations, which would restrict freedom of consent.

24 *De Franceschi* (n 23) 74, 115, 120; *Schmidt-Kessel/Grimm* (n 10) 91; *Graf von Westphalen/Wendehorst* (n 10) 2183–2814.

freely withdrawable and the right of the data subject to withdraw is protected under Art 8(2) CFR (and Art 7(3) GDPR).

This basic solution is in line with the specific thresholds for consent, established in particular by Arts 4(11), 7, 8 GDPR. The general enforcement deficit neglecting the extraordinary decision that pure information asymmetry as such could render the consent void (see Art 4(11) GDPR) should not lead to an underestimation of these thresholds. The right to withdraw consent mirrors the thresholds by releasing the data subject from the need to explain and prove the information asymmetry, in general, and the lack of information given, in particular.

Moreover, the right to withdraw is a consequence of the purpose limitation principle, Art 5(1)(b) GDPR. Other than Art 6(1)(b)–(d) GDPR, the legal basis of consent under Art 6(1)(a) GDPR is not restricted to a certain purpose or a certain set of purposes, but rather the purposes covered by the consent are within the decision of the data subject. This raises the risk of a delimitation of the protective function of Art 6(1) GDPR by consent to processing for a broad range of purposes. This risk is balanced by the limitation of the effects of consent inherent to the right to withdraw it, which aims to execute the purpose limitation principle not only by the – rather weak – specification requirement but also by limiting the binding nature of consent. This purpose limiting function of the right to withdraw would not be effective if the right to withdraw would not be mandatory.

On the other hand, the controller's trust in the consent given is protected not only by the significant factual rarity of withdrawal but also by the lack of retroactive effect (see Art 7(3) 2nd Sentence GDPR).[25] Practical needs to organize the cessation of data processing will additionally be satisfied by an application of Art 6(1)(f) GDPR under a transition period. Data protection law, therefore, safeguards the general interest of the controller of being protected in his expectation interest in the possibility to use personal data for the purposes consented to by the data subject at least until withdrawal. Contract law consequences – such as rights to end the contract via withdrawal or other means of expiration of the obligations of the controller as a party to the contract – may amend this protection.

As a consequence of these considerations, the right to withdraw consent constitutes a part of the *ordre public interne*.[26] The data subject does not

25 *Heckmann/Paschke* (n 3) para 87.

26 *Langhanke* (n 3) 118; *Langhanke/Schmidt-Kessel* (n 2) 221; *Metzger* (n 3) 825; *Specht* (n 3) 767.

have the capacity to waive the right to withdraw consent.[27] The mandatory nature of that right goes even further by also prohibiting the establishment of contractual obligations not to withdraw from consent.[28] Without this amendment, European law would allow the circumvention of the incapacity to waive the right to withdraw. Therefore, Art 8 CFR and Art 7(3) GDPR also prevent contractual obligations to that effect. Indirectly, this interpretation excludes fully enforceable obligations to establish a right to use personal data by way of consent.[29]

This result raises further questions: to what extent does the lack of an enforceable obligation limit the binding effect of a contract? In addition, to what degree does the free right to withdrawal determine the consequences of withdrawal? While the second question will be dealt with in the next section, the answer to the first focuses on the initial binding effect of such a contract and the obligations thereunder. With Art 3(1) subpara 2 DCD and the new Art 3(1a) Consumer Rights Directive 2011/83/EU[30] ('CRD'), EU law acknowledges the possibility of such a binding effect at least for the situations of data processing under Art 6(1)(a) and (f) GDPR:[31] for contracts for the supply of digital content or a digital service, the consumer may – validly – undertake to provide personal data to the supplier and confer upon him the right to use the data,[32] which enables the consumer to profit from the standards on conformity for digital content or digital service supplied (Arts 6ff DCD) and from remedies for nonconformity (Art 14 DCD) established by the Digital Content Directive 2019/770. The same holds true for the consumer protection instruments enacted in transposing the Consumer Rights Directive 2011/83/EU into national law. Therefore, EU law prohibits an obligation enforceable in kind, but does not (aim to) prohibit valid contracts including such data-related obligations. This is in line with the fact, that under European private law(s) enforceability in kind is – from a comparative point of view – not self-evident. On the contrary, national legal orders know of many concepts

---

27 *Klement* (n 11) para. 92.

28 *Langhanke/Schmidt-Kessel* (n 2) 220; *Schmidt-Kessel/Grimm* (n 10) 92; contra *Klement* (n 11) para. 92.

29 *Langhanke/Schmidt-Kessel* (n 2) 221; *Riehm* (n 5) 187–189.

30 As amended by the Directive (EU) 2019/2161 of the European Parliament and of the Council of 27 November 2019 amending Council Directive 93/13/EEC and Directives 98/6/EC, 2005/29/EC and 2011/83/EU of the European Parliament and of the Council as regards the better enforcement and modernisation of Union consumer protection rules [2019] OJ L238/7.

31 *Metzger* (n 3) 824.

32 *Langhanke* (n 3) 108 et seq.; *Metzger* (n 3) 833.

to handle non-enforceable duties and obligations under a – valid – contract, such as natural obligations, *Obliegenheiten*, exception of contradictory behaviour *(dolo agit)*, justified non-performance or excused non-performance.[33] Most are dealt with in the discussion on *Datenschuldrecht* and data-related obligations from 2015 onwards.[34] On the other hand, authors discussing the exact legal construction of data-related obligations agree in generally accepting the validity of the respective contracts.

VI. Consequences of withdrawal under an existing contract

A necessary point of consideration concerns the consequences of withdrawal under Art 7(3) GDPR on an existing contract. While the provision deals with the main consequences of withdrawal for the lawfulness of data processing (1), so far no obligatory consequences are expressly regulated either in data protection law or in contract law. However, a set of implied consequences based on the effectiveness of data protection will certainly emerge to protect freedom of consent and the free withdrawal from consent (2). Moreover, the EU recently established two special rules on restitutionary effects of ending a contract entailing data-related obligations (3), which have to be evaluated as to whether they could serve as a model for restitution after withdrawal under Art 7(3) GDPR (4).

1. Consequences under data protection law

Art 7(3) 2nd Sentence GDPR establishes a rough structure of the consequences of withdrawal under data protection law: Withdrawal of consent has no retroactive effect. Therefore, the lawfulness of processing based on consent before withdrawal is not affected.[35]

What remains open to discussion, however, is whether another legal basis for the data processing could apply after withdrawal or to the conse-

---

33 Cf the discussion in *Langhanke* (n 3) 125–129; *Langhanke/Schmidt-Kessel* (n 2) 221.

34 Natural obligations are considered by *Langhanke/Schmidt-Kessel* (n 2) 221; *Riehm* (n 5) 192. *Obliegenheiten* are considered by *Riehm* (n 5) 192. A dolo agit-exception is argued by *Langhanke* (n 3) 127. The concept of justified non-performance may be found with *De Franceschi* (n 23) 121; *Langhanke/Schmidt-Kessel* (n 2) 218, 221; *Metzger* (n 3) 834ff., 855; *Schmidt-Kessel/Grimm* (n 10) 103ff. Excused non-performance is argued in favour of by *Specht* (n 3) 767.

35 See *ex multis De Franceschi* (n 23) 116.

quences of withdrawal.[36] In the general discourses on data protection law this mainly concerns the case of a parallel legal basis and, in particular, whether withdrawal would bar their applicability. However, the structure of Art 6(1) GDPR is very clear as to the parallel applicability of all legal bases mentioned in the provision,[37] which excludes a general solution of withdrawal always barring the other legal bases. Art 17(1)(b) GDPR provides for the decisive systematic argument.[38] On the other hand, at least in case of Art 6(1)(f) GDPR the controller in the individual case may be prevented from pleading a legitimate interest because of contractual obligations to the contrary, of waiver, or of estoppel by inconsistent behaviour *(venire contra factum proprium)*. Such an exclusion may be based in the individual case on Art 5(1)(a) GDPR.[39]

For the questions at hand, it is of much more interest whether withdrawal could lead to an additional application of other legal bases just for dealing with the consequences of withdrawal. For example, the winding-up of the contract – in case this becomes necessary because of the withdrawal of consent – should at least provide the controller with a legitimate interest (Art 6(1)(f) GDPR) for that purpose. Moreover, the general contract privilege of Art 6(1)(b) GDPR would apply for new contractual duties, e.g. restitution after termination or modification(s) of the contract.[40]

2. *Consequences in contract law*

In contract law, a broad variety of questions of contracting over privacy and *Datenschuldrecht* emerge because of withdrawal of consent. If the right to use personal data forms the object of an obligation under the contract, the original aim of the performance of the contract will be disarranged by the withdrawal. This will lead in many cases to consequences for the other obligations under the contract. The Digital Content Directive 2019/700 deliberately abstains from establishing rules on the consequences of with-

36 See *Buchner* (n 21) 272–274.

37 *Schulz* (n 8) para 10.

38 *Schulz* (n 8) para 11; Phillip Hacker, 'Daten als Gegenleistung: Rechtsgeschäfte im Spannungsfeld von DS-GVO und allgemeinem Vertragsrecht' [2019] ZfPW 148, 160; *Klement* (n 11) para. 34.

39 *Schantz/Wolff* (n 23) para 475.

40 *Schulz* (n 8) para 28; *Riehm* (n 5) 180. Contra *Schantz* (n 10) para 30; *Schantz/Wolff* (n 23) para 558.

drawal in contract law leaving them to national law (for the time being).[41] Of the variety of possible echoes of withdrawal in the contract, the following will only deal with the replacement by another obligation of the data subject, and with termination.

However, those consequences are not always inevitable: where the controller has drawn his earnings (or the overwhelming part thereof) out of the right to use the personal data, before the data subject withdrew consent, there might be no need to change anything of the rest of the contract. For example, this might be the case where a consent without time limit[42] is withdrawn years later or where the amortization for the controller takes place within the first days after consent was given.

a) Replacement by an obligation to pay?

Some discussions in the context of the bundling prohibition in Art 7(4) GDPR suggest that replacing the data-related obligation by an obligation with a different content could be a suitable contractual consequence of withdrawal of consent. This suggestion originates in the idea that a bundling prohibition may be overcome by offering alternatives to consent, e.g. an extra payment.[43] However, would replacing the use of the personal data with another obligation of the data subject (e.g. additional payment, losing a discount, compensation for value) be in conformity with the free right to withdraw?[44] Any detriment to the data subject could be interpreted as a restriction of the – mandatory – right to withdraw from consent. Therefore, the answer correlates to a large extent with the meaning of Art 7(4) GDPR: Initially using an obligatory alternative money consideration as a fallback position in case of withdrawal would be in line with GDPR. Therefore, the weaker Art 7(4) GDPR is, the more the compensatory solution would be on the table.

---

41 See Recital 40 DCD.

42 If not anyway such a consent would be qualified usury, cf Martin Schmidt-Kessel, *Lehrbuch Verbraucherrecht* (2018) para 127.

43 See *Hacker* (n 38) 178; *Metzger* (n 3) 823 and 824; *Pertot* (n 12) 55; *Schwamberger* (n 12) 58; Shaira Thobani, 'Il mercato dei dati personali: tra tutela dell'interessato e tutela dell'utente' (2019) 3 Rivista di diritto dei media 131, 140ff. Contra *Lindratos* (n 10) para 49.

44 Cf *Specht* (n 3) 769.

b) Termination of the contract?

As withdrawal leads to a termination of the right to use the personal data under data protection law, the connotation with a right to terminate the contract is rather obvious.[45] However, neither the GDPR nor the Digital Content Directive 2019/770 give a hint into that direction. Recital 40 DCD is sometimes understood as a mandate for Member States to establish a right of the controller to end the contract for withdrawal of consent by the other party. However, it was a wise decision by the EU legislator not to go into the regulatory details here and Member States should follow by applying general contract law instead of establishing new rules. This is not only true because of the divergence of Member States' legal orders as to termination the contract disturbed by breach or other events. For the situations at hand, there may have been no uniform policy decision to take.

Whether the controller should be allowed to bring the contract to an end if the data subject withdraws from consent, depends on many factors. Dogmatically, the exact interpretation of Art 7(4) GDPR would be substantially influenced by such a decision. From a policy point of view, the (subjective) equilibrium of values of the reciprocal performances is not necessarily touched upon by the end of the right to use the personal data. Finally, the right to terminate the contract must also be calibrated with the counter-performance by the controller, which might be a single act of supply or a continuous supply.

3. Relevant restitutionary rules within the acquis

EU law is rather reluctant to deal with the detailed consequences of termination for breach. References to national law prevail. Arts 16 and 17 DCD therefore represent the exception. For the first time ever in EU law, Art 16(2) DCD now deals with the restitution of data provided by one party in fulfilling the contract: 'In respect of personal data of the consumer, the trader shall comply with the obligations applicable under Regulation (EU) 2016/679.' Art 13(4) CRD establishes the same rule (with identical

45 This consequence is argued by several authors: *De Cristofaro* (n 17) 171; *Metzger* (n 3) 864; *Specht* (n 3) 768. Cf *Langhanke/Schmidt-Kessel* (n 2) 222 and Gerald Spindler, 'Digitale Wirtschaft – analoges Recht: Braucht das BGB ein Update?' (2016) 17 JZ 805, 807.

wording) for the restitution after a withdrawal by a consumer from a consumer contract under the Directive.

Probably, the cross-reference to the GDPR not only covers the rights and remedies of the data subject established by Arts 12–23 GDPR (information, access, erasure, restriction of processing, notification, data portability, etc.) but also those dealt with by Arts 77–84 GDPR (including effective judicial remedy against controller, monetary compensation). However, at present it is not entirely clear whether these obligations are conclusive in the sense that neither additional rights of the consumer may be deduced from the Directive(s) nor may the Member States add rules, e.g. for the restitution of profits gained by using the personal data. The question is not without importance bearing in mind that not all rules in Arts 12–33, 77–84 GDPR are meant to apply in circumstances of restitution. Moreover, ending the contract under the Digital Content Directive 2019/770 and the Consumer Rights Directive 2011/83/EU does not necessarily trigger the rights and remedies to which the articles refer.

4. *No generalization of the rules so far established!*

The aforementioned articles with rules for two different means of ending the contract raise the question whether they represent more general principles of data protection law, of *Datenschuldrecht* in general or of the principles governing restitution in case of data-related contractual obligations in particular. From a general data protection perspective one could even ask whether Art 16(2) DCD and Art 13(4) CRD cause a paradigm shift for the whole GDPR: do these provisions generally lead to a commercialization of the GDPR in the sense that the Regulation according to the European legislator also protects the commercial interests of the data subject in the use of his personal data? At least both articles here provide a valuable argument.[46]

On a more technical level, one could discuss whether the GDPR-remedies generally serve as a model solution on restitution after failure of contract. Expressed more dogmatically: does the GDPR serve as a functional *re vindicatio* for personal data?[47] The answer to this last question is – tentatively – 'no': Art 16(2) DCD and Art 13(4) CRD serve rather as a stopgap-solu-

46 See *Schmidt-Kessel* (n 3) paras 37–39.

47 Some authors seem to argue that way, see *De Franceschi* (n 23) 124; *Metzger* (n 3) 864; *Specht* (n 3) 768.

tion[48] in the sense of a *Datenschuldrecht avant la lettre*. Such an analysis is completely in line with the classical experiences with restitution after termination in other uniform law texts (e.g. the CISG). Usually such rules consist of some last minute formulas, in which only German lawyers seem to be significantly interested. The German particularities include a denser control of first instance judges by the German Federal Court of Justice *(Bundesgerichtshof)* in the realm of restitution, the fault principle, which largely prevents judges from solving restitutionary issues within the calculation of damages and the sharp dichotomy between the separate kinds of termination, the termination *ex tunc (Rücktritt)* and termination *ex nunc (Kündigung)*.

The solutions enacted in Art 16(2) DCD and Art 13(4) CRD should therefore not be taken too seriously. In particular, the provisions do not represent a binding interpretation of GDPR. First and foremost, however, Art 16(2) DCD and Art 13(4) CRD should not be used as a model for further legislation.

VI. Seven short conclusions

1) The GDPR is (inter alia) based on freedom of contract, but contains some restrictions in terms of illegality and legal impediments of performance.
2) The GDPR prevents data-related duties and obligations of the data subject from being enforceable in kind.
3) The GDPR does not prevent a contract including such duty or obligation from being binding as such on both parties.
4) Withdrawal of consent by the data subject is followed by consequences in data protection law mainly organized by the GDPR.
5) Consequences in contract are determined by GDPR only to a limited extent.
6) Art 16(2) DCD and Art 13(4) Directive CRD do not represent a binding interpretation of GDPR.
7) Art 16(2) DCD and Art 13(4) Directive CRD should not be used as a model for further legislation.

48 *Schmidt-Kessel* (n 3) para 39.

Article 16(2) of the 'Digital Content and Digital Services' Directive on the Consequences of Termination of Contract, or the Difficult Articulation between Union Law on Consumer Contract and Union Law on the Protection of Personal Data

Juliette Sénéchal[*]

According to a preliminary analysis, the right to terminate a consumer contract due to a failure of performance and the reciprocal restitutions, as a consequence of this termination, have the function of combating contractual imbalances resulting from this failure, while the law on the protection of personal data conveys the idea of the necessary protection of a fundamental right that is inextricably linked to the person whose data are collected: two distinct sets of rules, each with its own logic.

Nevertheless, this clear-cut distinction is Manichean.

Art 16 of the Directive 2019/770 of 20 May 2019 on certain aspects concerning contracts for the supply of digital content and digital services[1] is precisely the sign of the porosity between contractual rules and rules on the protection of personal data.

This new Directive enshrines the idea that personal data collected in connection with the contract for the provision of digital content and services contribute to the remuneration of the digital service provider, and enable him to no longer systematically charge consumers a price for the supply of that service.

Art 16 of this Directive deals with the question of the termination of this contract in the event of lack of conformity or failure to supply and raises the question of the trader's restitutions and abstentions in case of termination.

And the rules vary widely depending on whether the consumer has paid a price for receiving the digital service or digital content or whether the consumer has provided only data.

---

* Associate Professor of Private Law, University of Lille.

1 Directive (EU) 2019/770 of the European Parliament and of the Council of 20 May 2019 on certain aspects concerning contracts for the supply of digital content and digital services [2019] OJ L136/1.

Where the consumer has paid a price, Arts 16(1) and 17 Directive 2019/770, based exclusively on a contractual logic, and precisely on the logic of the termination of a synallagmatic contract, provide for reciprocal restitutions and abstentions in case of termination: the trader shall reimburse the consumer for all sums paid under the contract and the consumer shall refrain from using the digital content or digital service and from making it available to third parties. In cases where the digital content was supplied on a tangible medium, the consumer shall, at the request and at the expense of the trader, return the tangible medium to the trader without undue delay.

However, where the consumer has provided only data and in particular personal data[2], two distinct logics are to be articulated. The trader cannot reimburse a price that he has not received. Therefore, Art 16(2) Directive 2019/770 simply specifies that '[a]s regards the consumer's personal data, the trader shall comply with the obligations applicable under Regulation (EU) 2016/679'. In other words, this paragraph recalls that the consumer may exercise his rights under the General Data Protection Regulation (GDPR) of 27 May 2016, such as the right to erasure (Art 17) or the right to data portability (Art 20), two rights which are not at all a consequence of the termination of the contract, which are totally independent of the question of the termination of the contract. Then, the contractual logic reappears in Art 17 Directive 2019/770, which provides that the consumer shall refrain from using the digital content or digital service and from making it available to third parties. And where the digital content was supplied on a tangible medium, the consumer shall, at the request and at the expense of the trader, return the tangible medium to the trader without undue delay.

Art 16(2) Directive 2019/770 has not always been drafted in this way. The first version of this article, Art 13(2) of the Proposal for a Directive of 9 December 2015, opted for a pure contractual logic and provided reciprocal restitutions or abstentions even if the consumer had only provided per-

---

2 The data collected from the consumer are mainly, if not exclusively, personal data. However, Arts16(3) and 16(4) Directive 2019/770 also raise the question of the status of content other than personal data in the event of termination.

sonal data, did not pay a price, in order to receive the digital content or the digital service[3].

Where the consumer has provided only personal data, the logic of reciprocal restitutions or abstentions, specific to synallagmatic consumer contracts, has now disappeared from the Art 16(2) Directive 2019/770 and reflects the complexity of the articulation between contract law and data protection law.

The complexity is not only present in Art 16(2), but also in some other recitals and articles of the Directive 2019/770. For example, while the recitals of the Directive 2019/770 recall that the protection of personal data is a 'fundamental right' (Recital 24) and that the GDPR provides for 'non-contractual remedies' which prevail over the logic of the contractual remedies proposed in the Directive 2019/770 (Recital 48), these recitals also acknowledge that 'facts leading to a lack of compliance with requirements provided for by Regulation (EU) 2016/679, including core principles such

---

3 Art 13(2) of the proposal of the Directive of 9 December 2015: 'Where the consumer terminates the contract:

(a) the supplier shall reimburse to the consumer the price paid without undue delay and in any event not later than 14 days from receipt of the notice;
(b) the supplier shall take all measures which could be expected in order to refrain from the use of the counter-performance other than money which the consumer has provided in exchange for the digital content and any other data collected by the supplier in relation to the supply of the digital content including any content provided by the consumer with the exception of the content which has been generated jointly by the consumer and others who continue to make use of the content;
(c) the supplier shall provide the consumer with technical means to retrieve all content provided by the consumer and any other data produced or generated through the consumer's use of the digital content to the extent that data has been retained by the supplier. The consumer shall be entitled to retrieve the content free of charge, without significant inconvenience, in reasonable time and in a commonly used data format;
(d) where the digital content was not supplied on a durable medium, the consumer shall refrain from using the digital content or making it available to third parties, in particular by deleting the digital content or rendering it otherwise unintelligible;
(e) where the digital content was supplied on a durable medium, the consumer shall:
   (i) upon the request of the supplier, return, at the supplier's expense, the durable medium to the supplier without undue delay, and in any event not later than 14 days from the receipt of the supplier's request; and
   (ii) delete any usable copy of the digital content, render it unintelligible or otherwise refrain from using it or making it available to third parties.'

as the requirements for data minimisation, data protection by design and data protection by default, may, depending on the circumstances of the case, also be considered to constitute a lack of conformity of the digital content or digital service with subjective or objective requirements for conformity provided for in this Directive' (Recital 48).

This complexity can be explained by the duality of the objectives pursued by the texts concerning personal data protection. The European texts on the protection of personal data, and in particular the General Data Protection Regulation (GDPR) of 27 April 2016, which entered into force on 25 May 2018[4], follow two different objectives which are exposed in their title: 'protection of natural persons with regard to the processing of personal data', in the one hand, and 'free movement of such data' in the other hand[5].

These two objectives, partially contradictory, needed therefore to be articulated in the provisions of the GRPD.

This articulation has taken different forms[6]. Some provisions of the GDPR can be seen as the result of the articulation between the two contradictory objectives[7]. Some rights or prerogatives enshrined in a provision of the GDPR can be analysed more as the expression of one or of the other of the two objectives.

For example, Art 6 GDPR concerning the lawfulness of processing contains some basis for processing, for instance, the consent of the Art 6(1)(a)[8] that pursues the objective of the protection of the personal data of the data subject as a fundamental right. On the contrary, the legal basis of Art 6(1)(f), the notion of the legitimate interests, pursues the objective of the free

4 Regulation (EU) 2016/679 of the European Parliament and of the Council of 27 April 2016 on the protection of natural persons with regard to the processing of personal data and on the free movement of such data, and repealing Directive 95/46/EC (General Data Protection Regulation) [2016] OJ L119/1.

5 M Delmas-Marty, *Les forces imaginantes du droit (I), le relatif et l'universel* (Seuil 2004) 148ff: The author describes the race between human rights law and commercial law.

6 Other types of articulation can be found in foreign texts, such as in the California Consumer Privacy Act, which has the particularity of merging consumer and personal aspects into a single text: California Consumer Privacy Act, June 28, 2018, Title 1.81.5 (commencing with Section 1798.100) to Part 4 of Division 3 of the Civil Code, relating to privacy.

7 A Sen, *Development as Freedom* (Oxford University Press 1999): far from opposing human rights to the market, the economist A Sen proposes to integrate human rights into economic analysis.

8 Art 6(1)(a) GDPR: 'The data subject has given consent to the processing of his or her personal data for one or more specific purposes'.

flow of personal data, but limited to the respect of the fundamental rights of the data subject[9].

For other illustrative purposes, the right to erasure of Art 17 GDPR or the right to withdraw consent (Art 7 GDPR) certainly pursue the first objective of protecting the personal data of the data subject as a fundamental right. In this regard, this first objective is closely linked to non-contractual rights, obligations and remedies. Conversely, the right to data portability (Art 20 GDPR) pursues the objective of free movement of data and competition law issues[10]. The aim is to enable the data subject not to remain locked in the ecosystem of an economic operator and to be able to leave this first ecosystem by bringing his or her data with him or her to a second economic operator. In this regard, this second objective is linked to the notion of contract[11], which is a concept recognised by the GDPR, explicitly in Art 6(1)(b) referring to the contract concluded by the data controller, or in Art 28 referring to the contract between the controller and the processor, implicitly in Art 6(1)(f) through the notion of 'legitimate interests pursued by the controller or by a third party'.

To some extent, the new Directive 2019/770 concerning the contract for the supply of digital content and digital services and the General Data Protection Regulation, raise, both of them, the question of the relationship between the contract for the provision of digital content and digital services and the question of the collection of data from users of these digital contents and digital services.

But there are still uncertainties concerning the way to articulate contract law and data protection law, due to the duality of the main objectives of the GDPR, uncertainties that the European Data Protection Supervisor has

9 Art 6(1)(f) GDPR: 'Processing is necessary for the purposes of the legitimate interests pursued by the controller or by a third party, except where such interests are overridden by the interests or fundamental rights and freedoms of the data subject which require protection of personal data, in particular where the data subject is a child'.

10 RH Weber, 'Data Protection in the Termination of Contract' in R Schulze, D Staudenmayer, S Lohsse (eds), Contracts for the Supply of Digital Content: Regulatory Challenge and Gaps (Nomos 2017) 202: 'Having been a topic of competition law investigations for several years, the right to data portability is now also enshrined in Art 20 GDPR'.

11 The same logic of the right to portability as a means of guaranteeing competition law objectives and using contract law to achieve them can be found in Art 6 'Porting of data' of the Regulation (EU) 2018/1807 of 14 November 2018 on a framework for the free flow of non-personal data in the European Union [2018] OJ L303/59.

only partially resolved, by reminding the European legislator on 14 March 2017[12] and 5 October 2018[13] of the primacy of the General Data Protection Regulation over consumer law, but also the need to exclude consumers' personal data from the qualification of counter-performance in the contract for the provision of digital content and digital services.

At the end of this dialogue at European level, if the harmonisation of the regime of the contract for the supply of digital content and digital services, in terms of remedies in the event of lack of conformity or failure to supply, has seemingly been achieved in the Directive 2019/770, the conceptualisation of the contract for the provision of digital services have not yet been completed in this text (Part I).

As stated in Recital 12 of the Directive 2019/770, the task of determining the nature of the contract for the provision of digital content and digital services will be left to the Member States. However, the nature and regime of the contract for the provision of digital content and services are not two separate aspects. Consequently, the definition of the nature of the contract for the supply of digital content and digital services, at the national level, will necessarily have an impact on the regime of this contract, in particular with regard to the questions of the termination of the contract and the reciprocal (or non-reciprocal) restitutions following this termination (Part II).

I. The incompleteness of the conceptualisation of the contract for the supply of digital content and digital services, at the European level

The dialogue at European level took place on two stages. The Proposal of a Directive of 9 December 2015 concerning contracts for the supply of digital content, confronted with the question of the place of data collection within the contract for the provision of digital content and digital services, firstly, pursued an objective of equal treatment between economic operators, regardless of how they are remunerated (with a price or via data) (1). Finally, The Directive of 20 May 2019, according to the opinions of the

---

12 European Data Protection Supervisor, 'Opinion 4/2017 on the Proposal for a Directive on certain aspects concerning contracts for the supply of digital content' <https://edps.europa.eu/sites/edp/files/publication/17-03-14_opinion_digital_content_en.pdf> accessed 12 August 2019.

13 European Data Protection Supervisor, 'Opinion 8/2018 on the legislative package "A new deal for consumers"' < https://edps.europa.eu/sites/edp/files/publication/18-10-05_opinion_consumer_law_en.pdf> accessed 12 August 2019.

European Data Protection Supervisor, adopted an incomplete solution by considering that the collection of consumer data cannot be analysed as a counter-performance for the digital content or service provided under the contract for the provision of digital content and digital services, while implicitly suggesting that this contract remains a synallagmatic contract (2).

1. *First stage of the dialogue: the competition law's objective of equal treatment between economic operators*

The first text that enshrined the important idea that personal data collected in connection with the contract for the provision of digital content and services contributed to the remuneration of the digital service provider, and allowed the latter to no longer systematically charge consumers a price for the provision of that service, was the proposal for a Directive of 9 December 2015 on the contract for the provision of digital content[14].

As originally drafted, this text did not focus on the issue of the protection of consumers' personal data, but on some objectives of competition law. In addition to the pursuit of consumer welfare, which is very different from the protection of fundamental consumer rights, one of the main objectives of the 2015 proposal was in particular to pursue equal legal treatment between economic operators providing digital content and digital services to consumers.

The observation made in 2015 was that, in the digital age, economic operators providing digital content and services are financed in two alternative and/or cumulative ways, i.e. sometimes by receiving a price from the consumer, sometimes by collecting data from the same consumer, when providing digital content and services[15]. Data collected can have various uses, as the development of targeted behavioural advertising, or as the development of artificial intelligence contributing to the improvement of the services provided by the operator and the corresponding strengthening of its economic position with regard to other operators on the market. In this context, the 2015 proposal, in its Art 3, envisaged the contract for the supply of digital content and digital services as a synallagmatic contract, and

14 European Commission, 'Proposal for a Directive of the European Parliament and of the Council on certain aspects concerning contracts for the supply of digital content' COM(2015) 634 final.

15 Recital 13 COM(2015) 634 final (n 14).

the price and the data collected from the consumer as alternative or cumulative counterparties to the digital service or digital content provided[16].

In line with Art 3, Art 13(2) of the proposal of Directive opted for a pure contractual logic and provided reciprocal restitutions or abstentions even if the consumer had only provided personal data, did not pay a price, to receive the digital content or the digital service[17].

In doing so, in the version of the proposal for a Directive on the contract for the provision of digital content of 9 December 2005, the data entered into the contractual field could be of a three-fold nature. It could be found in the digital content provided, in the digital service provided, but also in the data collected from the consumer in counterparty of the digital services or digital content provided.

This analysis by the European Commission, which was partially maintained in a second proposal for a Directive of 11 April 2018[18], a directive on a new deal for consumers, called for a reaction from the European Data Protection Supervisor.

2. *Second stage of the dialogue: personal data are not tradeable commodities…*

The European Data Protection Supervisor, by two opinions dated 14 March 2017[19] and 5 October 2018[20], first of all affirmed the primacy of the General Regulation on data protection over consumer law. This first statement was underpinned by the observation that the data collected from the consumer were mainly, if not exclusively, personal data. The Data Protection Supervisor further clarified that personal data could not be considered as contractual counterparty since such data, because of the fundamental

16 Art 3 COM(2015) 634 final (n 14): 'This Directive shall apply to any contract where the supplier supplies digital content to the consumer or undertakes to do so and, in exchange, a price is to be paid or the consumer actively provides counter-performance other than money in the form of personal data or any other data'.

17 See above (n 2).

18 European Commission, 'Proposal for a Directive of the European Parliament and of the Council amending Council Directive 93/13/EEC of 5 April 1993, Directive 98/6/EC of the European Parliament and of the Council, Directive 2005/29/EC of the European Parliament and of the Council and Directive 2011/83/EU of the European Parliament and of the Council as regards better enforcement and modernisation of EU consumer protection rules' COM(2018) 185 final.

19 Opinion 4/2017 (n 12).

20 Opinion 8/2018 (n 13).

rights attached to them, could not be considered as tradeable commodities[21].

Taking these observations into account, the Directive 2019/770 of 20 May 2019 (as well as the proposal for a Directive on a new deal for the consumer, as adopted by the European Parliament at first reading on 17 April 2019[22]) has made a very complex distinction between the scope of the text relating to contracts for the provision of digital services and the conceptual definition of the contract for the supply of digital content and digital services.

Concerning the scope of the Directive 2019/770, Art 3 still continues to stipulate that both contracts for the provision of digital content and digital services concluded in counterparty of the payment of a price and contracts in which consumers data is collected, without being asked to pay a price, must fall within their textual scope and receive the same legal regulation[23].

From the point of view of the conceptual definition of the contract for the provision of digital content and digital services, the Directive 2019/770 has abandoned any implicit or explicit reference to the notion of contractual counterparty in order to qualify the data collected from the consumer. The reference to the counterparty is only maintained in the event of the payment of a price by the consumer.

And finally, at the interface between the scope of the directive and the conceptual definition of the contract, Art 3 Directive 2019/770, implicitly referring to the legitimate basis for processing of Art 6(1)(b) GDPR con-

---

21 § 14, p. 9 et § 29, p. 13 of the Opinion 4/2017 (n 12).

22 European Parliament, 'Legislative resolution of 17 April 2019 on the Proposal for a Directive of the European Parliament and of the Council amending Council Directive 93/13/EEC of 5 April 1993, Directive 98/6/EC of the European Parliament and of the Council, Directive 2005/29/EC of the European Parliament and of the Council and Directive 2011/83/EU of the European Parliament and of the Council as regards better enforcement and modernisation of EU consumer protection rules' COM(2018) 185 final.

23 Art 3(1) Directive 2019/770: 'This Directive shall apply to any contract where the trader supplies or undertakes to supply digital content or a digital service to the consumer and the consumer pays or undertakes to pay a price.
This Directive shall also apply where the trader supplies or undertakes to supply digital content or a digital service to the consumer, and the consumer provides or undertakes to provide personal data to the trader, except where the personal data provided by the consumer are exclusively processed by the trader for the purpose of supplying the digital content or digital service in accordance with this Directive or for allowing the trader to comply with legal requirements to which the trader is subject, and the trader does not process those data for any other purpose'.

cerning the contractual necessity[24] and 6(1)(c) GDPR concerning the compliance with legal obligations, specifies that if 'the personal data provided by the consumer are exclusively processed by the trader for the purpose of supplying the digital content or digital service in accordance with this Directive or for allowing the trader to comply with legal requirements to which the trader is subject', without a price being paid by the consumer or data collected from him for any other purposes (targeted advertising, service improvement, development of artificial intelligence, etc.), this is a truly free contract which does not fall within the scope of the Directives on consumer contracts in the digital age.

On the contrary, where the collection of consumer's data is implicitly made on the basis of the legitimate bases for processing, that are the consent of Art 6(1)(a) GDPR and the legitimate interests of the controller and of third parties of Art 6(1)(f) GDPR, the contract for the supply of digital content and digital services is in the scope of the Directive 2019/770.

In other words, the Directive 2019/770 intends implicitly to deal only with contracts for the supply of digital content and digital services that are synallagmatic and onerous, and not those that are purely free. However, the directives now completely ignore the nature of the counterparty of the digital content or digital service when it is not expressed in terms of a price.

The only certainty is that this counterparty cannot be analysed in terms of the personal data collected from the consumer, since the latter, because of the fundamental rights attached to them, are not tradeable commodities.

This incomplete definition thus leaves open a central question from the point of view of consumer contract law: what is the counterparty of the content or digital service provided, when no price is paid by the consumer?

---

24 On this notion of contractual necessity within the meaning of Art 6(1)(b) GDPR, see the guidelines of the European Data Protection Committee dated 9 April 2019: < https://edpb.europa.eu/our-work-tools/public-consultations/2019/guidelines-22019-processing-personal-data-under-article-61b_en > accessed 12 August 2019.

II. *Impact of the definition, at the national level, of the nature of the contract for the supply of digital content and digital services on the contractual rules concerning termination*

As stated in Recital 12 of the Directive 2019/770, the task of determining the nature of the contract for the provision of digital content and services will be left to the Member States (II.1).

However, the nature and regime of the contract for the provision of digital content and services are not two separate aspects. Consequently, the precision of the nature of the contract for the supply of digital content and digital services, at the national level, will necessarily have an impact on the regime of this contract, in particular with regard to the questions of the termination of the contract and the restitutions following this termination (II.2).

1. *Definition of the nature of the contract for the supply of digital services at the national level: the contribution of three recent decisions of the Paris Court of First Instance*

Recital 12 of the Directive 2019/770 states: 'This Directive should not affect national law to the extent that the matters concerned are not regulated by this Directive, such as national rules on the formation, validity, nullity or effects of contracts or the legality of the digital content or the digital service. This Directive should also not determine the legal nature of contracts for the supply of digital content or a digital service, and the question of whether such contracts constitute, for instance, a sales, service, rental or sui generis contract, should be left to national law'.

In this context, several recent decisions of the Paris Court of First Instance, in particular a first decision dated August 7, 2018 in a *UFC Que choisir versus Twitter* case[25], a second decision dated February 12, 2019 in a *UFC Que choisir versus Google +* case[26], then a third decision dated April 9,

---

25 TGI Paris, decision of the 7 August 2018, UFC-Que choisir / Twitter; < https://www.legalis.net/jurisprudences/tgi-de-paris-jugement-du-7-aout-2018/ > accessed 12 August 2019.

26 TGI Paris, decision of the 12 February 2019, UFC-Que choisir /Google Inc.; < https://www.legalis.net/jurisprudences/tgi-de-paris-jugement-du-12-fevrier-2019/ > accessed 12 Augsut 2019.

2019 in a case *UFC Que choisir versus Facebook* case[27] contribute, via the fight against unfair terms, to the development of the nature and regime of the contract for the supply of digital services.

These decisions converge to establish a prerequisite for the implementation of the provisions of consumer law (concerning unfair terms and conditions): the assertion that the contract for the supply of digital services contract is onerous (but not yet synallagmatic).

The decisions of the Paris Court of first Instance of 7 August 2018, 12 February and 9 April 2019, using the new definition of the onerous contract in the Art 1107 Code civil resulting from the French reform of the law of obligations of 10 February 2016, according to which 'A contract is onerous where each of the parties receives a benefit from the other in return for what he provides'[28], state that the contract for the supply of digital services is an onerous contract, even in cases where the consumer does not pay a price. For the court, this contract is an onerous contract, where the digital service provider receives a benefit induced by the collection of data of the consumer. This benefit derives precisely from the fact that this service provider 'sells personal or non-personal data to partner companies, advertisers or merchants, data that they are deposited free of charge by the user at the time of registration or during browsing and use of the digital service'.

However, the decisions of the Paris Court of First Instance do not go so far as to recognise the synallagmatic nature of the contract for the supply of digital services, within the meaning of the new Art 1106 Code civil, according to which 'A contract is synallagmatic where the parties undertake reciprocal obligations in favour of each other'[29].

---

27 TGI Paris, decision of the 9 Avril 2019, UFC-Que choisir /Facebook Inc.; < https://www.legalis.net/jurisprudences/tgi-de-paris-jugement-du-9-avril-2019/ > accessed 12 August 2019.

28 Art 1107 Code civil: 'A contract is onerous where each of the parties receives a benefit from the other in return for what he provides. It is gratuitous where one of the parties provides a benefit to the other without expecting or receiving anything in return', in 'The law of contract, the general regime of obligations, and proof of obligations, The new provisions of the *Code civil* created by *Ordonnance* n ° 2016-131 of 10 February 2016 and including revisions made to the text by *Loi* n° 2018-287 of 20 April 2018 translated into English by J Cartwright, B Fauvarque-Cosson, S Whittaker', < http://www.textes.justice.gouv.fr/art_pix/Translationrevised2018final.pdf > accessed 12 August 2019.

29 Art 1106 Code civil: 'A contract is synallagmatic where the parties undertake reciprocal obligations in favour of each other. It is unilateral where one or more

The choice of the reference to Art 1107 Code civil, and not that of Art 1106 Code civil by the Paris TGI, calls for reflection. What is precisely the 'benefit' received by the trader? What is the link between this notion of 'benefit' and the notion of 'reciprocal obligations'?[30]

This reflection should be conducted because many rules of consumer law are based on the notion of a consumer contract, understood both as a synallagmatic and onerous contract (for instance, rules concerning unfair contractual terms, pre-contractual obligations to provide information on the essential and reciprocal elements of the contract).

But beyond the specific discipline of contract and consumer law, it is also important to stress the anthropological issue at stake behind the characterisation of a contractual relationship of a synallagmatic type, an anthropological issue that has been highlighted by anthropologists such as Marcel Mauss or Claude Levi-Strauss and brought to the attention of lawyers by Doyen Carbonnier[31].

---

persons undertake obligations in favour of one or more others without there being any reciprocal obligation on the part of the latter', id.

30 Concerning this notion of 'reciprocal obligations', cf C von Bar, E Clive and H Schulte-Nölke et al (eds), *Principles, Definitions and Model Rules of European Private Law, Draft Common Frame of Reference (DCFR) Outline Edition*, prepared by the Study Group on a European Civil Code and the Research Group on EC Private Law (Acquis Group), based in part on a revised version of the *Principles of European Contract Law* (Sellier 2009), Book III: Obligations and corresponding rights; Chapter 1: General; Article III. – 1:102: Definitions:

(1) ' An obligation is a duty to perform which one party to a legal relationship, the debtor, owes to another party, the creditor.
(2) Performance of an obligation is the doing by the debtor of what is to be done under the obligation or the not doing by the debtor of what is not to be done.
(3) Non-performance of an obligation is any failure to perform the obligation, whether or not excused, and includes delayed performance and any other performance which is not in accordance with the terms regulating the obligation.
(4) An obligation is reciprocal in relation to another obligation if:
  (a) performance of the obligation is due in exchange for performance of the other obligation;
  (b) it is an obligation to facilitate or accept performance of the other obligation; or
  (c) it is so clearly connected to the other obligation or its subject matter that performance of the one can reasonably be regarded as dependent on performance of the other'.

31 J Carbonnier, *Flexible droit, Pour une sociologie du droit sans rigueur* (8th edn, LGDJ 1995) 309 who recalls the strength of the primitive, magical, prelogical mentality sitting in the gift understood as the primitive form of exchange.

Behind this major challenge, lies in particular the possibility for consumers to become aware of the importance, both for their contracting partner and for the digital economy as a whole, of the data, activities and traces of all kinds they provide when using the digital service.

And the difficulty lies in asking whether it is possible to characterise this counterparty, to preserve the synallagmatic nature of the contract, while avoiding the prism of property law that would reify the person of the consumer, holder of the collected data[32].

In this respect, it is worth noting the analysis of sociologists Antonio Casilli and Dominique Cardon[33], who propose to analyse the activity, data and traces transmitted by the user of the digital service in terms of 'digital labour', a renewed form of human service at the digital age.

In so doing, making the synallagmatic nature of the contract for the supply of digital services reappear could make it possible to consider it as an exchange between, on the one hand, the algorithmic service provided by the digital service provider and, on the other hand, the human service, the service provided by the consumer consisting of the activity, data, traces produced by him when subscribing to and using the digital service.

Whether or not this counterparty is finally enshrined, reflecting on it highlights the great specificity of the contract for the supply of digital content and digital services and the need for vigilance that this contract requires with regard to the protection of the consumer, as a natural person.

2. *Future impacts on the contractual rules concerning termination*

The contribution of the three decisions of the Paris Court of First Instance of 7 August 2018, 12 February and 9 April 2019, concerning the qualification of the digital service contract, has potentially an impact on its regime.

If some national laws recognise the onerous (or synallagmatic) nature of the contract for the supply of digital content and digital services, it will have an impact on the question of the restitutions in case of termination of this contract.

---

32 J Rochfeld, 'Contre l'hypothèse de la qualification des données personnelles comme des biens' in Emmanuel Netter and Aurore Chaigneau, *Les biens numériques* (Cerprisca 2015) 214ff.

33 A Casilli, *En attendant les robots, Enquête sur le travail du clic* (Seuil 2019); A Casilli, D Cardon, *Qu'est-ce que le digital labor?* (Edition de l'Ina 2015).

The main question will be the question of the identification of the 'benefit' that the trader has to give restitution in case of termination of the contract[34]

34 For source of inspirations, see von Bar, Clive and Schulte-Nölke et al (n 30) Article III. – 3:510: Restitution of benefits received by performance:

(1) On termination under this Section a party (the recipient) who has received any benefit by the other's performance of obligations under the terminated contractual relationship or terminated part of the contractual relationship is obliged to return it. Where both parties have ob- ligations to return, the obligations are reciprocal.
(2) If the performance was a payment of money, the amount received is to be repaid.
(3) To the extent that the benefit (not being money) is transferable, it is to be returned by transferring it. However, if a transfer would cause un- reasonable effort or expense, the benefit may be returned by paying its value.
(4) To the extent that the benefit is not transferable it is to be returned by paying its value in accordance with III. – 3:512 (Payment of value of benefit).
(5) The obligation to return a benefit extends to any natural or legal fruits received from the benefit.

Article III. – 3:512: Payment of value of benefit:

(1) The recipient is obliged to:
    (a) pay the value (at the time of performance) of a benefit which is not transferable or which ceases to be transferable before the time when it is to be returned; and
    (b) pay recompense for any reduction in the value of a returnable benefit as a result of a change in the condition of the benefit between the time of receipt and the time when it is to be returned.
(2) Where there was an agreed price the value of the benefit is that proportion of the price which the value of the actual performance bears to the value of the promised performance. Where no price was agreed the value of the benefit is the sum of money which a willing and capable provider and a willing and capable recipient, knowing of any non-conformity, would lawfully have agreed.
(3) The recipient's liability to pay the value of a benefit is reduced to the extent that as a result of a non-performance of an obligation owed by the other party to the recipient:
    (a) the benefit cannot be returned in essentially the same condition as when it was received; or
    (b) the recipient is compelled without compensation either to dispose of it or to sustain a disadvantage in order to preserve it.
(4) The recipient's liability to pay the value of a benefit is likewise reduced to the extent that it cannot be returned in the same condition as when it was received as a result of conduct of the recipient in the reasonable, but mistaken, belief that there was no non-conformity.

Due to the importance of the competition laws objective of equivalent treatment for all economic operators, this question goes beyond the sole case of the contract for the supply of digital content or digital services for which no price is paid by the consumer.

Indeed, consumer data are generally collected, even when a price (relatively low and not necessarily in relation with the value of the product, content or service provided) is paid to receive the content, the digital service or the 'good with digital elements' within the meaning of the new Directive 2019/771 of 20 May 2019 on certain aspects concerning contracts for the sale of goods[35].

See also, in 'The law of contract, the general regime of obligations, and proof of obligations, The new provisions of the Code civil created by Ordonnance n° 2016-131 of 10 February 2016 and including revisions made to the text by *Loi* n° 2018-287 of 20 April 2018 translated into English by J Cartwright, B Fauvarque-Cosson, S Whittaker', < http://www.textes.justice.gouv.fr/art_pix/Translationrevised2018final.pdf > accessed 12 August 2019;

Chapter V Restitution
Art 1352: 'Restitution of a thing other than a sum of money takes place in kind or, where this is impossible, by value assessed at the date of the restitution'.

35 Art 2(5)(b) Directive 2019/771: 'goods' means: (…)
any tangible movable items that incorporate or are inter-connected with digital content or a digital service in such a way that the absence of that digital content or digital service would prevent the goods from performing their functions ("goods with digital elements").

Termination of the Contract for the Supply of Digital Content and Services, and Availability of Data: Rights of Retrieval, Portability and Erasure in EU Law and Practice

*Sergio Cámara Lapuente**

I. Contract extinction and contract termination

The Directive on contracts for the supply of digital content and digital services, hereinafter DCDC[1], only deals with the consumer's rights on the use of his or her data, whether personal in nature or otherwise, in case the contract is *terminated.* In contracts covered by the Directive, which embraces also some contracts concluded without a price paid in money but with personal data involved[2], termination may be due to three causes: failure to provide (Art 13)[3], lack of conformity (Arts 14–18) or a modification in the contents or services that negatively affects the consumer (Art 19(3)). In all three cases, the trader can use personal data and any other non-personal data uploaded by the consumer up until termination of the contract. The normal effect of termination in private law is the restitution of the counter-performances exchanged by the parties in the contract.

Certainly, because the scope of the Directive focuses only on the remedies of the three cases mentioned, it limits the aspects subject to full harmonisation in the European Union. But when the Member States transpose the Directive, there are a number of questions that will need answering, since as per Art 3(10), it is their competence to regulate contract law,

---

* Professor of Civil Law, University of La Rioja. This chapter is a result of the research project DER2017-84748-R, funded by the Spanish Ministry of Economy, Industry and Competitiveness.

1 Directive (EU) 2019/770 of the European Parliament and of the Council of 20 May 2019 on certain aspects concerning contracts for the supply of digital content and digital services [2019] OJ L136/1.

2 See Art 3(1) and recitals 25 and 67.

3 And see recital 20 as for the application of the remedies established in Directive 2011/83/EU, instead of the ones in DCDC, in case of supply of digital content in a tangible medium.

including the effects of these contracts, as well as the consequences of termination unforeseen in the European regulation. Specifically, the Member States may need either to expand the rules of the Directive on the destination of the data to cases of *contract extinction other than termination* or to create different rules for such cases. This leads to a number of questions: a) Does the cause of extinction affect the rules on the availability of the data? For example, if said cause is attributable to the consumer rather than to the trader. b) Should the consumer have the same rights over such data/contents regardless of the grounds for ending the contract? In particular, given that the DCDC bestows rights of retrieval and refraining from use in the event of breaches by the trader, should the consumer not be guaranteed similar rights at least in cases where he legitimately exercises his right to cancel or otherwise terminate the contract? c) Should the same right to data retrieval (and, where appropriate, portability) not be legally guaranteed while the contractual relationship is in force, given that this is what all consumers reasonably expect, for example in *cloud computing* and social networking services? This result could be deemed to derive already from Art 8(1)(b) DCDC. d) The national legislations will have to pronounce on the destination of 'other data' or, in the final version of the Directive, on '*content other than personal data, which was provided or created by the consumer when using*' the digital content or service supplied by the trader (Art 16(3) and 16(4) DCDC) in a different context for termination other than the aforementioned three cases. In relation to the disposal of personal data, European harmonisation has already taken place through the General Data Protection Regulation (GDPR)[4]: namely, the consumer of digital services and content (ie, the 'data subject' in GDPR terms) shall have the rights of access, erasure and portability, not only upon termination of the contract and not even only, more generally, when the contract is ended, but also during the validity period of the contract (even if there is none or it has finished). d) Should the trader have a right to retain the user's non-personal data in case of user breach or non-payment as a measure of guarantee or pressure to obtain what is owed? The GDPR does not protect this right for personal data, nor does the DCDC create it for user-generated content (UGC)[5]. But it could be established in the adhesion contracts or

4 Regulation (EU) 2016/679, of 27 April 2016.

5 Recital 15 of the Directive recalls that Member States may regulate whether the consumer may suspend payment of the price until conformity or whether the trader may withhold refunds until the tangible medium is returned to him. But that recital fails to mention the possibility of the trader's withholding of data, thereby preventing its deletion, recovery or portability by the user.

done by de facto means, thereby giving the trader an advantageous position to put pressure on the user, renegotiate or attempt to charge penalties or fees for deletion or retrieval[6]. In principle, such withholding based on a non-negotiated term is likely to be considered unfair on the grounds of a lack of proportionality[7] and the consumer's expectation, even in free contracts, is that the trader must fulfil his essential obligation to return to him what has merely been deposited[8].

Even before this Directive is passed, some Member States have already started to regulate the availability of non-personal data in the digital services environment following the example of the rights established in the GDPR (and, significantly, portability): some States did so originally in their consumer protection laws; France was a pioneer, since its Digital Republic Act of 2016 introduced new laws on data 'retrieval and portability' (personal and non-personal alike) 'at all times' (not only upon contract extinction) as part of its Consumer Code[9], although those dispositions were later repealed by the new French regulations in late 2018)[10]. Other Member States such as Spain directly regulated the right of portability of non-personal data ('contents') for any user of social networks when they passed new rules on personal data protection[11]. Transposition of the Directive will require revising the subsistence or consistency of those rules with the new DCDC.

In order to determine the cases to which to extend the users' new rights of data recovery and of preventing them from being used by the trader, a closer look should be taken at the very different *causes for ending contracts* for the provision of digital content and digital services, which can be classi-

---

6 Rolf H Weber, 'Data Protection in the Termination of Contract' in Reiner Schulze, Dirk Staudenmayer and Sebastian Lohsse (eds), *Contracts for the Supply of Digital Content: Regulatory Challenges and Gaps* (Nomos 2017) 201 and 207.

7 It was the conclusion of the 'Expert Group on Cloud Computing' set by the European Commission, *Synthesis* 5/6 March 2014 (available online under <https://ec.europa.eu/info/business-economy-euro/doing-business-eu/contract-rules/cloud-computing/expert-group-cloud-computing-contracts_en> accessed 5 August 2019).

8 With due nuances regarding the legitimate interests of the trader or rights of third parties, in this sense see Francisca María Roselló Rubert, *Cloud Computing. Régimen Jurídico para Empresarios* (Aranzadi 2018) 365–369.

9 Art 48 of the *Loi* n° 2016-1321, of 7 October 2016, creating in the *Code de la Consommation* the new articles L-224-42-1/4 on *portabilité et récupération des données*.

10 Section L-224-42 of the Consumer Code was derogated by *Loi* n° 2018-493 of 20 June 2018 on the protection of personal data (Art 33).

11 Art 95 of the Organic Law 3/2018, of 5 December 2018 on 'Protección de Datos Personales y garantía de los derechos digitales', with a referral to Art 20 GDPR (in Art 17 of the Spanish Law).

fied as *natural* and *pathological*. The former may include reaching the end in fixed-term contracts, the cancellation of open-ended contracts[12], the unilateral withdrawal right of the consumer[13], the mutual dissent of both parties, etc. Among the pathological causes for putting an end to a contract, one may think of nullity or annulment of the contract due to different grounds (lack of capacity, defective consent...), unjustified withdrawal by either party, termination also by the trader in the event of qualified breaches of contract by the consumer, etc.

Special mention should be made of the extinction of the contract for the supply of digital content and services due to the death of the user. This case could well be framed as another case of natural end of the contract, as most of the general conditions of the main traders in the sector expressly contemplate, except that it is possible to conceive certain digital content as part of the inheritance of the deceased user, so that their heirs could have access to their social network accounts, email services, cloud storage services, and so on[14].

In conclusion, when transposing the new Directive (DCDC), Member States will need to address a number of legislative policy questions on contract extinction and use of data that fall short of the full harmonisation on one hand by the GDPR with respect to personal data, and on the other hand with respect to other non-personal data (UGC), both by the DCDC and by the 2019 reformed Directive 2011/83/EU. But let us focus now on the new rights established by the DCDC just in the cases of termination.

---

12 See Art 16 of the 2015 Commission's Proposal for the DCDC (for contracts with a duration of more than 12 months).

13 See Arts 13(5), 13(6) and 13(7) of the Directive 2011/83/EU on consumer rights as modified by the new Directive 2019/2161 of the European Parliament and of the Council of 27 November 2019 amending Directives 93/13/EEC, 98/6/EC, 2005/29/EC and 2011/83, as regards better enforcement and modernisation of Union consumer protection rules [2019] OJ L328/7 which establishes rights to retrieve content and to prevent its use by the provider after withdrawal, similar to the ones designed in Art 16 DCDC.

14 See comparative law approaches on the topic of digital inheritance and the faculties of heirs, executors and relatives against the platforms in different countries in Giorgio Resta, 'Personal Data and Digital Assets after Death: a Comparative Law Perspective on the BGH Facebook Ruling' (2018) 5 EuCML 201; Sergio Cámara Lapuente, 'La sucesión *mortis causa* en el patrimonio digital' (2019) Anales de la Academia Matritense del Notariado 375–432.

II. Rights in play on data upon contract termination

1. Comparison between access/portability/erasure in the GDPR and retrieval/ impeding use in the DCDC

The consequences for data (personal and non-personal) in the event of termination due to lack of conformity are set out in Art 16 DCDC[15]. Given that for the consumer's personal data, DCDC Art 16(2) refers to the 'obligations' established for the trader in the GDPR, it is hard to avoid comparing the 'rights' of the consumer as a contracting party to other non-personal data that he provided or created during the duration of the contract (DCDC) with the rights as a data subject (GDPR). And this is necessary not only for conceptual boundaries, but also to differentiate the scope and exceptions of each right, to verify whether the disparities are justified and thus, once again, to be able to say whether national lawmakers should replicate the solutions of the Directive or whether or not they should go any further in the non-harmonised areas.

According to the GDPR, the main rights involved in a contract termination with regard to the consumer's personal data are the traditional right of access (Art 15), the new right of portability (Art 20) and the partially reformed right to erasure or the 'right to be forgotten' (Art 17). Once the criticism has been overcome of portability being a mere extension of the right of access or some sort of 'premium' version thereof, it becomes evident that portability has its own nature and that there are clear differences between the two[16]. The right to portability comprises three rights: first, 'the right to receive the personal data concerning him or her, which he or she has provided to a controller, in a structured, commonly used and machine-readable format'; second, 'the right to transmit those data to another controller without hindrance from' the previous controller; and third, 'the right to have the personal data transmitted directly from one controller to another, where technically feasible'.

---

15 Referred to in Art 13(3) (lack of supply) and Art 19(3) (detrimental modifications of the content); the same rule is replicated for withdrawal in Art 13 of the Directive 2011/83/EU as modified by Directive 2019/2161/EU.

16 The right of access is more related to information, transparency and knowledge than to the use or control of data; in addition to accessing personal data and extensive information on eight different items, the data subject has the right to receive a copy of the data (Art 15(3)).

The differences are clear[17]: in terms of its object, the right of access includes any personal data and various kinds of additional information, while the right of portability only includes data 'provided' by the subject and concerning him. In terms of purposes and faculties, the right of access (recital 63) aims to 'be aware of, and verify, the lawfulness of the processing' which is why it includes the possibility of obtaining a copy of the data. However, the copy does not have to be interoperable. In contrast, it does in the right to portability, which, in accordance with the purpose of heightening competition, ensures the possibility of transferring his data directly or indirectly to another controller. In this case, the format of the copy must be structured and machine-readable[18], not just be in electronic form. For example, a mere 'pdf' (mere electronic text) without metadata may satisfy the right of access, but not the portability to another platform or provider that, in the case of very specific standards, must be able to process and reuse the data that was in the possession of the first controller (eg, going from *Facebook* to *Google+* with the entire profile, information, tags, etc.; or migrating messages, contacts, shared files, etc. from *WhatsApp* to *Line* or *Telegram*).

The renamed 'right to be forgotten' (Art 17 GDPR) entails 'the right to obtain from the controller the erasure of personal data concerning him or her without undue delay', when circumstances occur that make processing that data unlawful, among which are that 'the personal data are no longer necessary in relation to the purposes' or 'the data subject withdraws consent on which the processing is based (…), and where there is no other legal ground for the processing'[19].

17 See Paul De Hert, Vagelis Papakonstantinou, Gianclaudio Malgieri, Laurent Beslay and Ignacio Sánchez, 'The right to data portability in the GDPR: Towards user-centric interoperability of digital services' (2018) Computer Law and Security Review 201; Wenlong Li, 'A Tale of Two Rights: the Clash and Collaboration of Right to Data Portability and Right to Be Forgotten' in BA Juanpere, JB Padullés et al (eds), *Managing Risk In the Digital Society* (UOC/Huygens 2017) 176 (see also in International Data Privacy Law [2018] 1); Radina Stoykova, 'The right to Data Portability' (2018) 3 Computer Law Review International (CRi) 66.

18 According to Paul Przemysław Polański, 'Some thoughts on data portability in the aftermath of the Cambridge Analytica scandal' (2018) 4 EuCML 143, the sole legal mention of 'machine-readable' format actually implies the usage of an electronic, structured and commonly used format, although it should not be equated with achieving interoperability; see there examples of common electronic formats which might fulfil both aims.

19 In addition, if the controller is obliged to delete the data he must take reasonable measures to inform other controllers that the data subject also requests the deletion 'of any links to, or copy or replication of, those personal data'. The exercise

If we now look at the new rights established in the Directive with respect to UGC other than personal data[20], there is a temptation to pair 'erasure' with 'right to prevent further use of the data' and 'portability' with 'right to retrieve' the data. On one hand, in the event the contract is terminated, Art 16(3) establishes that 'the trader shall *refrain from using*' these user-generated contents, with four exceptions. This obligation will therefore entail the user's corresponding right to '*prevent any further use*' of his non-personal data despite the fact that the trader has this legal burden or obligation even if the consumer does not request it of him. On the other hand, according to Art 16(4), at the request of the consumer (here the right must be expressly exercised), 'the trader shall (...) make that non-personal data available to the consumer'; in this case, the Directive makes positive the consumer's right to retrieve that digital content free of charge, without hindrance from the trader, within a reasonable time and in a commonly used and machine-readable format.

The parallels between the rights guaranteed in the GDPR and the DCDC are clear, but this does not mean they are the same. For example, the new Directive may be said to consecrate certain rights (of retrieval, of preventing further use) that are buffered or softened with respect to their reference models in the GDPR, in terms of both the lesser control granted by the faculties of the Directive and the breadth of the exceptions added in the last stage of negotiations on the Directive.

Thus, if the right to erasure (GDPR) is compared with the right to prevent further use (DCDC), several substantial differences become apparent (in addition to the obvious ones on the type of data involved and the existence of the right for any cause of extinction or only for termination):

a) Whereas the GDPR consolidates an obligation of result (and *in faciendo*) of deleting the personal data (equivalent to anonymisation), the DCDC does not make deletion obligatory, but rather, it sets an obligation *de non faciendo*, ie, the trader 'shall refrain from using' those contents; it may suffice to make them inaccessible to other users as well as

of the right of portability does not imply deletion of the data, which must be expressly requested (see Art 20(3) and recital 68 GDPR).

20 Art 16(3) DCDC: 'any content other than personal data, which was provided or created by the consumer when using the digital content or digital service supplied by the trader'.

to his own employees[21]. It may at least be said that this negative obligation is also one of results, not means, taking into account the removal of the original formulation by the Commission ('the supplier shall take all measures which could be expected in order to refrain from the use')

b) The exceptions are also very different in scope: compared to causes that justify further processing of personal data (Art 17(3) GDPR) based on legal obligations or for reasons of public interest and fundamental rights such as freedom of expression and information, Art 16(3) DCDC consolidates a cause similar to the latter (the content must have been generated jointly by several different people), but adds three new causes that only aim to safeguard the interests of the trader in favour on data mining, the use of big data techniques and, if applicable, improvement of the services provided. This approach deserves criticism[22].
c) Although apparently the data subject must exercise his right in order to have his personal data deleted, the principles in force in the GDPR lead to the same result without having to ask for the deletion if the data are no longer necessary for the business purpose they were collected for, by virtue of the principles of limiting the term of storage and minimisation (Art 5(1)), since their processing would no longer be necessary to execute the contract (Art 6(1)(b)). For its part, the DCDC enshrines the refraining from use directly as a duty of the trader, but there must be also a corresponding right of the consumer to demand that the obligation be fulfilled. On this point, despite the differences in formulation, the legal configuration is very close.

The differences between the portability right (GDPR) and the retrieval right (DCDC) are quite evident[23] (in addition, again, to the data affected and the situations that justify the emergence of each right):

---

21 The obligation would be fulfilled, *ad extra*, by disabling access to that content by other users (ceasing public communication or ceasing to make it available, in the case of original works) and, *ad intra*, by not using that content for their business purposes (excluding it from both personalised analysis and *big data* techniques, eluding the processing of their associated metadata, not ceding its use to other traders, etc.).

22 See below at III.1.a) and III.2.b).

23 Further comparisons on the versions prior to the approved Directive in Ruth Janal, 'Data Portability – A Tale of Two Concepts' (2017) JIPITEC 59ff; Axel Metzger, Zohar Efroni, Lena Mischau and Jakob Metzger, 'Data-Related Aspects of the Digital Content Directive' (2018) JIPITEC 102–105.

a) The GDPR allows requesting that personal data be transmitted 'directly' from one controller to another new controller, if technically feasible (Art 20(2)). This rule is not provided for in the DCDC.
b) The GDPR allows requesting the portability of the data from any controller that has processed them and not only of the user's contractual counterpart, which is the contractual scenario contemplated in the DCDC.
c) The only exception in the GDPR is that portability must not adversely affect the rights and freedoms of others (Art 20(4)) and, when exercised in conjunction with the right of erasure, must not affect processing necessary for missions in the public interest or in the exercise of public powers (Art 20(3)). In contrast, the DCDC – which could also have included the clause safeguarding the rights and freedoms of third parties, but has not done so – only provides for three exceptions which, without any real justification, undermine the consumer's control over data generated by him.
d) The way of retrieving or receiving the data, the absence of cost and the term are similar in the GDPR and DCDC, in a calculated legal parallelism. However, although the electronic format in both cases is 'machine-readable'[24], which will favour interoperability and the transfer of content to another platform or provider (it is not a mere electronic format as in the right of access), it is missing the 'structured' feature. This lack should not be interpreted as an obstacle to retrieved content being transferred as is to another trader.
e) Does the consumer have a right to 'indirect' portability, ie, to do it himself by sending the retrieved content to another trader? With the DCDC silent on this matter, it encourages leaving the decision up to the traders by means of their general contractual conditions instead of intervening legislatively, as would have been desirable, to promote the full portability of UGCs and non-personal data as well in order to foster real competition in the digital single market. In fact, Art 16(4) DCDC does not say, as Art 20(1) GDPR does, that the consumer will have 'the *right to transmit* those data to another controller *without hindrance* from the [previous] controller'; it stops at the right to retrieve the contents. The European Parliament passed an amendment (No 47) in 2017 to ex-

24 This feature was not in the original proposal by the Commission, but was introduced in the versions of 2017 approved both by the EU Parliament and the Council. As for the meaning of the omission of the feature of the structured format see n 18.

pressly include this right, but the text of the Directive as finally adopted does not contain it.

In fact, most digital service providers usually have provisions that highlight the non-exclusive nature of the license granted by the user to the trader for the dissemination of content that the user uploads, creates or shares with other users, so that a change of trader (be it at the time of or after the first contractual relationship) is guaranteed. These same general conditions also tend to highlight the 'perpetual' or 'indefinite' nature of that licence, which, on the other hand, will conflict with the duty of the trader to refrain from using once the rules of the directive have been transposed. For example, this is the case with *Apple Stores*, *Google*, *Spotify*, *Twitter* or *WhatsApp*. For its part, *YouTube* explains that the license granted by the consumer on the content generated by him is cancelled when he deletes the videos. However, other traders state that this license of use is exclusive (for the duration of the relationship and, in some cases, they proclaim—with doubtful legality—even after that) or that the consumer may not delete certain content despite ending the relationship (such as with comments on blogs or in online markets).

Therefore, in order to weigh the balance of what is stipulated (non-negotiated) in the contract, the clause must be contrasted with the objective parameter of legitimate expectation of the average user. For example, in cloud computing services, the reasonable expectation of every user is to be able to retrieve the content deposited on the server and transfer it to wherever he or she deems appropriate. Not stipulating it that way, for example, would thus be a clear lack of conformity because it does not have the functionality expected of services of this type (Art 8(1)(b) DCDC). In social networking services, not guaranteeing this self or indirect portability undoubtedly leads to the creation of captive markets, which are contrary to the aims proposed in the Digital Single Market Strategy. Therefore, if this is not upheld in consumer protection rules, it may deserve sanction from the European competition law[25]. Moreover, the European Commission raised the very same question from this perspective in its resolution on *Facebook's* acquisition of *WhatsApp*: potential portability problems were ex-

25 Inge Graef, 'Mandating Portability and Interoperability in Online Social Networks: Regulatory and Competition Law Issues in the European Union' (2015) 39-6 Telecommunications Policy 502–514; and for some proposals, Inge Graef, Damian Clifford and Peggy Valcke, 'Fairness and enforcement: bridging competition, data protection, and consumer law' (2018) 8-3 International Data Privacy Law 200.

pressly analysed, such as network effects that could be harmful to competition (by making it difficult for users to rebuild their network of contacts in the event of a change of provider)[26].

Having pointed out the differences between the rights granted by the GDPR and the DCDC, it is useful to look into some of the key elements of the Directive's gestation process that may explain the basis for the legislative decisions taken.

2. *Legislative evolution, basis and criticism*

The Proposal for a Directive on contracts for the supply of digital content presented by the European Commission on 9 December 2015 still contained a single definition for all types of digital content, and included the well-known, highly criticised and finally deleted phrase that the trader supplies the content and 'in exchange, a price is to be paid or the consumer actively provides counter-performance other than money in the form of personal data or any other data' (Art 3(1)). At this point in the legislative process, the 'counter-performance' comprised every type of data (personal or non-personal) and the consumer's rights in terminating the contract were the same (retrieving and preventing further use) with respect to data of any kind.

This approach underwent changes mainly due to two turning points: on one hand, after the Commission's proposal, the GDPR was approved on 27 April 2016 with its rights of erasure and portability; the tortuous proceedings of the right of portability are well known: introduced in the European Commission's proposal in January 2012, eliminated in the European Parliament in 2014 and reintroduced in the version approved by the Council in 2015, ending in the text definitively approved in 2016 with changes with respect to the original proposal. In this context, it is easy to understand the reluctance to duplicating portability whole in the new Proposal for a Directive. On the other hand, the European Data Protection Supervisor (EDPS) report of March 2017 on the Proposal for a Directive on digital content rejected 'any new provision introducing the idea that peo-

---

26 European Commission, Case nº COMP/M.7217 – *Facebook/Whatsapp*, 3 October 2014, see § 113 and 127–142 (available online under: <http://ec.europa.eu/competition/mergers/cases/decisions/m7217201410032031039621 32EN.pdf> accessed 5 August 2019). See Jorge Vilarino Marzo, *La privacidad en el entorno del cloud computing* (Reus 2018) 117.

ple can pay with their data in the same way as they do with money'[27]; the impact of banishing the idea of counter-performance in personal data was such that even the currently adopted recital 24 of the DCDC borrows one of the phrases from EDPS report as its own: 'the protection of personal data is a fundamental right and (...) therefore personal data cannot be considered as a commodity'.

From then on, the versions of the Directive approved in 2017 respectively by the Parliament and the Council adopted two major changes: firstly, they split up the consumer's rights in the event of termination, with rights relating to personal data being governed by the GDPR and rights relating to 'other data' (ie, non-personal) by the Directive. Secondly, they differentiated between 'digital content' and two types of 'digital services'. They also adopted other relevant distinctions, such as supplying in a single act, in several acts or as a continuous supply.

In short, the question is this: is it justified that in the event of termination of a contract the consumer has such different rights with respect to his personal data and other, non-personal data, such as content he either provides or creates by using the provider's digital content and service? It is clear that the identity aspect of the person contained in personal data justifies enhanced protection, as opposed to the (intellectual) property aspects of his or her creations and the ownership of mere data (if they can be spoken of that way)[28]. At play here is the dichotomy between inherent personal rights and property rights over goods, with different standards of protection in the European tradition. However, in the case of the portability of personal data, one of its objectives, along with enhancing user control over his or her data (GDPR recital 68), is to avoid any *lock-in* effects, to promote competitiveness and the change of service providers[29]. That same objective

27 European Data Protection Supervisor (EDPS), 'Opinion 4/2017 on the Proposal for a Directive on certain aspects concerning contracts for the supply of digital content', 14 March 2017, 3 and 10.

28 On this trending and discussed issue see, for instance, Herbert Zech, 'Information as Property' (2015) 5 JIPITEC 192–197; Eric Tjong Tjin Tai, 'Data ownership and consumer protection' (2018) 4 EuCML 136–140.

29 As the European Commission stated: 'with increasing use of certain online service, the amount of personal data collected in this service becomes an obstacle for changing services, even if better, cheaper or more privacy friendly services become available. This could mean the loss of contact information, calendar story, interpersonal communication exchanges and other kinds of personally or socially relevant data which is very difficult to recreate or restore': European Commission, 'Commission Staff Working Paper. Impact Assessment Accompanying the Document on the General Data Protection Regulation', SEC (2012)72 final 28.

can (and should) also be pursued, once declared desirable (as it was throughout the processing of the DCDC) in relation to exactly the same contracts for the provision of digital content[30], with the promotion of portability (and not only retrieval) of content provided or created by users other than personal data. The exceptions to retrieval of this type of data along with a failure to mention that obstacles must not be put in the way of any consumers wishing to migrate their content to other platforms only jeopardise the goal of a competitive digital market. It should also be remembered that not even for direct portability did it go so far as to obligate controllers, since consumers will only have the right 'where technically feasible'; moreover, in general, interoperability does not become obligatory but only 'suggested': according to recital 68 GPDR, 'data controllers should be *encouraged* to develop interoperable formats that enable data portability'; the only obligatory thing are the three requirements for the format (Art 20.1 GPDR)[31]. In addition, the European Commission's initial proposal to act as an institution imposing certain formats and promoting interoperable standards disappeared from the GPDR (Art 18.3). Nevertheless, suitably, this role of the Commission reappears, albeit attenuated, in DCDC recital 50 concerning the development of international standards and codes of conduct on the format for retrieving content other than personal data.

3. *Kind of data included in the new rights: 'personal data provided' vs. 'any content other than personal data provided or created'*

The initial version of the Directive presented by the Commission differentiated between 'personal data' and 'other, non-personal data'. The European Data Protection Supervisor's suggestion[32] of removing that difference and redirecting it all to the broad concept of personal data in Art 4(1) GDPR and to the rights listed in the Regulations was, fortunately, only

---

30 See recital 46 of the Commission's Proposal of the Directive. Currently, recital 70 DCDC only refers to safeguard consumer's right of termination. References to the aim of fostering competition and switch of providers have been deleted (see n 58–61). The potentialities of portability of personal data as regards to a more competitive market environment were also underlined by WP29, 'Opinion 06/2014 on the notion of legitimate interests of the data controller under Article 7 of Directive 95/46/EC', adopted on 9 April 2014 (844/14/EN WP 217) 48.

31 De Hert et al (n 17) 197 and 200; Stoykova (n 17) 68.

32 EDPS (n 27) 11.

partially heeded, since it would have completely eliminated the rights of retrieval and of preventing further use of 'non-personal data'. Instead of this, it was decided to refer to 'any content other than personal data provided or created by the consumer when using the digital content or digital service supplied by the trader' (Art 16). This, in fact, theoretically covers the same situations as 'non-personal data in general'. However, the exceptions added during the Directive proceedings considerably lessen the scope of the contents covered, as will be seen next.

The concept of 'personal data' in Art 4(1) GDPR is well known. It refers to any information that may be tied to a specific individual. Article 29 Data Protection Working Party (WP29) provides a thorough interpretation of the concept and examples to clarify questionable cases. Thus, unless certain 'metadata' (data that give information about other data) are completely anonymous, they would also be considered as personal data. However, some companies have privacy policies that expressly classify some data as non-personal data in ways that would hardly meet the definition of the GDPR[33].

If we now try to imagine generally what those 'other non-personal data' could be in a contract for the provision of digital content or services, at least three categories of data seem important: a) Data that do not identify a person and cannot be connected to an identified or identifiable person[34], in short, when it comes to 'anonymised' data (for 'pseudonymisation', see Arts 4(5) and 11(2) and recital 26 GDPR) or data *aggregated*[35] with other data by the trader that cannot be separated and do not allow identification of the individual. b) Non-personal data constituting *digital content acquired* by the user from the provider: think of videos, films, songs *downloaded or transferred to a server* from which the user could download or view them at any time. c) *User-generated contents* that do not constitute personal data.

---

33 One such example is *Apple*: 'We also collect data in a form that does not, on its own, permit direct association with any specific individual. The following are *some examples of non-personal information (…) such as occupation, language, zip code, area code, unique device identifier, referrer URL, location*, and the time zone… *Aggregated data is considered non-personal information* for the purposes of this Privacy Policy' (accessed in June 2019).

34 Thus, WP29, 'Opinion 4/2007 on the concept of personal data', adopted on 20 June 2007 (01248/07/EN WP 136) 26.

35 For an instance of this kind of data, see section 3.5 of *Twitter*'s privacy policy, entitled as 'non personal information': 'We share or disclose non-personal data, such as aggregated information like *the total number of times people engaged with a Tweet, the number of people who clicked on a particular link* or voted on a poll in a Tweet (even if only one did)' (accessed in June 2019).

With respect to anonymised data, there is a well-known concern that they can revert to personal data through reverse engineering and data mining techniques, so that even with regard to the erasure and portability aspects of the GDPR to which the Directive refers, such a possibility should nevertheless be envisaged[36]. The same applies to data combined and aggregated with other data from the provider in such way that they lose their personal nature, but can regain it later[37]. The EDPS has clarified on several occasions that metadata and anonymous data are covered under the GDPR[38] (*see* Art 11(2)).

In order to qualify which specific contents have finally been covered in the rights regarding termination in Art 16 DCDC, a number of conceptual premises must be taken as a starting point. Firstly, a distinction must be made between the *data necessary to establish the contractual relationship* (such as the user's identity, e-mail address, country of residence and language, credit card number, etc.) *and the data necessary to execute the contract* in accordance with what has been offered (for example, for a physical workout app: the evolution of body weight during the use of the application, information on the food eaten every day, monitoring the distances travelled, etc.). Just as the latter group of personal data must disappear from the trader's sphere of control once the relationship has ended –simply by applying the principle of limitation of the storage period in Art 5(1)(e) GDPR–, sometimes the former could be retained for a time by him for legitimate purposes, such as claiming liabilities (due to insults in a social network, fraudulent use of the service, collection of non-payments, etc.).

In principle, the consent to process both types of personal data is the same and as long as the processing is 'necessary'[39], it will last for as long as the contractual relationship lasts[40]. According to Art 3(1) DCDC, the Di-

---

36 cf Weber (n 6) 201–202; Rafał Mańko and Shara Monteleone (EPRS), 'Contracts for the supply of digital content and personal data protection' (European Parliament 2017) 5; Roselló Rubert (n 8) 225 and 391.

37 See recital 26 GDPR; and WP29, 'Opinion 05/2014 on Anonymisation Techniques', adopted 10 April 2014 (0829/14/EN WP216) 10.

38 Mańko/Monteleone (n 36) 6.

39 See recently, European Data Protection Board (EDPB), 'Guidelines 2/2019 on the processing of personal data under Article 6(1)(b) GDPR in the context of the provision of online services to data subjects', adopted on 8 April 2019.

40 See Art 7(3) GDPR on withdrawal of consent; see also Arts 6(1)(b) and 13(2)(e) GDPR. But as EDPB (n 39) 10 underlines, if 'the contract is terminated in full, then as a general rule, the processing of that data will no longer be necessary … and thus the controller will need to stop processing… Hence, it is generally unfair to swap to a new legal basis when the original basis ceases to exist'.

rective shall not be applied 'where the personal data provided by the consumer is exclusively processed by the trader for the purpose of supplying the digital content or digital service in accordance with this Directive or for allowing the trader to comply with legal requirements to which the trader is subject, and the trader does not process that data for any other purpose'. Therefore, the first category of data (personal and non-personal) that are excluded from the scope of the Directive will be the data needed to enter into a contract and to perform it, if they are not processed for other uses – which, as experience shows, will exclude very few contracts, as they are used for other uses, mainly commercial ones, whether or not they are reported.

Secondly, a difference can be made between '*primary data*' and '*secondary data*', the latter understood as data observed by the data controller, with which he or she creates profiles and patterns of behaviour and interests, thus generating knowledge-data and not mere raw material-data. Social science studies show that allowing consumers to retrieve the further flow of their data would help consumers understand the scope of their consent[41].

Thirdly, a deeper distinction can still be made between *'data provided', data 'generated or created' by the user, 'data collected'* and even '*processed or produced*' by the trader. Others prefer to distinguish between data received, observed, inferred or predicted by companies[42]. One of the most controversial concepts of the right of portability in Art 20 GDPR is precisely the reference to '*data* concerning him or her, *which he or she has provided* to the controller'. This concept clearly includes any data supplied 'actively' by the consumer, such as contact information, content generated by him and uploaded to a platform (video, photo, etc.), comments in forums, etc. At this point, 'facilitated' and 'generated' data overlap, but can 'facilitated' also be understood as data collected by the trader with a 'passive' attitude of the user or even clearly unconscious or concealed, as happens with user activity logs (eg, knowing the links of the emails you click on, the types of

---

41 Bernadette Kamleitner and Vincent W Mitchell, 'Can consumers experience ownership for their personal data? From issues of scope and invisibility to agents handling our digital blueprints' in Joann Peck and Suzanne B Shu (eds), *Psychological ownership and consumer behavior* (Springer 2018) 91; Iris van Ooijen and Helena U Vrabec, 'Does the GDPR Enhance Consumers' Control over Personal Data? An Analysis from a Behavioural Perspective' (2019) Journal of Consumer Policy 103.

42 Gianclaudio Malgieri, 'Property and (Intellectual) Ownership of Consumers' Information: A New Taxonomy for Personal Data' (2016) 6 Privacy in Germany (PinG) 133 (version available online under: <https://papers.ssrn.com/sol3/papers.cfm?abstract_id=2916058> accessed on 5 August 2019).

movies you stop before you see the end, the user's blood pressure)? To cut to the chase in a long controversy with arguments for[43] and against an expansive interpretation of the term 'provided'[44], the generous interpretation of WP29 seems to have prevailed in practice: 'the term 'provided by' *includes personal data that relate to the data subject activity or result from the observation* of an individual's behaviour, *but does not include* data resulting from *subsequent analysis* of that behaviour'[45].

Therefore, according to those categories, the right of portability in Art 20 GDPR includes data provided and created by the user as well as data observed/collected by the trader, provided that they have not been subject to any additional processing that gives them added value[46]. The Directive, *only* with regard to personal data, takes this approach and these categories, as recital 24 includes in its scope the data provided '*either at the time when the contract is concluded or at a later time*', such as when uploading or creating digital content; and recital 38 recalls that the rights of erasure and of portability (both) under the GDPR apply in case of termination of contract with regard to 'any personal data *provided* by the consumer to the trader *or collected by the trader* in connection with any contract falling within the scope of this Directive'.

Next, however, is to delimit *what content other than personal data* can be retrieved by the user under the new right granted by Art 16(4). Here we find that the user can only retrieve data that he has 'provided or created' when using the services. He is not entitled to data collected or observed by the trader. The exception in Art 16(3)(b) specifically excludes these when referring to the content that '*only relates to the consumer's activity* when using the digital content or digital service supplied by the trader'. Therefore, of the three types of non-personal data that could potentially be retrieved by the consumer (anonymised and aggregated data, acquired third-party content and user-generated content or UGC), Art 16(4) will only allow for the retrieval of the latter and even then with a very restrictive interpretation. In fact, recital 69 exemplifies them exclusively that way: 'such content could include digital images, video and audio files and content created on mobile devices'. This restriction, mainly generated by the new exceptions of Art 16 (see below), is a legislative policy decision that, in my view, is

43 cf recitals 60 and 68.

44 eg, see arguments in De Hert et al (n 17) 199–200.

45 WP29, 'Guidelines on the right to data portability', adopted on 13 December 2016, revised 5 April 2017 (16/EN WP 242 rev.01) 10–11.

46 WP29 (n 45) 11.

wrong and contrary to the generation of a high level of consumer protection as required by Art 169 TFEU.

III. Comparison and interaction between the new rights

1. The right to erasure and the right to prevent further use of the data

a) Rules and exceptions

If the contracting party of digital content or services withdraws his consent to the processing of personal data, as will typically occur upon termination of the contract, he may demand that all his personal data held by the controller be deleted or erased unless there are other legal grounds for not doing so (Art 17(1)(b) GDPR). Furthermore, he may require the latter to inform other parties who are processing these data of the interested party's request for the removal of any link to them or any copy or replica[47].

Article 17(3) GDPR sets out five exceptions or limits to the exercise of the right to erasure. The two most relevant in the scenario of termination of a contract for the provision of digital content and services are as follows. The first is when the data processing is necessary 'for the establishment, exercise or defence of legal claims' (17(3)(e)), which is especially applicable when the contractual parties do not agree on the breach of the obligations that led to the termination, or when termination was initiated by the trader. In the second scenario, despite termination, data processing continues (17(3)(a)) 'for exercising the right of freedom of expression and information'. Thus, the voluntary disclosure of personal data or public posts on social networks (such as *Facebook* or *Twitter*) will find in this limit an important barrier to their total disappearance when they shared or commented in exercise of freedom of expression or when the media broadcast them under the protection of freedom of information.

The trader's obligation to refrain from using user-generated digital content other than personal data presents the essential difference in the DCDC of not requiring that said data be removed or erased. The considerable technical difficulty involved in erasing or deleting data absolutely is

47 Art 17(2) and recital 66. This regulation in fact is the transposition of the 'right to be forgotten' online, inspired by well known judicial decisions such as CJEU Case C-131/12 *Google Spain SL, Google Inc. v Agencia Española de Protección de Datos (AEPD), Mario Costeja González* [2014] ECLI:EU:C:2014:317.

well known. The lawmaker has not sought to impose unduly heavy burdens on social networks and storage services when no personal data are involved. The main exception to this right to prevent further use can be found in the Directive initially proposed by the European Commission: if what should be understood as two different requirements are fulfilled cumulatively, both the trader and the other users of his digital services have the right to continue using the UGCs. Those requirements are that a) the content 'has been generated jointly by the consumer and others' and that b) 'other consumers are able to continue to make use of the content'. This use by other consumers should be interpreted as a cause for rather than a consequence of the exception. Basically, the grounds for the exception are based on considerations similar to those of Art 17(3)(a) GDPR, also related to freedom of expression and information, as well as to basic principles of intellectual property. Thus, for example, it will not be possible to remove content that is considered derivative work when the copyright holder previously authorised the transformation (eg, of a video or photograph), or to delete comments or social network posts in conversation threads, messages received in instant messaging applications such as *WhatsApp* and emails received.

However, three more exceptions were introduced in the European Parliament and Council versions that considerably limit what would otherwise have been reasonable consumer rights to full restitution of a sort of counter-performance once the consumer leaves the contractual relationship due to breach of contract by the trader. According to Art 16(3) DCDC, the employer need not refrain from using this content when:

'(a) has *no utility outside* the context of the digital content or digital service supplied by the trader;
(b) *only* relates to the *consumer's activity* when using the digital content or digital service supplied by the trader;
(c) has been aggregated with other data by the trader and *cannot be disaggregated* or only with disproportionate efforts'

With regard to these three exceptions, which, for even less apparent reason[48] in some cases, also apply to the consumer's right to retrieval of content, the following considerations should be made:

48 Restrictions can make any sense in relation to the trader's obligation to refrain from using them, since the user's (non-personal) activity data may be useful to improving his service or act as a basis for combining and processing them with other data for various purposes, but it is hard to understand the reason for such a reduction in the right to retrieve non-personal data.

(a) Interestingly, as loquacious and illustrative and full of specific examples as they are, the recitals of the Directive provide absolutely none for these three exceptions (recitals 69 and 71), which they reproduce verbatim, nor do they explain their justification. Only regarding the right to retrieve data, for example, recital 71 states that 'in such cases, *the content does not have significant practical use or interest for the consumer* while taking into account also the interests of the trader'. The first statement is a manifest excess by presuming that absence of interest *iuris et de iure*: the consumer can have many different reasons for wanting to know his activity history (overcoming an addiction, reconstructing his movements to prove them someone else, writing memoires, demonstrating to third parties his active participation in the online world or his ability with certain computer programs, etc.); the lack of usefulness outside of the original digital service is true if the intended purpose of the retrieval is to transfer or port the content to a different platform if the format is not interoperable (eg, an avatar in a digital game, gems or accessories acquired in a game, the *likes* or *ratings* regarding contents specific to a platform, the drawings or designs in a closed-code program), but for the consumer it may be useful, even emotional or sentimental, to somehow retrieve those contents constructed over time and, in its case, with money, even if he may not be able to 'use' them interactively in another context.
(b) The approved version is very similar to the one suggested by the Council[49]. In the version passed by the European Parliament, the three exceptions at least included the 'balancing clause' that such content 'cannot be refrained from using [or made available] without disproportionate and unreasonable effort'[50].
(c) Therefore, in configuring these exceptions, the scale has tipped too far in favour of the trader's interests: this is also the case by not requiring that it be impossible to disaggregate the data, but rather, if they cannot be disaggregated with disproportionate efforts, the interest of the trader prevail. This limit may even give rise to unsavoury business practices, as it will suffice merely to add on data, which will be habitual, for example, in the Internet of things.

---

49 Council of the European Union, 'General Approach on the Proposal for a Directive of the European Parliament and of the Council on certain aspects concerning contracts for the supply of digital content (First reading)' ST 9901 2017 ADD 1 – 2015/0287, 1 June 2017.

50 European Parliament, 'Report on the proposal for a directive…' (A8-0375/2017), 27 November 2017.

In conclusion, from the point of view of the balance of interests, these three exceptions make more sense in terms of the right to prevent further use than they do in terms of the right to retrieve content. User activity and aggregation with other data both have their usefulness in business activity. Indeed, less justification is found in continuing to use all sorts of user content on the platform if its format is closed and not interoperable, as this denies the consumer a reasonable pseudo 'right to be forgotten' once the contract is terminated, when not generated jointly with other content. Any prejudging of the lack of usefulness for the consumer of the contents that he generated with his activity is a regulatory excess that practically affronts the dignity of the person: the fact that this person cannot be identified through these contents does not mean that they do not have an undeniable value and usefulness for him. While the possibility of continuing to use the UGG jointly created and used by various consumers has constitutional support, all the other limits are actually meant not to hinder big data business models.

b) *How*

The current state of technology reveals the difficulties of achieving total and definitive deletion or erasure of data. Obviously, the most definitive way would be to destroy or otherwise render unusable the hardware (hard disks) on which the trader stores the information; but aside from being uneconomical, this action does not ensure the disappearance of data elsewhere on the Internet, given that periodic copies are usually made of websites not only by their creators but by third parties, copies in the cache memory, and so on. Three factors therefore make total elimination difficult: data persistence, redundancies and backup[51]. The most commonly used technique consists of *overwriting the data*: the data to be removed is overwritten by new data stored on the same hardware device, such that the more the initially deleted data are overwritten (which does not make them disappear completely), the more difficult it will be to recover them[52]. Oth-

51 Mark Henriques, James Ding, 'Purging the Cloud: Data Destruction in the Age of Cloud Computing', Womble Carlyle, 23 June 2014; Khalid Aissaoui, Hafsa Ait, Hicham Belhadaoui, and Mounir Rifi, 'Survey on data remanence in Cloud Computing environment' (2017) International Conference on Wireless Technologies, Embedded and Intelligent Systems (WITS) 1–4.

52 See on those measures Roselló Rubert (n 8) 385.

er techniques such as 'degaussing' are also used (a device generates a magnetic field that purges a media efficiently).

As regards personal data, erasure may be equivalent to their absolute and irreversible anonymisation. In contrast, 'pseudonymisation'[53]—which consists in replacing one datum for another attribute in a file or register, although the data could become identifiable again with a specific person if the process is reversible—does not entail erasure, although it may still be a useful in shoring up the right to be forgotten (ie, making it more difficult to access) in search engines and third-party websites.

Similarly, the trader's obligation to refrain from using content other than personal data can also be fulfilled using the techniques of destruction, erasure and overwriting described above; the NIST (National Institute of Standards and Technology) lists techniques for so-called 'sanitisation', including these three methods: cleaning, purging and destroying the data. Likewise, the legal obligation may also be fulfilled simply by 'blocking' the data, which consists of identifying them and reserving them to prevent their processing except to comply with legal obligations, so that the personnel who would normally have access to them within the company would no longer have access; only a person with maximum responsibility would and only with a court or administrative order to that effect. In short, it is a matter of using techniques from the 'right to restriction of processing' (Art 18 GDPR), as could be, for example, 'temporarily moving the selected data to another processing system' (recital 67 GDPR).

As for the time limit for erasing personal data, Art 17(1) GDPR establishes that it must be done 'without undue delay' and by application of the general criterion of Art 12(3) GDPR, within one month at most from the reception of the request, extendable to two months. In practice, a number of major operators do not meet these deadlines by freezing data longer than necessary and including some sort of extraordinary period of regret[54].

---

53 For a detailed explanation of both techniques see WP29 (n 45) 11ff. On its application by *Google* see next footnote and <https://policies.google.com/technologies/anonymization?hl=en> accessed 5 August 2019.

54 *Google* policy's terms are apparently transparent as for the timings foreseen to erase data and as regards to the distinction between what is conserved, what is fully deleted and what is just progressively eliminated: see <https://policies.google.com/technologies/retention?hl=en> accessed 5 August 2019. *Twitter*, for instance, fixes too long deadlines and other companies use a notable vagueness (*Apple*).

c) Proof

Fulfilment of the duty to erase or the duty to refrain from using the data is not only difficult to prove, it is also unconvincing unless third parties intervene to vouch for the effectiveness of the trader's measures.

Some techniques, such as data rewriting, leave documentary evidence of the process, while other erasure mechanisms are more difficult to certify[55]. Proof of *non facere* (of refraining from using) is even more difficult than that of *facere* (of erasure) without some sort of third-party computer audit to endorse the controller's claims, unless the infraction arises precisely because of accrediting the use of the contents and the traceability of its origin. The approach of the GDPR (Arts 42 and 43) is therefore appropriate and virtually the only one possible, by urging the creation of certification mechanisms and of seals and hallmarks to demonstrate compliance with obligations such as these. For this very reason, the failure of the new Directive to foresee this is a major lack. In any case, to date, national supervisory authorities have been firm in sanctioning controllers of digital content and services when they have not erased personal data despite being legitimately requested by users[56].

2. The right to portability and the right to retrieve data

a) Rules and exceptions

Although in the finally approved versions of the GDPR and DCDC recitals the grounds for both rights seem to separate[57], an examination of the recitals and claims during the legislative process of both regulations reveals similar purposes: encouraging competition between market operators, avoiding captive markets and closed platforms[58], encouraging the creation of interoperable formats[59]; guaranteeing the consumer's right to terminate the contract in the event of non-compliance without fear of losing data or

55 Roselló Rubert (n 8) 397–398.

56 For example, the Spanish Data Protection Agency fined *Facebook* 1.2 million euros in a 2017 ruling for maintaining *cookies* from deleted accounts that continued to collect and process information for 17 months after the supposed deletion.

57 See now only recital 69 GDPR and recital 70 DCDC.

58 Recital 46 of the Proposal by the Commission for a DCDC.

59 Recital 68 GDPR.

content of value to him[60], which, in the final analysis, in the field of personal data means bolstering his control over his own data[61]. Along these lines, recital 70 DCDC clarifies that the trader should 'at the request of the consumer, make such content available to the consumer *following* the termination of the contract'; therefore, also *after* the contract has been extinguished this way and not only prior to termination, although no time limit is set for such post-contractual retrieval.

The right to portability had successful predecessors at the European level: the portability of telephone numbers was first approved in the telecommunications sector (Directive 2002/22/EC). From another perspective, Regulation (EU) 2017/1128 on cross-border portability of online content services removed the obstacles to enjoying these services on account of the territorial limitations of the licenses for use of copyrighted material.

The right to portability affects the personal data ('concerning him or her') that the data subject 'provided', in the broad sense explained above, to the controller. Both this delimitation of the type of data involved and the provision that the right of portability 'shall not adversely affect the rights and freedoms of others' represent an important limit to a common situation in social network services: shared contents featuring personal data from different users, such as photos or videos in which several identifiable subjects appear, whether or not they are all users of the social network; forums in which the opinions of different users are recorded, etc., as well as cases of UGC created jointly by several users but containing personal data. A strict reading of Art 20(4) GDPR could lead to the conclusion that portability can never be achieved in such cases, because the rights of others are involved. However, the article does not establish a total prohibition, but only that portability must not negatively affect the rights of others. Therefore, the solution proposed by WP29 is balanced: controllers should establish tools to allow data subjects to select relevant data and exclude data from third parties. Controllers should also implement the necessary mechanisms to obtain the consent of the latter and only in this case allow online portability[62]. Another interpretation that would keep third-party rights from being used in any case as an impediment to the right to portability could be to turn to the rest of the rules and principles of the GDPR and, in particular, to understand that the user who wants to change from one social network to another has a 'legitimate interest' in the sense

60 Recital 39 of the Proposal by the Commission for a DCDC.

61 Recital 68 GDPR, *ab initio*.

62 WP29 (n 45) 17 and 21.

of Art 6(1)(f) GDPR[63]. Such an interest is one against which the rights of others do not prevail in any case if all the circumstances are examined case by case (such as how data are used, reasonable expectations about data usages, additional safeguards applied by the controller, etc.)[64]. Furthermore, the notion of 'reasonable expectation' can play an important role, because depending on the how closed or open the core of content recipients is within a platform, a user might expect that his data can only be accessed on that platform but not on others or vice versa[65].

In short, several other rights have a different degree of prevalence over the right to portability: the right to be forgotten, which cannot be impaired by the right to portability (Art 20(3) GDPR); the rights of third parties, which should not be negatively affected by portability (Art 20(4)) and the public interest, which will prevail over portability in any case (Art 20(3)).[66]

As for the right to retrieve content that is not personal data provided or user-generated, the new Directive makes no objection to retrieving content generated jointly by the consumer and other persons (Art 16(4) DCDC *a contrario)*, even if they continue to make use of the content, as it presumes that all co-authors can request such retrieval, but none may request the trader to destroy it or refrain from allowing access as long as there are consumers who can use it (Art 16(3)(d) DCDC). On the other hand, with excessive restriction, as has already been criticised[67], it prevents the retrieval of these UGCs in three other situations (lack of usefulness outside, addressing only the activity of consumer use and not being able to be easily disaggregated from other data).

b) How?

In both the GDPR and in the DCDC, data retrieval implies the possibility of it being downloaded directly by the user 'free of charge, without hindrance from the trader, within a reasonable time and in a commonly used and machine-readable format' (Art 16(4) DCDC); Art 20(1) GDPR only

63 Thus, Stoykova (n 17) 70, who tries to safeguard the portability reinforcing it with other general rules such as the household exemption of Art 2(2)(c) GDPR. See also De Hert et al (n 17) 198.

64 See De Hert et al (n 17) 198 and WP29 (n 30) 34ff.

65 See Janal (n 23) 62.

66 On this scale of degrees of prevalence see De Hert et al (n 17) 198.

67 See above III.1.a).

adds that it must be a 'structured' format. The aim is for the data format to become interoperable, but there is no strict obligation to make it so. Though there may not be any standardised formats that allow the transfer of some data (such as the *likes* in a particular social network), the fact is that some of the main operators have already implemented user-friendly systems that allow this retrieval by downloading a .zip file with subfolders for the different contents/data/formats involved, such as the option to download all the data that *Google* has of a user[68]. Others send the consumer to various pages of its interface to download (and, where appropriate, delete) the contents, starting with the account setup page and from there on a odyssey through various links. As for the direct portability from one controller to another, it is technically feasible with the creation of a specific API (*application programming interface*). In the absence of any legal obligation in this respect, however, the promotion of a single digital market will need other incentives. The example of *WhatsApp* is illustrative, allowing messages and their attachments to be copied to the most popular cloud storage platforms of the three most widely used operating systems[69], but it does not provide for migration to other free Internet messaging competitors.

As for the *free nature* of the right to retrieval and the right to portability (Art 12(5) GDPR and 16(4) DCDC), it is guaranteed in both regulations, although in terms of personal data, the GDPR also provides for the possibility of a 'reasonable fee' or of refusing to act 'where requests are manifestly unfounded or excessive, in particular because of their repetitive character'. This exception must be understood in relation to requests from one particular user, but not from all user requests as whole, since the magnitude would involve costs that the provider would be unable to charge to the specific users[70].

The *time frame* for handling the user's request is left open in the Directive ('within a reasonable time'), while the Regulation specifies it as one month, extendible to two in case of complexity or a high number of requests[71]. Today's state of technology makes it easy to fulfil the request automatically in short time, despite the fact that many provider contracts

---

68 <https://takeout.google.com> accessed 5 August 2019.

69 ie, *Android, Windows* y *MacOs*; in particular, it allows to make a back up of the contents in *Google Drive, One Drive* and *iCloud* (see the process in <https://faq.whatsapp.com> accessed 5 August 2019).

70 WP29 (n 62) 17.

71 Art 20 GDPR does not fix a period; Art 12(3) GDPR would be applicable.

set it as taking days to several months, or they reserve the right to set the time at the end of the contract.

c) Proof

Conflicting situations may arise when the provider claims that he complied but did so, for example, in an unreadable format or through a broken link and attributes the non-compliance to the user's lack of skill or to his operating system environment. However, the biggest problems with proof lie in checking that the digital content or services provider returned *all* the consumer's data, personal and non-personal, in his possession. Once again, without trustworthy third-party certification, the user must rely on a mere unilateral statement from the provider/controller without complete certainty of having received all the data collected or observed by the provider, for example, or of the techniques having fully anonymised his data or whether the provider passed data or contents to third parties without having received the user's consent, etc.

3. Relationship between the rights at the time they are exercised

From the time the Directive fails to require the elimination of all the non-personal data that the consumer wishes to take back, but rather only that the trader refrains from further use of it, the relationship between the two rights is simple and compatible. Unless a clause establishes otherwise (as occurs in *YouTube*), the consumer has no right to request erasure of these UGC. Therefore, as recalled in recital 70 DCDC, it is possible for the consumer to retrieve his contents *after* termination of the contract. This provision implicitly establishes an obligation for the provider to conserve these non-personal data. The question is, for how long? Not a hint is given in the Directive or in its recitals.

More troublesome is the relationship between the right to erasure and the right to portability in the GDPR. Clearly, the data subject that wishes to retrieve his data or port them to someone else needs to do so before exercising the right to erasure. Therefore, the two rights may be exercised jointly but also separately, provided that the portability is requested and undertaken before the erasure. Thus, a request for portability does no directly imply destruction of the personal data, which can only be at the data subject's express request[72]. Doctrine has interpreted mention of Art 20(3) GDPR that the right to portability 'shall be without prejudice to' the right to erasure, not as a hierarchy in the strict sense, but that portability is not an impediment to the erasure of the data[73]. Therefore, portability cannot be used by the controller as a way to delay or reject the user's request for erasure, nor does it require the agent responsible to conserve personal data for longer than truly necessary[74].

To assess all the potential of the right to portability, two different scenarios must be considered: that of the dissatisfied consumer and that of the consumer satisfied with his digital content and services provider. In the first case, socioeconomic studies show that the consumer will want to exercise both rights, switching companies in the smoothest way possible and eliminating all his personal data from the first company. This feature is characteristic of the so-called switching economy[75]. In contrast, a consumer satisfied with his provider may wish to port all his data to another provider without leaving off the first service and therefore without eliminating the data held by the first trader. In other words, not only using his data but also 're-using' them, which is the basis of portability (and this applies both to data provided as well as data observed, personal or not)[76]. The scenario of the satisfied consumer may arise in cases of 'substitutive markets' as well as and even more so in 'complementary markets'[77], when exporting all the data from one account facilitates keeping the same online identity in a completely different service. The consumer may, for example, have his reasons for having two social network accounts that update automatically, two blogs with the same content or a backup copy in the cloud that periodically ports to another provider of the same storage service. Even more understandably, the consumer may wish to transfer his creations, activity history, profiles, ratings, etc. from one social network to another platform that offers complementary but completely different services without quitting that social network (for example, from a general social

72 See Recital 60.
73 Li (n 17) 183; de Hert et al (n 17) 201.
74 WP29 (n 62) 8–9.
75 Li (n 17) 186 and 189.
76 De Hert et al (n 17) 202-203, making different suggestions for what they call the 'adieu scenario' and the 'fusing scenario'.
77 See empirical study by Barbara Engels, 'Data portability among online platforms' (2016) 5–2 Internet Policy Review 1. See also Radina Stoykova, 'The Right to Data Portability as a Market Tool' (2018) 2 Computer Law International (CRi) 47, with interesting examples.

network such as *Facebook* to a network of marriage contacts). An example of these complementary markets is the copying of *WhatsApp* contents onto cloud storage servers. Portability therefore does not always need to be exercised jointly with the right to erasure, nor is it always a tool that jeopardises client retention. Instead, it has great potential for creating new business models and a more dynamic digital market. That said, it is a matter for Competition Law rather than Consumer Law to determine which situations (such as the abuse of dominant position or in cases of complementary markets generated by small enterprises) should emphasise the obligations of direct portability of personal data and which should not.

Personal Data in Data Value Chains – Is Data Protection Law Fit for the Data Economy?

Christiane Wendehorst[*]

I. Introduction

Personal data are considered emanations of an individual's personality, and it is very much in this vein that their protection is recognised as a human right under the Charter. Yet, as everyone is aware, and economically speaking, personal data has also become an asset and a commodity that is being traded all over the globe. Between these two insights, there is obviously a degree of tension. This is illustrated by the debate around 'data as counter-performance' that was sparked, in particular, by the 2015 Proposal of the European Commission for a Directive on contracts for the supply of digital content.[1] Its Article 3 had stated that the proposed Directive should apply to any contract where the supplier supplies digital content to a consumer and, in exchange, a price is to be paid 'or the consumer actively provides counter-performance other than money in the form of personal data or any other data'. It was after the European Data Protection Supervisor, in his famous Opinion No. 4/2017,[2] had compared the concept to trade in live human organs and stated that the catchphrase of 'paying with data' could be dangerous if turned into a legal principle,[3] that the legislative technique was changed. Directive (EU) 2019/770 now makes payment of a price or provision of data by the consumer beyond what is necessary for the fulfilment of the contract or of legal duties an objective requirement for the Directive's legal regime to apply, thus avoiding any classification of data as 'counter-performance'. While comparison of data to live human or-

---

* Professor of Civil Law, University of Vienna.

1 European Commission, 'Proposal for a Directive of the European Parliament and of the Council on certain aspects concerning contracts for the supply of digital content' COM (2015) 634 final.

2 European Data Protection Supervisor (EDPS), 'Opinion 4/2017 of 14 March 2017 on the Proposal for a Directive on certain aspects concerning contracts for the supply of digital content' <https://edps.europa.eu/sites/edp/files/publication/17-03-14_opinion_digital_content_en_1.pdf> accessed 19 November 2019.

3 EDPS (n 2), para 17 (with endnote 27).

gans was flawed in various respects, this shift in the wording of the Directive was a big step forward, if only because it avoids any potential conclusion that terms about data could be exempt from unfairness control under national law implementing Directive 93/13/EEC[4],[5] or that the consumer could be liable for providing poor data[6]. However, the underlying tension remains, and at some point the elephant in the room[7] needs to be openly addressed. We cannot continue playing with words, such as by omitting the term 'counter-performance', pretending the data economy were only about non-personal data,[8] or repeating like a mantra in all sorts of contexts that protection of individuals under the General Data Protection Regulation (GDPR)[9] would remain unaffected. What is rather needed is a rigorous fitness check of the legal frameworks in force, ie whether they are fit to tackle the specific challenges of personal data in the data economy, and speedy legislative action if the fitness check reveals they are not.

II. The parties involved in data value chains

While the number of different ways in which data can be used is almost unlimited, it may prove to be useful, for purposes of data protection, to differentiate between different types of data utilisation in data value

---

4 Article 4(2) of Council Directive 93/13/EEC of 5 April 1993 on unfair terms in consumer contracts [1993] OJ L95/29.

5 The inapplicability of the unfairness control would also be in contradiction with Recital 42 GDPR, see III.3.b.

6 cf Axel Metzger, 'Dienst gegen Daten: Ein synallagmatischer Vertrag' (2016) 216 AcP 817, 848ff.

7 Christiane Wendehorst, 'Of Elephants in the Room and Paper Tigers: How to Reconcile Data Protection and the Data Economy' in Sebastian Lohsse, Reiner Schulze and Dirk Staudenmayer (eds), *Trading Data in the Digital Economy: Legal Concepts and Tools* (Nomos 2017) 327.

8 cf Regulation (EU) 2018/1807 of the European Parliament and of the Council of 14 November 2018 on a framework for the free flow of non-personal data in the European Union [2018] OJ L303/59; Commission, 'Building a European Data Economy' (Communication) COM(2017) 9 final; Commission, 'Building a European Data Economy' (Staff Working Document) SWD(2017) 2 final, 4, 11, 22, 33, 34.

9 Regulation (EU) 2016/679 of the European Parliament and of the Council of 27 April 2016 on the protection of natural persons with regard to the processing of personal data and on the free movement of such data, and repealing Directive 95/56/EC (General Data Protection Regulation) [2016] OJ L119/1.

chains, depending on the parties involved and the role these parties play within a value creation scheme.

1. *The main types of personal data utilisation schemes*

For the purposes of this analysis, utilisation schemes may be divided into four main types, depending on whether (A) the value is created exclusively within the sphere of control of one controller,[10] such as the controller who collected the data, or (B) that controller creates value for third parties who do not get access to the data, or (C) the first controller passes personal data on to third party controllers, or (D) a party just provides the technical framework that allows third parties the collection and further processing of data. These types do not strictly coincide with the different types of data transactions identified, eg, by the ALI-ELI Principles for a Data Economy[11] or the METI Contract Guidelines[12] but some types of transactions are more relevant than others for a particular type of data utilisation.

a) *Type A: use for the controller's own purposes*

Under schemes of what is here called type A utilisation the controller who has collected the data creates value by (re)using the data for commercial or

---

10 Where reference is made to a 'controller' this could always mean one party, or several parties who exercise control jointly.

11 See Part II on 'Data Transactions' of the recently finished Tentative Draft No. 1 of the 'Principles for a Data Economy'. The 'Principles for a Data Economy' are a joint project of the American Law Institute (ALI, <https://www.ali.org/projects/show/data-economy/> accessed 19 November) and the European Law Institute (ELI, <https://europeanlawinstitute.eu/principles-for-a-data-economy/> accessed 19 November), which identifies and analyses the existing legal rules and seeks to provide guidance as to how they could be further developed in order to provide both an enabling framework for the data economy and strong protection of individual rights, notably those stemming from data protection and trade secrets law. For an overview see Christiane Wendehorst, 'The ALI-ELI Principles for a Data Economy' in De Franceschi et al (eds) *Digital Revolution – New Challenges for Law: Data Protection, Artificial Intelligence, Smart Products, Blockchain Technology and Virtual Currencies* (C.H. Beck 2019) 43.

12 Japanese Ministry of Economy, Trade and Industry (METI), *Contract Guidelines on Utilization of AI and Data – Data Section*, English Translation [2018] <https://www.meti.go.jp/press/2019/04/20190404001/20190404001-1.pdf> accessed 19 November 2019.

similar purposes. Among the simplest ways of doing so are processing customer data for the analysis and optimisation of a controller's own business model, for the improvement of the controller's products or services, for the development of new products and services by the controller (such as smart services, or artificial intelligence trained with the help of data), or for direct marketing of the controller's own products and services.

b) *Type B: use for a service provided by the controller to third parties*

In what is here called type B utilisation of personal data processing personal data by the controller is a service provided by the controller to third parties. As in type A, none of the personal data leave the controller's sphere of control, ie none of the third parties to whom the service is provided get access to the personal data. However, in contrast to cases of type A utilisation, the purposes of the processing are defined by third parties. This situation is akin to a controller-processor relationship, but the party processing the data does so as an independent controller and not as a mere processor and the third parties would not be in a position to access the data. Among the most common scenarios is targeted advertising which, eg, the provider of a social network or search engine conducts for businesses or political parties. Another very common scenario is data analytics where, eg, another business requests the provider of a social network or search engine to analyse user behaviour in some sector that is relevant for the business, but where the analytics supplied to the other business consist of highly aggregated and fully anonymous data.

c) *Type C: use by third party controllers after a controller-to-controller transfer*

In what is here called type C utilisation the initial controller passes personal data on to another controller, ie data (re)use involves a controller-to-controller transfer. Such controller-to-controller transfers may be about supplied or observed personal data, such as where data concerning the browsing behaviour of identifiable customers is passed on to a third party that will then use the data for their own analytics, targeted advertising or similar purposes. They may equally be about refined or derived data, such as where whole customer profiles, possibly enriched by estimated data, are created and 'sold' to third parties. Finally, they may be about inferred data, ie data that is not even partly identical with, or generated by way of enrichment or aggregation of, any raw personal data but rather generated afresh from raw or refined data with the help of algorithmic systems and underlying assumptions, such as where conclusions with regard to a user's disposition to suffer from depression are drawn from data concerning his or her their typing pace.[13]

d) *Type D: provision of framework for collection of data by third party controllers*

Frequently, a party primarily provides the technical or other framework, such as by putting on the market a product with digital elements, digital content or a digital service, by means of which third parties are provided the possibility to harvest data, but where the first party does not (necessarily) itself access the data. For example, the provider of an online translation service allows a series of third parties to install cookies on users' devices and monitor the users' search interests, with or without ever storing data itself. Likewise, the manufacturer of a mobile phone may produce and market the phone with pre-installed apps that allow third parties the collection of user data. This scenario will be called type D utilisation.

2. *Identifying controllers*

It is often a challenging task to identify, in data value chains and data value networks, who is a controller, who a processor, and who is neither of the two. Recent case law of the Court of Justice has provided some more clarity in particular as to the notion of who counts as a joint controller, extending the concept to parties who do not themselves have access to the data in question.

---

13 cf Article 29 Data Protection Working Party (WP29), 'Guidelines on the right to data portability' WP 242, 10 <https://ec.europa.eu/newsroom/article29/item-detail.cfm?item_id=611233> accessed 19 November 2019.

a) Recent CJEU case law

In *Wirtschaftsakademie Schleswig-Holstein*,[14] the CJEU extended the concept of 'controller' to the administrator of a fan page hosted on the Facebook social network (type B scenario). The Court stressed that the creation of a fan page on Facebook involves the definition of parameters by the administrator, depending inter alia on the target audience and the objectives of managing and promoting its activities, which has an influence on the processing of personal data for the purpose of producing statistics based on visits to the fan page. Even if the data which the administrator of the fan page can ask for – such as trends in its target audience in terms of age, relationship occupation and lifestyles – are themselves in anonymised form, it remains the case that the administrator has a significant share in defining the means and purposes of processing personal data.

In *Jehovan todistajat*,[15] the CJEU held that a religious community is a controller, jointly with its members who engage in preaching, for the processing of personal data carried out by the latter in the context of door-to-door preaching organised, coordinated and encouraged by that community, without it being necessary that the community has access to those data, or to establish that that community has given its members written guidelines or instructions in relation to the data processing.

In *Fashion ID*,[16] the Court extended the concept of joint controller to an online clothing retailer that had embedded on its website the Facebook 'Like' button (type D scenario). By doing so, the retailer caused the browser of a visitor to that website to request content from the provider of the plugin and, to that end, to transmit personal data to that provider. The Court ruled that, insofar as Fashion ID actually determines the purpose and means of the processing of the personal data by knowingly enabling Facebook to process the data for particular purposes it can be considered to be a controller together with Facebook.[17] The Court equally clarified that any responsibility of a controller – such as concerning the seeking of consent or the provision of information under Articles 13 or14 GDPR – and any liability is, for each of several joint controllers, limited to the operation or set of operations involving the processing of personal data in respect of which it actually determines the purposes and means. In the case

14 CJEU, Case C-210/16 *Wirtschaftsakademie Schleswig-Holstein* [2018] EU:C:2018:388.

15 CJEU, Case C-25/17 *Jehovan todistajat* [2018] EU:C:2018:551.

16 CJEU, Case C-40/17 *Fashion ID* [2019] EU:C:2019:629 paras 64ff.

17 CJEU, Case C-40/17 *Fashion ID* [2019] EU:C:2019:629 paras 64ff.

of the party embedding the 'Like' button this was the collection and disclosure by transmission of the data at issue.

b) *Consequences for personal data utilisation in type B and type D scenarios*

While it is clear that there is only one controller in what has here been called data utilisation type A, and two independent controllers in what has been called data utilisation type C, the role of the parties involved in data utilisation types B and D is often difficult to determine. What is required, at the end of the day, is a case-by-case analysis.

It transpires quite clearly from *Wirtschaftsakademie Schleswig-Holstein* that third parties requesting data analytics qualify as controllers where they are somehow 'physically' close to data collection, such as by operating the fanpage and instigating users to visit the site, and *Jehovan todistajat* confirms that the same holds true for continuous encouragement of data collection. What remains unclear is whether determining the means and purposes of data processing is sufficient in a case where data have already been collected or would be collected anyway, such as where, in a type B scenario, a third party makes a contract with a social network about analysing the network users' political preferences and delivering fully anonymised data analytics. While CJEU case law would not exclude that party's qualification as a controller this might be going too far, considering, in particular, that such a third party would not even be in a position to provide the information under Articles 13 or 14 to data subjects, nor to seek consent. Similar questions arise in type D scenarios. Clearly, *Fashion ID* shows that a party operating a website whose design allows third parties to collect data qualifies as a controller, at least where this party knows that the third party will collect and process the data and has an economic interest in that processing. However, where a party merely produces a device that will allow, in the future, unspecified third parties to collect personal data, and where the party, after putting the device on the market, no longer plays any active part, the question arises to what extent it makes sense to qualify the producer of the device as a controller of data.

III. The legal basis for utilisation of personal data in data value chains (types A to D)

Any type of data utilisation in a value chains or value networks, be it a type A, B, C or D scenario, involves the use of personal data for a particular value creating purpose, which again requires, according to the GDPR, a legal basis for doing so.

1. The focus in the private sector: contract, legitimate interests, and consent

Legal bases of processing are listed in Article 6 GDPR, unless, where the data are of a particularly sensitive nature, the stricter rules of Article 9 GDPR apply. Article 49 GDPR contains special justifications for data transfers to third countries and international organisations where no more general justification, such as an adequacy decision, exists. A potential legal basis for the use of data will, at least in the private sector, usually be either of the following: (a) the data subject has given consent to the onward transfer of his or her personal data for one or more specific purposes; (b) onward transfer is necessary for the performance of a contract to which the data subject is party; or (f) onward transfer is necessary for the purposes of the legitimate interests pursued by the controller or by a third party. It is only in exceptional cases that other justifications may come into play, such as protection of the data subject's vital interests (eg in the context of safety features).

a) Contract

Where data are collected within the context of the supply of digital content or digital services, or of a similar arrangement, the legal basis for processing user data could be contract. Only recently, the EDPB has issued Guidelines on the processing of personal data in the context of a contract with the data subject for the provision of online services.[18] In these Guide-

18 EDPB, 'Guidelines 2/2019 on the processing of personal data under Article 6(1)(b) GDPR in the context of the provision of online services to data subjects – version adopted after public consultation – Version 2.0 of 8 October 2019' <https://edpb.europa.eu/sites/edpb/files/files/file1/edpb_guidelines-art_6-1-b-adopted_after_public_consultation_en.pdf> accessed 19 November 2019; Friedrich Graf von Westphalen and Christiane Wendehorst, 'Der Entwurf neuer Leitlinien des

lines, it has stated quite clearly that the legal basis of 'contract' must be seen against the background of both the purpose limitation and the data minimisation principles, which are particularly relevant in this context. The concept of what is 'necessary for the performance of a contract' is not simply an assessment of what is permitted by or written into the terms of a contract, but has an independent meaning. It does not cover processing which is useful but not objectively necessary for performing the contractual service or for taking relevant pre-contractual steps at the request of the data subject. The controller must demonstrate that the main subject-matter of the specific contract with the data subject cannot, as a matter of fact, be performed if the specific processing of the personal data in question does not occur. What is the 'main subject-matter' must be ascertained, in particular, from a reasonable data subject's perspective when entering into the contract. Taken together, and provided the strict approach rightly taken by the EDPB is confirmed by the Court of Justice, contract will hardly ever be a legal basis for creating additional value with the help of personal data, ie value that goes beyond the value of the service for the provision of which the data is necessary.

b) Legitimate interests

The legal basis of 'legitimate interests' requires three cumulative conditions for the processing of personal data to be lawful, namely, first, the pursuit of a legitimate interest by the data controller or by the third party or parties to whom the data are disclosed; second, the need to process personal data for the purposes of the legitimate interests pursued; and third, the condition that the fundamental rights and freedoms of the data subject whose data require protection do not take precedence.[19] In the past, reference to 'legitimate interests' has been used widely to justify data reuse. The Article 29 Data Protection Working Party (WP29) has recommended a pragmatic approach that allows the use of practical assumptions ('rules of thumb') based primarily on what a reasonable person would find acceptable under the circumstances ('reasonable expectations') and based on the

---

Europäischen Datenschutzausschusses 2/2019 betreffend die Auslegung von Art 6 Abs 1 lit. b DSGVO' (2019) 40 ZIP 1937; see also Christiane Wendehorst and Friedrich Graf von Westphalen, 'Das Verhältnis von Datenschutz-Grundverordnung und AGB-Recht' (2016) 69 (52) NJW 3745.

19 CJEU, Case C-13/16 *Rīgas satiksme* [2017] EU:C:2017:336, para 28; CJEU, Case C-40/17 *Fashion ID* [2019] EU:C:2019:629 para 94.

consequences of the data processing activity for data subjects ('impact') and taking into account any protection-enhancing safeguards in place ('care and diligence').[20] This opinion was still issued with regard to Directive 95/46/EC and is not among the list of opinions adopted by the European Data Protection Board (EDPB) at its first meeting in 2018, which is why it may not, at least not in all respects, continue to be relevant under the GDPR. However, also Recital 47 to the GDPR mentions direct marketing, alongside fraud prevention, as an example where legitimate interests could be invoked by a controller. Arguably, this is to be understood narrowly and to cover only type A constellations, ie where a controller uses personal data for direct marketing of its own products and services to its own customers.[21] In any case, reliance on legitimate interests triggers the data subject's right to object under Article 21 GDPR, which may be excluded only where there are compelling and overriding legitimate grounds for the processing.

c) Consent

Where neither contract nor legitimate interests serve as a legal basis for the processing, and none of the other statutory bases applies, processing must be based on the data subject's consent. Consent under the GDPR is defined as 'any freely given, specific, informed and unambiguous indication of the data subject's wishes by which he or she, by a statement or by a clear affirmative action, signifies agreement to the processing of personal data relating to him or her.' According to the Recitals and in the view of WP29 and the EDPB,[22] consent is not free if the data subject has no real choice, feels compelled to consent or will endure negative consequences if they do not consent. If consent is bundled up as a non-negotiable part of terms and conditions under a contract it is presumed not to have been freely given, Article 7(4). One exception might be that the controller offers data subjects a genuinely equivalent choice between a service that includes consenting

---

20 WP29, 'Opinion 06/2014 on the notion of legitimate interests of the data controller under Article 7 of Directive 95/46/EC' [2014] WP 217, 33, 56.

21 cf WP29 (n 25) 46; WP 29, 'Guidelines on Automated individual decision-making and Profiling for the purposes of Regulation 2016/679' [2018] WP 251 rev.01, 14ff.

22 WP29, 'Guidelines on Consent under Regulation 2016/679' [2018] WP 259 rev.01, 5f.

to the use of personal data and a service that does not,[23] and the future ePrivacy Regulation may provide for more far reaching exceptions under the heading 'legitimate interests'.[24] The WP29 and EDPB list a series of further, rather strict requirements that must be met in order to make consent valid, including the information provided, specificity of the purpose, granularity, and lack of ambiguity of the data subject's will.

2. *Compatible secondary use*

a) *The 'Recital 50 debate'*

A major point of controversy is whether a separate legal basis is required also where the controller intends to use the data for a purpose other than that for which the personal data have been collected (secondary use) but which is still 'compatible with' the first purpose within the meaning of Article 6(4). In order to ascertain whether processing for another purpose is compatible with the initial purpose, a controller must take into account any link between the purposes, the context in which the personal data were collected, the nature of the personal data, the possible consequences of the intended further processing for data subjects and the existence of appropriate safeguards for the data subject's rights. Recital 50 explicitly states that, where the 'compatibility test' is met, no legal ground is required, but authors who took part in the negotiations remember a different outcome and say Recital 50 fails to reflect the decision that was ultimately taken.[25]

---

23 OGH 6 Ob 140/18h JBl 2019, 101 – *Klauselprüfung Simpli-TV*; DSB DSB-D122.931/0003-DSB/2018 jusIT 2019, 88; Data Ethics Commission, 'Gutachten der Datenethikkommission' [2019] 105 <https://datenethikkommission.de/> accessed 19 November 2019. See also Sebastian Schwamberger, 'Reichweite des datenschutzrechtlichen Koppelungsverbots nach alter und neuer Rechtslage – Anmerkung zu OGH 31. 8. 2018 – 6 Ob 140/18h' (2019) GPR 57, 58ff.

24 Recital 21b, Council Document 6543/20 PUBLIC of 6 March 2020 suggesting revisions to the 'Proposal for a Regulation of the European Parliament and the Council concerning the respect for private life and the protection of personal data in electronic communications and repealing Directive 2002/58/EC (Regulation on Privacy and Electronic Communications)' COM(2017) 10 final.

25 Jan Philipp Albrecht, 'Das neue EU-Datenschutzrecht – von der Richtlinie zur Verordnung' (2016) Computer und Recht 88, 92; Peter Schantz, 'Die Datenschutz-Grundverordnung – Beginn einer neuen Zeitrechnung im Datenschutzrecht' (2016) Neue Juristische Wochenschrift 1841, 1844. See also WP29, Opinion 03/2013 on purpose limitation [2013] WP 203, 19, 36f.

Some take the view that the first controller who collected the data does not need a separate legal basis, but any second controller does.[26]

The answer to the question whether or not a new legal basis is required is particularly relevant where the new purpose is a privileged purpose under Article 5(1)(b): further processing for archiving purposes in the public interest, scientific or historical research purposes or statistical purposes shall, in accordance with Article 89(1), not be considered to be incompatible with the initial purposes. This means in effect, that it is only the 'appropriate safeguards test' within the meaning of Article 89(1) instead of the full 'compatibility test' under Article 6(4) that applies. The appropriate safeguards must ensure that technical and organisational measures are in place to ensure respect for the principle of data minimisation, and they may include pseudonymisation.

b) Arguments derived from the Open Data Directive

Some indications as to the role secondary use plays in controller-to-controller transfers can be derived from the recast Open Data and Public Sector Information Directive (Open Data Directive).[27] According to Article 1(4) and Recital 52 this Directive does not affect the protection of individuals with regard to the processing of personal data under the GDPR and other data protection law. While this statement may not come as a surprise, the further explanation given in Recital 52 is quite interesting: 'This means, inter alia, that the re-use of personal data is permissible only if the principle of purpose limitation as set out in point (b) of Article 5(1) and Article 6 of Regulation (EU) 2016/679 is met. ... Rendering information anonymous is a means of reconciling the interests in making public sector information as re-usable as possible ....' By mentioning only purpose limitation, and citing Article 6 only in this context, Recital 52 of the Open Da-

26 cf Philipp Richter, 'Datenschutz zwecklos? – Das Prinzip der Zweckbindung im Ratsentwurf der DSGVO' (2015) 39 (11) DuD 735, 736; Gero Ziegenhorn and Katharina von Heckel, 'Datenverarbeitung durch Private nach der europäischen Datenschutzreform – Auswirkungen der Datenschutz-Grundverordnung auf die materielle Rechtmäßigkeit der Verarbeitung personenbezogener Daten' (2016) NVwZ 1585, 1590ff.

27 Directive (EU) 2019/1024 of the European Parliament and of the Council of 20 June 2019 on open data and the re-use of public sector information [2019] OJ L172/56.

ta Directive could be read as confirming that Article 6(4) on reuse of data is sufficient for onward transfer and no additional legal basis is required.

What is as conspicuous is the fact that nothing in the Open Data Directive seems to impose specific duties on the supplier. Rather, Article 5(2) reiterates the principle of 'open by design and by default', meaning that disclosure of data should be the rule rather than the exception, and Article 8(1) even states that the re-use of documents shall not be subject to conditions, unless such conditions are objective, proportionate, non-discriminatory and justified on grounds of a public interest objective.[28]

3. *Lawfulness of processing and potential for harm*

In the majority of cases, use of personal data in data value chains needs to be based either on 'legitimate interests' or 'compatible secondary use' or on 'consent'. The two former justifications have a more substantive and risk-based focus, weighing the relevant interests of the parties involved, any potential harm that could result, and the safeguards in place, whereas the latter is more of a formal nature, looking at whether or not consent was free, informed, specific and unambiguous.

a) Consent to harmful processing

That begs the question what the situations are where data subjects would, without any kind of pressure or dark patterns and without facing any detriment if consent is withheld, still consent to the processing of their data and which are not already covered by contract, legitimate interests or compatible secondary use. Taking the EDPB's guidance papers seriously, the only situations could be that the data subject wishes to support a particular purpose, such as research, for altruistic reasons ('data donation') or believes the benefits of data processing for the individual data subject outweigh the risks. The latter could be the case, eg, where data subjects consent to targeted third party advertising because they expect attractive offers tailored to their specific preferences, or where – assuming the Court of Justice accepts

28 The Data Ethics Commission (n 238) has recently urged to take the tension between 'open by default' and 'privacy by default' seriously and to make sure, by way of technical as well as legal means, that the fundamental rights of data subjects are protected.

that offering pay models as a genuine alternative avoids a conflict with Article 7(4) GDPR[29] – the data subject wants to avoid a payment in money.

While, from the perspective of the data subject, correct assessment of the risks associated with data processing is absolutely key to the decision about whether or not to give consent, these risks do not play much of a role under the GDPR. Neither does the data subject have to be informed about the risks of data processing[30] nor is it possible for the data subject to estimate that risk from the information at hand, given that it is next to impossible to predict and gauge the impact of future cumulative effects, network effects and effects of scale, as well as of changing actor constellations.[31] What the data subject ideally receives as information is nothing but the purpose of processing the concrete piece of information at hand. At no point does it become clear to the data subject how these data may be linked and combined with other data, and how inferences may in the future be drawn from these data, and what it may mean to the individual. This is not to say that proper information about the risks would be an adequate solution to the problem. In the light of the number and complexity of consent decisions required the vast majority of data subjects tend to click 'OK' or 'I agree' as a matter of routine and without reading the terms.[32] However, the fact that no information needs to be given about the

---

29 See the references in supra 23.

30 Note that even the WP29, which goes already quite far, only requires the following information for obtaining valid consent: (i) the controller's identity, (ii) the purpose of each of the processing operations for which consent is sought, (iii) what (type of) data will be collected and used, (iv) the existence of the right to withdraw consent, (v) information about the use of the data for automated decision-making in accordance with Article 22(2)(c) where relevant, and (vi) on the possible risks of data transfers due to absence of an adequacy decision and of appropriate safeguards as described in Article 46, see WP29 (n 22) 13.

31 cf Jacques Crémer and Yves-Alexandre de Montjoye and Heike Schweitzer, 'Competition policy for the digital era' [2019] 19ff <https://ec.europa.eu/competition/publications/reports/kd0419345enn.pdf> accessed 19 November 2019; United Nations Conference on Trade and Development (UNCTAD), 'Digital Economy Report 2019 – Value Creation and Capture: Implications for developing Countries' [2019] 38ff <https://unctad.org/en/pages/PublicationWebflyer.aspx?publicationid=2466> accessed 19 November 2019.

32 cf Maartje Elshout et al, 'Study on consumers' attitudes towards Terms and Conditions (T&Cs) – Final report' [2016] <https://ec.europa.eu/info/sites/info/files/terms_and_conditions_final_report_en.pdf> accessed 19 November 2019; Jonathan A. Obar and Anne Oeldorf-Hrisch, 'The Biggest Lie on the Internet: Ignoring the Privacy Policies and Terms of Service Policies of Social Networking Services' (2018) 22 iCS 1: An experimental survey (N=543) assessed the extent to which individuals ignored privacy policy and terms of service when joining a fictitious so-

risks serves to underline that the concept of consent under the GDPR might be simply agnostic to risk. Where data subjects consent because they want to receive a service without having to worry about payment, or receive it more quickly, or simply to avoid hassle, a user could consent to the most detrimental consequences, such as to the disclosure of the most intimate details of their life to all current and future employers or to their competitors and personal enemies.

b) Unfairness control – revision of the GDPR or application of rules implementing Directive 93/13/EEC

However, consent must be seen against the background of the fairness principle enshrined in Article 5(1)(a) GDPR,[33] and it is in this vein that Recital 42 explicitly refers to the application of rules implementing Directive 93/13/EEC and stresses that pre-formulated consent forms must not contain any unfair terms. While explicit inclusion of substantive fairness tests in the GDPR would have been preferable, and while it still seems highly advisable to include such a substantive fairness test on the occasion of the imminent evaluation and possibly revision of the GDPR,[34] it would arguably also be possible to solve the problem at the level of national unfair standard terms control.

Alongside some blacklisted terms, which would both address some particularly conspicuous constellations and provide a benchmark for fairness control, there should be a more general prohibition of terms where consent would either be inconsistent with public policy or where the potential risk that comes with the envisaged data processing, as compared with the benefits which the data subject might derive from the transaction, are such that the controller could not reasonably believe the data subject would ever consent if that data subject had read all the terms and considered the consequences.

Solving the issue at the level of the GDPR would, of course, have the benefit that it could be combined with the introduction of a much more

---

cial networking service, NameDrop. Results reveal 74% skipped PP, selecting the 'quick join' clickwrap. Average adult reading speed (250–280 words per minute), suggests privacy policy should have taken 29–32 minutes and terms of service 15–17 minutes to read. For those that did not select the clickwrap, average privacy policy reading time was 73 seconds.

33 WP29 (n 22) 12ff.

34 cf Article 97 GDPR.

comprehensive and more specific regime for, in particular, profiling and scoring.[35]

IV. Controller-to-controller transfers (type C)

Data utilisation type C requires, in addition to use of the personal data for a particular value creating purpose, such as data analytics, that personal data are transferred from the controller who had initially collected these data (or who had collected the data that served as a basis for the data) to one or more other controllers.

1. Basic principles for controller-to-controller transfers under the GDPR

Transfers of personal data from one controller to another are not specifically addressed by the GDPR. Rather, the GDPR includes specific provisions only for the transfer of data from a controller to a processor of data and for the relationship between joint controllers, cf Articles 26ff. Controller-to-controller transfers are only indirectly covered by the general provisions on data processing.

a) Principle of direct effect and equal status of controllers

The GDPR relies on the idea of direct effect and equal status of controllers,[36] ie every controller has, in principle, the same rights and duties under the GDPR, irrespective of whether a controller had initially collected the data, or received the data from the controller collecting the data, or received it from somebody else and is but a remote link in a chain of transactions. There are but very few exceptions. The 'portability right' under Article 20 GDPR is available only against the controller to whom the data subject has provided the data, ie the first controller in the chain. [37] Also, information duties of the 'first' controller in the chain who collects the

35 Data Ethics Commission (n 238) 191ff; For a new data protection right, the 'right to reasonable inferences': Sandra Wachter and Brent Mittelstadt, 'A Right to reasonable Inferences: Re-Thinking data Data Protection Law in the age of Big Data and AI' [2019] 119 (2) Colum L. Rev. 494.

36 Wendehorst (n 7) 328ff.

37 WP29, 'Guidelines on the right to data portability' [2017] WP242 rev.01, 9f.

personal data from the data subject differ from the information duties owed by a controller who has otherwise obtained control of the data—while the former may follow from either Article 13 or Article 14 but will more often follow from Article 13, the latter always follow from Article 14 GDPR. However, even the controller who is the 99th link in the chain of transactions may still be under a duty to provide information to the data subject, and the data subject, on the other hand, is theoretically entitled to receive 99 times, by each controller who is a link in the chain, the information referred to in Article 14.[38] Accordingly, data subjects have, in principle, the same set of rights against any controller of data. It is irrelevant whether the data have been processed and have significantly changed since they were initially collected, or whether inferences have been drawn from data, as long as the resulting data, including inferences are still related to the identified or identifiable data subject.

b) *Dual legal basis*

According to Article 4(2) GDPR 'processing' means any operation performed on personal data, and this includes disclosure by transmission, dissemination or otherwise making available of personal data. Any making available of data by a supplier to a recipient in the data economy amounts therefore to a separate step of processing and, as such, is in need of a legal basis. It follows from the principle of direct effect and equal status of controllers, that both the supplier and the recipient of personal data need a legal basis for what they are doing,[39] ie each data transfer requires a legal basis at two levels: the level of the supplier of data and the level of the recipient. The legal basis at the level of the recipient need not be the same as at the level of the supplier. The most common scenario, however, will be that both onward transfer and processing on the part of the recipient are justi-

---

38 This is hardly ever spelt out explicitly but can be concluded from, eg, CJEU, Case C-201/14 *Bara and Others* [2015] EU:C:2015:638, paras 42–44; Annex II Sec. II. 1. and 3. a. to the EU-U.S. Privacy Shield Framework Principles (Commission, 'Implementing Decision (EU) 2016/1250' [2016] OJ L207/1); Annex A n. 3 of Commission, 'Decision 2004/915/EC' [2004] OJ L385/74); see also CJEU Case C-473/12 *IPI* [2013] EU:C:2013:715, para 23; CJEU, Case C-553/07 *Rijkeboer* [2009] EU:C:2009:293, paras 48–52, 68; WP29 (n 22) 7; Pascal Tavanti, 'Datenverarbeitung zu Werbezwecken nach der Datenschutz-Grundverordnung (Teil 2)' [2016] RdV 295, 299.

39 Wendehorst (n 7) 334ff: separate justification.

fied by a comprehensive consent given by the data subject.[40] Furthermore, the Court of Justice has indicated in *Fashion ID* that, where one controller allows the transmission of data to another controller in a situation that can be qualified as joint controllership, the legal basis of legitimate interests can be invoked only where the requirements are met for each of the controllers.[41]

Where a legal basis for the transfer is missing this raises the question whether a contract on the supply of personal data to an independent controller is still valid. This is for national contract law to decide. However, when applying national contract law, one will need to take into account that most transfers could theoretically still be ratified by the data subject's consent, which might serve as an argument against nullity of the contract under many legal systems.

c) *Limited responsibility of supplier*

Despite the fact that, under the GDPR, it is in principle for each controller to judge separately whether there is a legal basis and what are the duties with relation to personal data there are some limited duties of support for controllers who have passed data on to other controllers. Where the data subject makes a request for rectification or erasure of personal data or restriction of processing according to Articles 16 to 18 GDPR the controller who has received the request is under an obligation to communicate the request to any recipient to whom the personal data have been disclosed, cf Article 19 GDPR. However, this does not apply where such communication proves impossible or involves disproportionate effort. In a similar vein, Article 17(2) requires the controller who has made personal data public and who is now confronted with a request for erasure to take 'reasonable steps', ie to make best efforts in the circumstances, to inform other controllers who are processing the data.[42] Where the information about a request for rectification, erasure or restriction of processing reaches a recip-

40 cf CJEU, Case C-543/98 *Deutsche Telekom* [2011] EU:C:2011:279, paras 57–66.
41 CJEU, Case C-40/17 *Fashion ID* [2019] EU:C:2019:629, para 95.
42 This will mainly include steps that can be taken by automated means, cf Martin Braund and Hans-Georg Kamann in Eugen Ehmann and Martin Selmayr (eds), *Datenschutz-Grundverordnung* (2nd edn, C.H. Beck 2018) Article 17 paras 46ff; Oskar Josef Gstrein, 'Die umfassende Verfügungsbefugnis über die eigenen Daten – „Das Recht auf Vergessenwerden“ und seine konkrete Umsetzbarkeit' [2012] ZD 424, 425.

ient of data that recipient is not automatically under an obligation to follow the request because processing by the recipient of the data might be justified by a separate legal ground. However, the information that a request for rectification, erasure or restriction of processing has been made will certainly trigger an obligation to make double sure a separate legal ground exists.

2. *Controller-to-controller transfers to third countries or international organisations*

A somewhat different regime exists under the model contracts for data transfers outside the EU/EEA[43] as well as in the Privacy Shield Framework Principles,[44] which have replaced the Safe Harbor regime,[45] but are also under scrutiny by the Court of Justice (Case C-311/18). Said regimes have been drafted on the basis of Directive 95/46/EC, but the relevant provisions in the Directive and in the GDPR are largely identical, and the regimes are still being used.[46]

a) *Purpose Limitation, Notice and Choice Principles*

The standard contractual terms introduced by the Commission Decisions on data transfers outside the EU/EEA for controller-to-controller transactions permit the data importer (eg a U.S. based data business) to pass the

---

43 Commission, 'Decision 2001/497/EC of 15 June 2001 on standard contractual clauses for the transfer of personal data to third countries, under Directive 95/46/EC (notified under document number C(2001) 1539)' [2001] OJ L181/19; Commission, 'Decision 2004/915/EC of 27 December 2004 amending Decision 2001/497/EC as regards the introduction of an alternative set of standard contractual clauses for the transfer of personal data to third countries (notified under document number C(2004) 5271)' [2004] OJ L385/74; for controller-to-processor agreements see Commission, 'Decision 2010/87/EU of 5 February 2010 on standard contractual clauses for the transfer of personal data to processors established in third countries under Directive 95/46/EC of the European Parliament and of the Council (notified under document C(2010) 593)' [2010] OJ L39/5.

44 Commission, 'Implementing Decision (EU) 2016/1250' [2016] OJ L207/1.

45 See CJEU, Case C-362/14 – *Schrems* [2015] EU:C:2015:650.

46 cf EDPB, 'EU – U.S. Privacy Shield – Second Annual Joint Review' (2019) 12ff <https://edpb.europa.eu/sites/edpb/files/files/file1/20190122edpb_2ndprivacyshieldreviewreport_final_en.pdf> accessed 19 November 2019.

data on to other third country controllers (eg other U.S. based data businesses) without a separate legal basis.[47] Likewise, the EU-U.S. Privacy Shield Framework Principles only require that, for any onward transfer, an organisation has to comply with the Notice and Choice Principles.

The Notice Principle implies information duties largely identical with Article 14 GDPR. Each controller must comply with the Notice Principle when individuals are first asked to provide personal information to the relevant controller or as soon thereafter as is practicable, but in any event before the controller uses such information for a purpose other than that for which it was originally collected or processed by the transferring controller or discloses it for the first time to a third party. It is primarily the supplier who has to inform the data subject about 'the type or identity of third parties to which it discloses personal information', ie it is arguably within the discretion of the supplier to inform only about the categories of recipients. On the other hand, there is no exception from the Notice Principle where compliance with the information duties would cause disproportionate effort. Arguably this means that the parties to the controller-to-controller transaction have to make sure, in one way or another, that the Notice Principle can be complied with where that becomes necessary because the recipient intends to process the data for a new purpose or to make an onward transfer. In this case there is likewise no escape for the supplier, eg by omitting to keep records about the recipient's identity.

The Choice Principle means that data subjects must have the opportunity to choose (opt out) whether their personal information is (i) to be disclosed to a third party or (ii) to be used for a purpose that is materially different from the purpose(s) for which it was originally collected or subsequently authorised by the individuals.[48] There exists a special right to object also at a later point in the context of direct marketing.[49] At the end of the day, the Purpose Limitation Principle including the compatibility test and a right to object more or less replace the principle of dual legal basis.[50]

---

47 See point II of the Set II standard contractual clauses introduced by Commission, 'Decision 2004/915/EC (notified under C(2004) 5271)' [2004] OJ L385/74.

48 See Annex II, Sec. II 1.-3. to the EU-U.S. Privacy Shield Framework Principles (Commission, Implementing Decision (EU) 2016/1250, notified under document C(2016) 4176).

49 Annex II, Sec. II. 12.

50 Annex II, Sec. II. 5.

b) Accountability for onward transfer

A striking difference between the GDPR and the regimes for data transfer to the U.S. is that, according to the EU-U.S. Privacy Shield Framework Principles,[51] (future) suppliers within the U.S. must enter into a contract with the (future) recipient controllers, and this contract must provide that such data may only be processed for limited and specified purposes consistent with the consent provided by the data subject and that the recipient will provide the same level of protection as the Principles and will notify the supplier if it makes a determination that it can no longer meet this obligation. The contract shall provide that when such a determination is made the recipient controller ceases processing or takes other reasonable and appropriate steps to remediate. However, it is unclear to what extent the supplier can become liable if the recipient, who is not acting as an agent on the supplier's behalf,[52] is in breach of that contract.

3. Problems related to onward transfer

It is a well-known secret that data subjects' rights afforded by the GDPR are often close to worthless in practice because the data subject usually does not know the identity of controllers, finds it disproportionately difficult to exercise their rights vis-à-vis controllers, and because there is a lack of accountability of controllers for onward transfer.

a) Lack of central documentation

Already without any onward transfer of data, it is almost impossible for data subjects to find out the number and identity of controllers worldwide who are storing or using their data. This is so because there is no central mechanism for collecting consent declarations, let alone notifications under Articles 13 or 14 where a controller processes data on a statutory legal basis. While consumer contract law requires that for every single transaction involving payment of maybe less than one Euro requires information

51 Annex II Sec. I. 3.
52 For liability in cases of onward transfer to a party acting as an agent see Annex II Sec. 7. d.

is provided on a durable medium[53] there is no such requirement under the GDPR. Admittedly, it would be difficult to have such a requirement because it would mean that controllers need to collect data subjects' contact details, such as email address or phone number, which would be against the data minimisation principle and increase risks for data subjects. However, with the emergence of privacy management tools (PMT) and personal information management systems (PIMS)[54] it would be of the essence to have the technical features in place that allow for automated consent and notification management on the part of data subjects.

b) *Unknown identity of recipients*

What makes things worse is that there is, in practice, hardly a possibility for data subjects to know the identities of controllers where data are passed on. In cases of onward transfer of personal data, the supplier is under an obligation to provide data subjects with information concerning the recipients or categories of recipients of data, cf Articles 13(1)(e) and 14(1)(e), and definitely upon an access request, cf Article 15(1)(c) GDPR. On the part of a recipient of data, there is a corresponding duty under Article 15(1)(g) to identify, upon request of a data subject, the source from which the recipient has received the data. However, it is still unclear whether 'or categories' means that suppliers may, at their discretion, describe the recipi-

53 cf Article 2 nos 5, 10, Article 5ff of Directive 2011/83/EU of the European Parliament and of the Council of 25 October 2011 on consumer rights, amending Council Directive 93/13/EEC and Directive 1999/44/EC of the European Parliament and of the Council and repealing Council Directive 85/577/EEC and Directive 97/7/EC of the European Parliament and of the Council Text with EEA relevance [2011] OJ L304/64.

54 Data Ethics Commission (n 238) 135ff; On the notion of PIMS see, eg, Commission, 'An emerging offer of "personal information management services" – Current state of service offers and challenges' [2016] <https://ec.europa.eu/digital-single-market/en/news/emerging-offer-personal-information-management-services-current-state-service-offers-and> accessed 19 November 2019; EDPS, 'Opinion 9/2014 on Personal Information Management Systems. Towards more user empowerment in managing and processing personal data' [2014] <https://edps.europa.eu/sites/edp/files/publication/16-10-20_pims_opinion_en.pdf> accessed 19 November 2019. See also Stiftung Datenschutz, 'Neue Wege bei der Einwilligung im Datenschutz – technische, rechtliche und ökonomische Herausforderungen' [2017], including Policy Paper 'New ways of providing consent in data protection – technical, legal and economic challenges' <https://stiftungdatenschutz.org/index.php?id=132> accessed 19 November 2019.

ents only in a generic manner.[55] Information only about the 'categories' of recipients, such as 'other tourism service providers' or 'businesses who have a contractual relationship with us' is next to useless to the data subject. On the other hand, Article 30(1)(d) about the relevant recording duties of controllers only mentions the 'categories of recipients', so if there is no duty to keep records of the concrete identity of recipients it is difficult to argue that information duties go a step further. A different analysis may be justified for the second sentence of Article 19 GDPR[56] in the light of the obvious purpose of enabling the data subject to enforce rights directly against the recipients, but this is equally unclear.

It is primarily by virtue of information provided under 14(1)(a) that data subjects may gain knowledge of the identity and contact details of recipients in order to enforce their rights against recipients. In theory, the recipient has to give the information upon its own initiative, ie not only when contacted by the data subject, and the information has to be provided to the data subject within a reasonable time not exceeding one month after the data have been obtained, or when they are first used for communication with the data subject or disclosed to another recipient,[57] but information duties on the part of the recipient do not apply where and in so far as provision of such information proves impossible or would involve a disproportionate effort, Article 14(5)(b).[58] In this context, the question arises whether the supplier and/or recipient are under a duty to make sure that the data subject's contact details (such as email address or phone number) are passed on from the supplier to the recipient. This is arguably not the case as this would conflict with the data minimisation principle and also

---

55 For the controversial views taken on this matter see, eg, Boris P Paal in Boris P Paal and Daniel A Pauly (eds), *Datenschutz-Grundverordnung – Bundesdatenschutzgesetz* (2nd edn, C.H. Beck 2018) Article 15 paras 26ff on the one hand, and Schmidt-Wudy in Heinrich Amadeus Wolff and Stefan Brink (eds), *BeckOK Datenschutzrecht* (C.H. Beck 2019) Article 15 paras 58ff on the other.

56 Peter Bräutigam and Florian Schmidt-Wudy, 'Das geplante Auskunfts- und Herausgaberecht des Betroffenen nach Art 15 der EU-Datenschutzgrundverordnung' [2015] Computer und Recht 56, 60.

57 It is essentially unclear whether the maximum period of one month applies in any case or whether, where the recipient intends to use the data for communication with the data subject (eg targeted advertising) or for disclosing the data to others, the recipient may wait until such communication or disclosure occurs.

58 Despite the fact that the GDPR mentions the proportionality test in the immediate context of particular 'privileged' purposes the wording is broader and could include a situation where the recipient is not readily in a position to contact the data subject, cf Article 11(2).

with the idea underlying Article 11 because it would mean that significantly more personal data about each data subject need to be passed on than would be strictly necessary for the purposes for which the data will be processed. It is essentially unclear whether, in a situation where the contact details are not forwarded, the information does not have to be provided at all or whether the parties to the transaction must find a solution by which the supplier provides the information on the recipient's behalf.

c) *Disproportionate difficulties in exercising data subjects' rights*

It is only for withdrawal of consent that Article 7(3) provides that it shall be as easy to withdraw as to give consent, which arguably means that if consent can be given by clicking a button the same must hold true for withdrawal. However, there is no comparable provision for exercising the right to object under Article 21, nor for exercising any other of the data subject's rights. In practice, and in particular when seen together with controller-to-controller transfers which often lead to data being forwarded to a large number of companies, this leads to a situation where it is next to impossible even for sophisticated data subjects to effectively exercise their rights, let alone for the average data subject. What would be required also in this context is that the technical features be put in place to allow for automated tracing and automated exercise of all data subject's rights, at least where data processing exceeds a particular level of risk.

d) *Silence as to first controller's duties of due diligence*

In particular in light of the fact that the Privacy Shield Principles and the model contracts for data transfers outside the EU/EEA contain rules on a controller's responsibility for onward transfer of personal data it is all the more surprising that the GDPR does not contain anything of the sort. It is only for controller-to-processor transfers that Articles 28 and 29 contain a series of very detailed requirements, including that the controller shall use only processors providing sufficient guarantees to implement appropriate technical and organisational measures in such a manner that processing will meet the requirements of the GDPR and ensure the protection of the rights of the data subject. There is the requirement to have a written and binding contract, and Article 28(3) sets out in quite some detail a range of mandatory provisions which such a contract must contain. For joint controllers, Article 26 contains at least some requirements, namely that the joint controllers determine their respective responsibilities for compliance with the GDPR in a transparent manner, in particular as regards the exercising of the rights of the data subject and their respective duties to provide the information referred to in Articles 13 and 14, by means of an arrangement between them.

Given that the existence of controller-to-controller transfers cannot possibly have escaped the attention of the European legislator it will be difficult to apply the very detailed requirements which Articles 28 and 29 have set up for controller-to-processor transfers, or Article 26 for joint controllers, simply by analogy. This means, at least at first sight, that the GDPR does not contain any kind of due diligence requirements, ie a controller making a decision about the onward transfer of personal data does not have to check whether the next controller provides sufficient guarantees and will ensure the protection of the data subject's rights. It is only with some difficulties that one could derive such a duty from the general obligation under Article 24(1) according to which the controller shall implement appropriate technical and organisational measures to ensure and be able to demonstrate that processing is performed in accordance with the GDPR, or, where processing is based on Article 6(4), from the factor of 'appropriate safeguards' in place.

4. *Solutions*

a) *Revision of the GDPR*

Clearly, the appropriate answer to these problems would be a revision of the GDPR. In order to do so without creating excessive uncertainty, burdens and liability risks for everyone in Europe, a risk-based approach should definitely be taken. This could mean, for instance, that a new definition of 'data commerce' is introduced which captures only those types of onward transfer of personal data to another controller that occur, in one way or another, for commercial purposes. New and much stricter provisions for onward transfer of data to another controller can then be restricted to cases of data commerce. By doing so, the vast majority of data transferring activities that create a high risk for data subjects would be covered while avoiding that the average sports club or school is confronted with still more regulation. Where, by contrast, a school suddenly decides to improve their financial situation by selling students' and parents' personal data to other businesses, it would only be justified to include them.

At the heart of the new provisions on data commerce would be a new Article 26*bis* setting out, in a similarly detailed manner as does Article 28 for controller-to-processor transfers, duties of due diligence and minimum requirements as regards the contract between any controller and another controller to whom personal data are passed on for a commercial purpose. Were these duties of due diligence are not complied with the controller would become liable for resulting damages, and be exposed to other sanctions.

In addition, it would have to be made crystal clear in the wording of the GDPR that full documentation of the identity of all recipients of data is required for all data commerce activities, and that there is an uninterrupted and machine-readable line of communication between the data subject and every recipient of data. This would allow a data subject to use automated privacy management tools or personal information management services, reaching with just one click even the remotest recipient. It would be part of that package to introduce a general duty for controllers engaging in data commerce activities to fully cooperate, on the basis of standardised formats to be developed, with such tools and services in order to make the use of such tools or services fully effective.

b) Contract and tort law

Given that prospects of actually changing much in the current wording of the GDPR are pretty low for political reasons, the question arises whether the same or similar effects could be reached by way of changing national contract law. This could occur at two levels, at the level of the controller-to-controller contract and at the level of the data subject-to-controller contract.

What national contract law could do with regard to the controller-to-controller contract is define the obligations owed by the controllers to one another.[59] For example, contract law could introduce a rule saying that the supplier of personal data must provide to the recipient all the information that is necessary for the recipient to comply with their own duties under data protection law, and to support the recipient in dealing with data subjects and authorities. What national contract could not do, however, is define the duties owed by the supplier vis-a-vis the data subject. So national contract law could not introduce rules saying that the supplier needs to

59 See Part II on 'Data Transactions' of the 'Principles for a Data Economy' (n 11).

make sure it chooses only such recipients as provide sufficient guarantees for safeguarding the data subjects' rights. This is because, by doing so, national contract law would regulate issues that clearly fall within the scope of the GDPR, which would not be in conformity with EU law.

With regard to the contract between the data subject and the supplier as the first controller of personal data possibilities are equally limited. What national contract law can do is introduce data-related rules that are clearly designed to protect consumer interests other than personality rights, in particular economic interests, because the GDPR does not claim to include any kind of legal regime protecting data subjects' economic interests as consumers of products and services. Also, a national court could identify rights and duties that follow from the individual agreement of the parties (as contrasted with terms implied by law) because the GDPR does not prevent controllers from granting, by way of a contractual promise, more protection to data subjects than is required by the GDPR.

Potentially, national contract law could even blacklist contract terms and contractual practices according to which businesses take unfair advantage of the loopholes provided by the GDPR. So where a consumer entrusts a controller with personal data within the wider scheme of a contract for products or services, and the business abuses this trust by requesting consent to onward transfer of the personal data to a series of unidentified recipients, in particular recipients whose reliability the business has not scrutinised, this could be seen as on third term or contractual practice. In a similar vein, national tort law could possibly define new data-specific torts provided the situation underlying these torts is sufficiently specific so as to avoid conflicts with the general regulatory regime of the GDPR. For example, were a person recklessly sells personal data to third parties whose lack of reliability and failure to comply with the GDPR is evident it would be very difficult to argue that a Member State is not free to declare this a tort: the GDPR can hardly be interpreted as allowing such unacceptable practices for the sake of free flow of personal data within the Union.

V. The role of producers and developers (type D)

Under the GDPR, the addressees of data protection duties are controllers on the one hand and processors on the other. By contrast, the GDPR does not create any duties for producers of devices or for the developers of digital content and digital services as such, where these devices, digital content, or digital services merely allow for the collection of data by third parties. This even holds true for the requirements of privacy by design and privacy by default even though these requirements can most effectively be complied with at the level of producers and developers. Liability under Article 82 GDPR does not lie with producers or developers as such because, by producing and developing very privacy-unfriendly ecosystems, they do not themselves violate any duties under the GDPR. Cautious attempts to introduce some binding standards for particular software in the proposed ePrivacy Regulation[60] seem to have failed, as the latest Council documents[61] reveal the relevant provisions will most likely not make it into the final text.

1. *The situation under Directives 2019/770 and 771*

Rather unexpectedly, a first step towards a solution may lie in the new Directives 2019/770 and 771 on contracts for the supply of digital content and digital services to consumers and on the sale of goods. According to Recital 48 of Directive 2019/770 whether digital content or a digital service supplied by a trader is not in conformity with the supply contract and the consumer therefore has remedies against the supplier may depend, inter alia, on whether that digital content or digital service allows or even encourages data processing that is inconsistent with the principles of privacy by design and privacy by default under Article 25 GDPR. Arguably, the same must hold true for the sale of goods with digital elements, even though a corresponding Recital in Directive 2019/771 is missing. Depending on the extent to which courts are prepared to take this seriously the new regime created by Directives 2019/770 and 771 could prove to be rather effective in putting pressure on producers and developers, albeit indirectly through other links in the distribution chain.

2. *Data-specific product safety standards*

What would be a much better solution is the introduction of data-specific product safety standards across the board. This concerns not only privacy

60 Article 10 of 'Proposal for a Regulation of the European Parliament and the Council concerning the respect for private life and the protection of personal data in electronic communications and repealing Directive 2002/58/EC (Regulation on Privacy and Electronic Communications)' COM(2017) 10 final.

61 cf Council Document 6543/20 PUBLIC of 6 March 2020.

by design by default, but also data security and cyber security in general. It seems unacceptable, that there are loads of technical standards for all aspects of everyday goods around us, but only few, if any, that address digital product safety.[62].

3. *Product liability law*

In addition to the development and introduction of data specific product safety standards, the extension of the liability regime created by the Product Liability Directive to digital content and digital services seems to be overdue. So far, product liability is only about personal injury and damage to tangible property, but not about the kind of damage that typically results from the uncontrolled dissemination of personal data. While inclusion of such types of damage would be desirable at EU level, the Product Liability Directive arguably does not prevent Member States from creating a similar regime of no-fault liability at national level, given that the Court of Justice ruled in C-285/08 – *Moteurs Leroy Somer* – that the extension of the regime to types of damage not covered by the Directive (in the concrete case: damage to property used in a business) is not inconsistent with full harmonisation. Needless to say, liability can anyway follow from traditional national tort law.[63]

In addition to, or as an alternative to, the extension of the no-fault liability regime created by the Product Liability Directive it is worth considering the introduction of a new regime of quasi-contractual liability of producers at EU or national level. Such a new regime could ideally have been established at EU level together with the new consumer sales law,[64] but

62 cf OECD, 'Consumer product safety in the Internet of Things – OECD Digital Economy papers' [2018] <https://www.oecd-ilibrary.org/science-and-technology/consumer-product-safety-in-the-internet-of-things_7c45fa66-en> accessed 19 November 2019.

63 CJEU, Case C-40/17 *Fashion ID* [2019] EU:C:2019:629 para 74.

64 Christiane Wendehorst, 'Consumer Contracts and the Internet of Things' in Reiner Schulze and Dirk Staudenmayer (eds), *Digital Revolution: Challenges for Contract Law in Practice* (Nomos 2016), 189, 217f.; Christiane Wendehorst, 'Sale of goods and supply of digital content – two worlds apart?' (Directorate-General for Internal Policies, Policy Department C, Citizen's Rights and Constitutional Affairs, 2016), 18f.; Christiane Wendehorst, 'Besitz und Eigentum im Internet der Dinge' in Hans Micklitz et al (eds), *Verbraucherrecht 2.0 – Verbraucher in der digitalen Welt* (Nomos 2017), 367, 411f.

could also be established now at national level.[65] The 'Dieselgate' affair has demonstrated how poorly the existing liability is suited to deal with harm other than personal injury or damage to property that is caused to a very high number of consumers by way of a particular product design, and it is to be feared that such constellations will occur more and more frequently in the future.

VI. *Summary*

The law as it stands, by turning a blind eye on the huge economic potential of personal data for value creation and on the exploitation of this potential through various forms of data commerce, fails to protect individuals against the most high-risk processing activities. This failure is so significant and yet so surprising that it is hardly ever openly addressed. It could be the combined effect of three different forces: the economic interests of what have become the most powerful industries worldwide, the reluctance on the part of those who have successfully fought for the GDPR to admit its remaining weaknesses, and, ironically, the fundamental rights mantra of those with the greatest passion for privacy: 'One cannot monetise and subject a fundamental right to a simple commercial transaction ...'[66]

It is difficult under the GDPR or other data protection regulations to get hold of those players who act neither as controllers nor as processors but who simply facilitate the collection of data by third parties. This concerns mainly the producers of devices with digital elements as well as the developers of digital content and of digital services in so far as these producers or developers do not become controllers themselves. Recently, the Court of Justice has significantly extended the concept of 'controller', thus closing a number of gaps. The remaining gaps should be closed by digital product safety standards, a revised product liability scheme, and national tort law.

A major weakness of the GDPR is the absence of substantive fairness requirements with regard to consent. Given that the vast majority of data subjects are induced to give consent without ever having read the terms and conditions, and given that the data subject receives information only

65 cf Christiane Wendehorst, 'Updates und digitale Dauerleistungen' in Christiane Wendehorst and Brigitta Zöchling-Jud (eds), *Das neue europäische Gewährleistungsrecht* (Manz 2019) 111, 113ff.

66 EDPS (n 2) para 17.

on the concrete purpose of processing the particular data and not on any risks involved (eg long-term risks due to cumulative and network effects), the notion of free and informed consent amounts to sheer fiction. There has to be a substantive fairness test, ruling out from the outset any consent the terms of which are either inconsistent with public policy or where the potential risks involved are such that the controller could not reasonably have believed that consent was freely given. This problem does not necessarily have to be addressed at the level of the GDPR. It could well be addressed by national law, provided the reference to Directive 93/13/EEC in Recital 42 is taken seriously and understood to require full unfairness control of pre-formulated consent declarations, as well as to allow for the application of more far-reaching tools under national law such as invalidity for reasons of public policy and the prohibition of misleading or aggressive business practices.

Another conspicuous flaw in the GDPR is the absence of a controller's duties with regard to onward transfer of personal data to another controller, and on accountability for such transfer. Unless the Court of Justice will apply the rules on controller-to-processor transfers by analogy, or derive similar results from the general principles in Article 5 or Article 24(1) or, where applicable, from the 'appropriate safeguards' requirement, there is nothing in the GDPR to stop a controller from passing on personal data to the most dubious recipients. In particular, there seems to be no general duty to request plausible guarantees that the recipient will comply with the GDPR, and all that is required is some legal basis for the transfer (such as consent).

Furthermore, the way in which the rules in the GDPR on documentation, information and communication along a chain of data transactions are formulated data subjects are not in a position to effectively enforce their rights, not even if their name were Max Schrems, and certainly not if they are just average consumers who would have to rely on automated means to trace data flows and recipients and to make sure requests at least reach controllers. Without being able to rely on automated means, there will also be no effective enforcement by data protection authorities. This would need to be tackled at the level of the GDPR, and possibilities to improve the situation through changes in national contract law or tort law are limited.

Autonomy or Heteronomy – Proposal for a Two-Tier Interpretation of Art 6 GDPR

*Andreas Sattler**

I. Introduction

Growing up is a complex challenge for individuals and societies alike. Parents teach their children: Never take candy from strangers! Once matured, most people have learned the lesson that 'there is no such thing as a free lunch'. However, if sweets are narrowed down to so-called 'cookies' and 'free lunch' is exchanges for 'free digital content' many consumers suddenly regress to unexperienced infants.

Experts in the area of behavioral economics have demonstrated it is not only children that find it hard to resist sweets and seemingly 'free digital content'. Experimental research reveals human biases, information asymmetries and a so-called privacy paradoxon,[1] thus shattering faith in human rationality and the efficient market hypothesis. Bounded rationality has not only become a descriptive feature of the *conditio humana*, the insights of behavioral economics are accepted as justification for legislation that aims at 'nudging' citizens to make better decisions. Accordingly, the foundation on which human dignity was originally based i.e. *Kant's* idea of a liberation from self-imposed immaturity, has increasingly been complemented by ideas of participatory empowerment.[2] Formal autonomy to conclude contracts and thereafter be bound by them (*pacta sunt servanda*) has – sometimes for good reason – been 'materialized' in order to enable

---

* Senior Lecturer, Ludwig-Maximilians-University, Munich.

1 As regards the 'price for privacy': Sören Preibusch, Dorothea Kübler and Alastair R Beresford, 'Price versus privacy. An Experiment into the competitive advantage of collecting less personal information', 2012 (available at: <http://test.preibusch.net/publications/Preibusch-Kuebler-Beresford__Price_versus_privacy_experiment.pdf> accessed 5 August 2019.

2 As regards privacy: Christoph Krönke, 'Datenpaternalismus – Staatliche Interventionen im Online-Datenverkehr zwischen Privaten, dargestellt am Beispiel der Datenschutz-Grundverordnung' [2016] 55 Der Staat 319.

superior individual choices (decision architecture) and to promote concepts of fairness.[3]

This article cannot provide a detailed analysis of the different philosophical theories that support the notions of autonomy and heteronomy. Nevertheless, both terms can function as opposite beacons. As an analysis of the General Data Protection Regulation (GDPR) and the Directive on Certain Aspects concerning Contracts for the Supply of Digital Content and Digital Services (DCSD) illustrates, the European legislator has found shelter in a halfway house along the route between these two beacons. However, this halfway house is not built on solid middle ground nor on balanced compromise. Instead, the European legislator introduced two conflicting sets of rules[4] and entrusted the national courts and eventually the CJEU with the task of synchronization.

Academia in general and the fascinating volumes of *Münster Colloquia on EU Law and the Digital Economy* in particular can support such future synchronization. Hoping that it will contribute to such a prolific volume, this article commences with a short analysis of a current gap that is left by the GDPR and the DCSD (II). Hereafter, three prerequisites will be identified as starting point when trying to bridge this gap (III). Any new proposal would be redundant if existing options could provide for such synchronization therefore current options and their respective disadvantages will be illustrated (IV). Finally, this article proposes a two-tier interpretation of Art 6 (1) GDPR[5] that could help the judiciary or the European legislator to reconcile the rules stipulated by the GDPR, the DCSD and general contract law (V).

3 Criticizing the principle of freedom to conclude contracts as 'mystifying beacon' Anne Röthel, 'Privatautonomie im Spiegel der Privatrechtsentwicklung: ein mystifizierendes Leuchtfeuer', in Christian Bumke and Anne Röthel (eds), *Autonomie und Recht. Gegenwartsdebatten über einen rechtlichen Grundbegriff* (Mohr Siebeck 2017) 91ff. In response and defending such freedom of contract: Karl Riesenhuber, 'Privatautonomie – Rechtsprinzip oder „mystifizierendes Leuchtfeuer"' [2018] ZfPW 352ff.

4 This is probably a result of the fact that two different Directorates General were responsible for the respective proposal. GDPR: Directorate General JUST (Justice and Consumers), for the DCSD: Directorate General CONNECT (Communication Networks, Content and Technology).

5 Hereafter all articles without further specification refer to the GDPR.

II. Mind the gap: between fundamental right and economic commodity

Currently, there is an almost ideological conflict between proponents and opponents of rigid data protection. One side emphasizes that privacy is rooted in human dignity and is therefore sacrosanct. The other side, principally enterprises, search for correlations in huge sets of data thus exploiting the semantic level of personal data to increase knowledge. The business models of powerful platforms and the current legal framework illustrates this conflict between economic reality (1) and the legal framework (2).

1. Fundamentals of platform economies

In recent years, multi-sided platforms (more generally referred to as intermediaries) have been the object of intense discussion. Many innovative platforms rely on a – at least – two-sided market structure. Currently, US enterprises, in particular *Google (Alphabet), Amazon, Facebook, Apple and Microsoft* (GAFAM) and their Chinese counterparts *Baidu, Alibaba and Tencent* (BAT) are the most successful intermediaries and have thus become synonyms for 'the platform economy'.

Many of the current business models of GAFAM and BAT – although to a different extent – depend on the processing of personal data. If viewed from a data subject's perspective, most two-sided platforms collect personal data at the front end and subsequently exploit and monetize it at the platform's back end. Targeted advertisement is based on personal data, which is aggregated according to certain social and economic criterions. The possibility of targeted advertisement and customer attention is auctioned against remuneration in money, thus financing the offer of digital content and digital services (DCS) at the platform's front end. Only if viewed naïvely can these offers be considered 'for free' because users do not pay a monetary price. As personal data is provided as remuneration that understanding is erroneous. *Facebook's* statement that its services 'remain free' amounts to misleading advertisement[6] as it supports such misinterpretation.

6 Art 6(1) Unfair Commercial Practices Directive (2005/29/EC). With a different opinion: District Court Berlin [2018] MMR 328 (330).

Due to the effects of economies of scope, economies of scale and direct/ indirect network effects,[7] multi-sided intermediaries tend to rapidly increase their share in a particular market and subsequently expand into other sectors. Economic analysis reveals that platform economies have a strong tendency towards highly concentrated markets. This poses the danger that only a few competitors will be left and barriers for new market entrants become prohibitively high.[8] Most anti-trust agencies fear that intermediaries with a dominant market position might reach a so-called 'tipping point', thus, posing the risk that one 'winner takes all'.[9]

Although the economic prowess of GAFAM and BAT enables and incentivizes an abuse of their respective dominant position in some markets, it should, nevertheless, be acknowledged that GAFAM and BAT offer valuable products to individual consumers and society as a whole.[10] Some of the services are commonly considered to be essential infrastructure of modern society.[11] Thus, it is important to bear in mind that many data subjects would have to invest a significant portion of their monetary in-

---

7 Nestor Duch-Brown, Bertin Martens and Frank Mueller-Langer, 'The economics of ownership, access and trade in digital data', JRC Digital Economy Working Paper 2017-01, 40ff, available at: <https://ec.europa.eu/jrc/sites/jrcsh/files/jrc104756.pdf> accessed 5 August 2019.

8 Jean-Charles Rochet and Jean Tirole, 'Two-sided markets: A Progress Report', [2006] 35 RAND Journal of Economics (645ff; Wolfgang Kerber, 'A New (Intellectual) Property Right for Non-Personal Data? An Economic Analysis' [2016] GRUR Int. 989; Jacques Crémer, Yves-Alexandre de Montjoye and Heike Schweitzer, 'Competition policy for the digital era, Report for the EU Commission' (2019) 19ff/54ff, available at: <http://ec.europa.eu/competition/publications/reports/kd0419345enn.pdf> accessed 5 August 2019.

9 Executive summary of the Working Paper 'The Market Power of Platforms and Networks' by the German Bundeskartellamt, 2016, available at: <https://www.bundeskartellamt.de/SharedDocs/Publikation/EN/Berichte/Think-Tank-Bericht-Zusammenfassung.pdf?__blob=publicationFile&v=4> accessed 5 August 2019; see also Joint Report of the Autorité de la concurrence and the Bundeskartellamt on 'Competition Law and Data', 10.5.2016, 26ff, available at: <https://www.bundeskartellamt.de/SharedDocs/Publikation/DE/Berichte/Big%20Data%20Papier.pdf?__blob=publicationFile&v=2> accessed 5 August 2019; applied at: Bundeskartellamt, Beschluss v. 6.2.2019, B6-22/16 – *Facebook*, paras 432ff.

10 Presumably of different opinion: Vanessa Mak, 'Contract and Consumer Law', in Vanessa Mak, Eric Tjin Tai and Anna Berlee (eds), *Research Handbook in Data Science and Law* (Edward Elgar 2018), 20 ('After all, why should Google be allowed to make money on my data, while I receive nothing?').

11 Such characterization as essential infrastructure usually relates to examinations of anti-competitive behavior and a potential abuse of dominant position. However, if overstated this might raise the question on a government's responsibility to

come in order to maintain the level of consumption of DCS currently enjoyed on the basis of granting access to personal data for targeted advertisement. Despite the great difficulty of attributing a price to personal data,[12] it could even be argued that – until now and thanks to regulation[13] – cautious data subjects receive good value for personal data.[14]

2. *Legal framework*

Currently all branches of the legal profession struggle with the challenges posed by the platform economy in general and the role of personal data in particular.[15] The regulatory framework is complex and can be compared to a patchwork rug.[16] In addition to the GDPR and the DCSD – the topic of this article – exist multiple other European and national rules that have an

---

safeguard the availability of such infrastructure. In short: Providing the infrastructure for traditional telecoms required public funding and state-owned companies that were only thereafter privatized. Contrastingly, the current infrastructure is increasingly provided by private companies – although based on partially publicly funded networks – and are only thereafter regulated, similar to traditional telecoms. See for example Art 7(4) GDPR as expansion of Art 102 TFEU and the specific § 95(5) German TKG (telecom sector).

12 The choices provided by media websites such as the Austrian 'Standard' (6 €/month) or the 'Washington Post' ($ 90/year) provide for a near to market expectation of the value of an average website user.

13 This will be different if personal data is processed for other means than personalized advertisement such as calculating individual premiums for health insurances.

14 Companies paying for targeted advertisement on platforms are themselves subject to information asymmetries. Intermediaries might be able to trace the impact of marketing efforts more accurately. However, as long as these intermediaries use 'walled gardens' to shield their customers from direct marketing access, advertisers might still be paying prices for derivatives of aggregated data beyond real impact. The famous adage that 'Half the money I spend on advertising is wasted; the trouble is I don't know which half', that is credited to John Wanamaker (1838–1922) might, although on a much lower level – still hold true in the age of the platform economy.

15 The European Data Protection Board (EDPB) tends to turn a blind eye on the platform economy. Its 'Guidelines 2/2019 on the processing of personal data under Article 6 (1)(b) GDPR in the context of the provision of online services to data subjects' (8.10.2019) discusses the (lack of) applicability of Art 6 (1)(b) GDPR in specific situations. However, the business models of GAFAM and BAT are hardly mentioned (https://edpb.europa.eu/sites/edpb/files/files/file1/edpb_guidelines-art_6-1-b-adopted_after_public_consultation_en.pdf).

16 Using this image in the context of laws protecting industrial data: Malte Grützmacher, 'Dateneigentum – Ein Flickenteppich' [2016] CR 485.

impact on data-based business models. To mention but a few: The law of monopolies,[17] the directive on the protection of databases,[18] the directive on the protection of trade secrets,[19] the directive on unfair contract terms,[20] the directive on unfair commercial practices,[21] the directive concerning misleading and comparative advertising,[22] and the directive on privacy and electronic communications.[23] Almost all of these acts have recently been, are currently or will soon be under revision due to the challenges posed by digitalization. Additional legislation on consumer protection[24] and even on the protection of businesses[25] have been proposed and will impact data-based business models once passed as laws.

17 Access to (personal) data leads to new economic theory and subsequently different legal approaches as regards merger control (Art 101 TFEU) and the abuse of dominant market position (Art 102 TFEU). For recent changes of the German Act against Restraints of Competition (Competition Act – GWB) to factor in data as counter-performance and the impact of intermediaries, see Art 18(2)(a) and (3)(a) GWB respectively (<http://www.gesetze-im-internet.de/englisch_gwb/englisch_gwb.html#p0024> accessed 5 August 2019). For an overview on the impact of digitization on the law against anti-competitive behavior: Jacques Crémer, Yves-Alexandre de Montjoye and Heike Schweitzer, 'Competition policy for the digital era', Report for the EU Commission, 2019.

18 Directive 96/9/EC of the European Parliament and of the Council of 11 March 1996 on the legal protection of databases, OJ L77, 27.3.1996, 20–28.

19 Directive (EU) 2016/943 of the European Parliament and of the Council of 8 June 2016 on the protection of undisclosed know-how and business information (trade secrets) against their unlawful acquisition, use and disclosure, OJ L157, 15.6.2016, 1–18.

20 Council Directive 93/13/EEC of 5 April 1993 on unfair terms in consumer contracts, OJ L95, 21.4.1993, 29–34.

21 Directive 2005/29/EC of the European Parliament and of the Council of 11 May 2005 concerning unfair business-to-consumer commercial practices in the internal market (Unfair Commercial Practices Directive), OJ L149, 11.6.2005, 22–39.

22 Directive 2006/114/EC of the European Parliament and of the Council of 12 December 2006 concerning misleading and comparative advertising, OJ L376, 27.12.2006, 21–27.

23 Directive 2002/58/EC of the European Parliament and of the Council of 12 July 2002 concerning the processing of personal data and the protection of privacy in the electronic communications sector, OJ L201, 31.7.2002, 37–47.

24 Proposal for a directive on representative actions for the protection of the collective interests of consumers, and repealing Directive 2009/22/EC, COM(2018) 184 final.

25 Regulation of the European Parliament and of the Council on promoting fairness and transparency for business users of online intermediation services, available at: <https://eur-lex.europa.eu/legal-content/EN/TXT/PDF/?uri=CONSIL:PE_56_2019_REV_1&from=EN> accessed 5 August 2019.

The protection of privacy has only recently gained momentum. Legal protection of information relating to an identified or identifiable natural person (personal data) has followed a calm and steady stream until May 2018 when the GDPR became applicable. While the reasons for new legal challenges are manifold, the single most important is a combination of money and enforcement. The option of fining a company with up to EUR 20 million or 4 % of its global annual turnover has catapulted the GDPR onto the agenda of management boards worldwide.

However, the debate on data protection law seems to be dangerously biased. The discussions leading up to the GDPR were partially impacted due to an excessive focus on GAFAM. The requirements for valid consent (Art 7), the right to erasure (Art 17) and the right to data portability (Art 20) can be perceived as effective instruments to restrict primarily US IT Companies. However, such regulation appears excessive when considering that it is equally applicable to small retail businesses or non-profit organizations. The approach of 'one size fits all' can be justified due to privacy rooting in fundamental rights.[26] However, Art 7 (3) and (4) in particular might lack proportionality if interpreted strictly, as currently proposed by most data protection authorities and some courts.[27] Such interpretation follows a perspective that takes little account of the commercialization of personal data and it overemphasizes the fundamental right to the protection of personal data (Art 8 ECHR, Art 16 TFEU) at the risk of neglecting the freedoms to choose an occupation (Art 15 ECHR) and to conduct business (Art 16 ECHR) and the general principle to conclude contracts (Art. 6(3) TEU).[28]

In contrast to the final wording of the DCSD, the EU Commission originally proposed a draft which brought personal data under the material scope of the DCSD, and also accepted that personal data can be commercialized. Consequently, it identified personal data as a type of counter-performance.[29] However, such an approach – which the European Data Pro-

---

26 Ironically, it is very likely that GAFAM will be able to cope with the strict regulation. The real cost will be borne by start-ups and companies which have to comply with the same rules, although their business model is not focused on personal data. Put short: The GDPR will help GAFAM to strengthen their market positions as it raises barriers of market entrance for competitors.

27 Austrian OGH, Urt. v. 31.08.2018 – 6 Ob 140/18h = [2018] BeckRS 30960 = [2019] ZD 72, para 47 – decided based on former Austrian law.

28 On Art 16 ECHR see CJEU, 21. 12. 2016 – C-201/15 = [2017] EuZW 229 (para 66f); CJEU, 22. 1. 2013 – C- 283/11 = [2013] EuZW 347 (para 42ff) – Sky Austria.

29 Art 3(1) of the proposal for a directive on certain aspects concerning contracts for the supply of digital content, COM(2015) 634 final.

tection Supervisor polemically compared to trading organs of a living person[30] – was unacceptable for members of the EU Parliament. As a result, all references to the term 'counter-performance'[31] were deleted. Contrastingly, the final wording includes the utopian proclamation that personal data is 'no-commodity'.[32] In order to achieve a level playing field for all providers of DCS, the directive remains applicable, irrespective of whether consumers provide remuneration in money or grant access to personal data.

Art 16(1) sentence 2 DCSD illustrates that both categories of remuneration cannot be treated equally. A right to reduction is only granted as a remedy to defective DCS if consumers have paid a monetary remuneration. If consumers grant access to personal data instead, they are entitled to terminate the contract even if the lack of conformity of DCS is minor under Art 14(6) DCSD. Thus, the absence of a right to reduction is partly compensated by a lower threshold as regards the termination right.[33]

As an attempt to avoid disputes, the DCSD stipulates that in any case of conflict the GDPR shall prevail, Art 3 (8) and Art 16 (2) DCSD. However, such superiority hardly provides solutions as the GDPR ignores the commercialization of personal data. Moreover, deleting the term 'counter-performance' in the DCSD has no impact on the persistent tension between GDPR, DCSD and general contract law. While a contract is defined by its reliable and binding mutual nature (*quid pro quo – do ut des*), the GDPR provides no such reliability as Art 7(3) generally allows a data subject to withdraw consent at any time without cause. Put short: The European legislator has not provided a solution to the challenges stemming from an approval of personal data as remuneration (DCSD) and the right to withdraw consent (GDPR), yet.[34]

---

30 Speech of Giovanni Buttarelli (EU-Data Protection Supervisor), available at: <https://edps.europa.eu/sites/edp/files/publication/17-01-12_digital_content_directive_sd_en.pdf> accessed 5 August 2019.

31 Recitals 13, 14, 37, 42 of the Commission's proposal.

32 Recital 24 DCSD. Repeating this mantra: Guidelines 2/2019 of the EDPB (n 15) para. 54.

33 It is difficult to reduce the volume of personal data provided once the digital content or service is defective. However, this approach saves courts from the difficult task of determining the value of the personal data.

34 Instead, an evasive recital 40 provides that the DCSD 'should not regulate the consequences for the contracts covered by this Directive in the event that the consumer withdraws the consent for the processing of the consumer's personal data. Such consequences should remain a matter for national law' (see below IV.3).

III. Bridging the gap

Only a superficial observation might suggest that European law contains an unambiguous decision that personal data is no object of trade. The policy statement that personal data is 'no commodity' is the result of political compromise. Nevertheless, reality proves such proclamations wrong. Public opinion and most data protection authorities neglect the fact that the GDPR has two regulatory purposes (1). Moreover, personal data has been an object of trade for decades. This reality is not sufficiently taken into account (2). The sheer amount of 87 verbose recitals illustrates that the few mandatory articles of the DCSD represent the lowest common denominator. The European legislator was unable to strike a balance between the protection of privacy and economic reality. Consequently, the DCSD delegates the task of synchronizing GDPR and DCSD to the judiciary (3).

1. Acknowledging the other side of the coin

According to its subject-matter and objectives, the GDPR lays down rules relating to the protection of natural persons with regard to the processing of personal data *and* rules relating to the free movement of personal data, Art 1(1) GDPR. Of course, there is not a single article within the GDPR that focuses on the free flow of data. Its regulatory emphasis is almost exclusively on the protection of privacy. Such disparity encourages an interpretation that represses the second rationale of enabling the free movement of personal data within the EU.[35] Obviously, any adjustment of diverse national laws reduces transaction costs and therefore removes market barriers. Thus, harmonization automatically facilitates the EU internal market. However, the objective of enabling a free flow of personal data should not be misunderstood as a mere factual consequence or by-product of the adjustments provided for by the GDPR, nor as paying mere lip service to the principle of conferred powers, Art 114(1) and Art 115 TFEU.

The equal status assigned to the aim of removing obstacles to trade in the internal market and the right to the protection of personal data is an ambiguous starting point and has to be considered by both the courts and data protection authorities when applying the GDPR. This is particularly important when the European Data Protection Board (EDPB) provides interpretative guidelines and adopts a decision that is binding for national

35 See also rec. 5 GDPR.

supervisory authorities, Art 65 (1).[36] While such decisions by the EDPB are essential for supervisory authorities to achieve a homogeneous interpretation, courts should consider these guidelines very carefully. It is the task of the judiciary to scrutinize these guidelines and decisions, especially if the EDPB neglects the free flow of personal data as second objective of the GDPR.

2. *Personal data as object of trade*

The EU Commission's proposal of the DCSD (2015)[37] was – when compared to the wording of the final DCSD – straightforward. Recitals 13, 14, 37 and 42 of the proposal mentioned that personal data should be considered as 'counter-performance'. According to Art 3(1) of the proposal, the directive was applicable to any contract under which a provider of digital content received either a price or a 'counter-performance other than money in the form of personal data or any other data'.[38] The proposal initiated a discussion on how the *de facto* commercialization of personal data should be treated in the context of contract law. As already mentioned, all references to personal data as 'counter-performance' were eventually deleted. Contrastingly, recital 24 DCSD proclaims that personal data is 'no commodity'. However, such wording is wishful thinking in the context of economic reality.

Firstly, there is an obvious tension stemming from the freedom of contract and the approach taken by the GDPR. Derived from its historic evo-

36 While such decisions by the EDPB are essential to achieve a homogeneous interpretation amongst supervisory authorities, courts should consider these guidelines carefully, but should not hesitate to reject their findings.

37 European Commission, 'Proposal for a directive on certain aspects concerning contracts for the supply of digital content' COM(2015) 634 final.

38 Furthermore, the EU-Commission did foresee a post-contractual conflict if a consumer provided user generated content (UGC), including personal data (Doc: ST 14827 2016 INIT 1.12.2016, 11 (no. 29) available at: <http://eur-lex.europa.eu/legal-content/EN/TXT/?uri=consil:ST_14827_2016_INIT> accessed 5 August 2019). Upon termination of the contract, the provider had to stop the processing of all personal data. However, Art 13(2)(b) of the proposal provided an exception for such UGC and personal data, which the consumer had generated jointly with other customers, who continue to make use of such multi-relational data.

lution as a legal defense against oppressive government,[39] privacy law is based on a prohibition of processing personal data unless consent or a formal legislative act allows otherwise, Art 6(1) and Art 9(1) GDPR. Conversely, contract law roots in the freedom of contract. Thus, voiding a contract is an exception.

Secondly, it is good law – at least in Germany – that a consent allowing the processing of personal data cannot be withdrawn at any time without cause. German courts held that a consent to produce and publish nude photography against remuneration in money could not be withdrawn because the pictured person opted for a more 'serious' lifestyle.[40] More recently, and in the context of labor law and therefore a legal field that is traditionally perceived as an area that safeguards employees, the German Federal Labor Court denied an employee the right to freely withdraw a given consent. The employee had consented to being filmed for a marketing video of his employer. This video was publicly available on the employer's website. A few months after termination of the labor contract, the former employee withdrew his consent and sued for an injunction, damages and erasure of the relevant video clip. Balancing the interests at stake, the court decided against such a right to withdraw consent, thus, decoupling the labor contract from the consent to a processing of personal data.[41] The video clip – including the image of the former employee – could remain on the website.

Despite the right to withdraw consent according to Art 7(3) and the right to erasure ('be forgotten') according to Art 17, both judgements are arguably still good law after May 2018. They fall within the scope of the so-called opening clauses for national law stipulated in Art 85 (freedom of expression and information) and Art 88 (processing in the context of employment) respectively. However, both decisions illustrate that a strict and verbatim interpretation of Art 6 and Art 7 can easily lead to contradictory decisions under the GDPR and national law.

Let us presume that the GDPR was applicable to the aforementioned facts. In the first example, sensitive personal data is concerned and such a situation would therefore not be open to a balancing of interests by a

---

39 Andreas Sattler, 'Personality to Property? – Revisiting the Fundamentals of the Protection of Personal Data' in Mor Bakhoum et al (eds), *Personal Data in Competition, Consumer Protection and Intellectual Property Law* (Springer 2018), 27ff.

40 District Court Munich, 17.3.1989 – 21 U 4729/88 [1990] NJW-RR 999.

41 German Federal Labor Court (BAG), 11.12.2014 – 8 AZR 1010/13 [2015] ZD 330.

court.[42] As regards the second example, processing would not be possible under the GDPR either if the interpretation of Art 6(1)(a) as proposed by the Art 29 Working Group is correct. According to its Working Paper 259,[43] the Art 29 Working Group proposes an interpretation of Art 6 that would bar data controllers from relying on more than one legal basis when processing personal data for a specific purpose. Consequently, all data controllers would be prohibited from switching to a different legal basis once a data subject withdraws consent.[44] According to that understanding, a court would be prevented from applying Art 6(1)(f) GDPR (balancing of interests) once consent has been withdrawn.

This interpretation of the Art 29 Working Group bluntly contradicts the wording of Art 6 (1) which requires that *at least one* legal basis justifies the processing. Therefore according to the verbatim law, controllers are free to rely on several justifications for the same data processing.[45] The narrow interpretation of the Art 29 Working Group would only be feasible if the respective legal justifications provided in Art 6(1) were sufficiently precise and easy to apply.[46] As none of these conditions are met, such restrictive interpretation is not convincing from a legal perspective and utterly unrealistic from an economic standpoint.[47]

---

42 Processing of sensitive data for commercial purposes requires – in general – either a consent or a public interest, Art 9(2) GDPR.

43 Article 29 Working Party, WP259 rev.01, 'Guidelines on consent under Regulation 2016/679', adopted on 28.11.2017, as last revised and adopted on 10.4.2018.

44 Article 29 Working Party, WP259 rev.01, 22: 'It is important to note here that if a controller chooses to rely on consent for any part of the processing, they must be prepared to respect that choice and stop that part of the processing if an individual withdraws consent. Sending out the message that data will be processed on the basis of consent, while actually some other lawful basis is relied on, would be fundamentally unfair to individuals'.

45 This understanding is confirmed by Art 17(1)(b) GDPR which stipulates that withdrawal of consent is not sufficient to constitute a right to erasure if such data processing can be based on another justification.

46 The EDPB seems less strict on this issue. According to recital 20 of the Guidelines 2/2019 (n 15) the controller can rely on different legal basis but 'should make sure to avoid any confusion as to what the applicable legal basis is'. Thus, instead of promoting exclusivity of the legal basis the EDPB seem to emphasize the principle of transparency.

47 Despite the relevance of the guidelines of the former Art 29 Working Group – which was succeeded by the European Data Protection Board –, courts and antitrust offices should, nevertheless, be cautious when referring to these guidelines, as the EDPB tends to take a perspective that focuses on the rights of data subjects and might therefore neglect other interests involved. Strongly relying on the Working Papers of the Art 29 Working Group: Bundeskartellamt, Beschluss v.

Thirdly, the GDPR largely blanks out celebrity merchandising that reaches beyond cheesy tabloid 'stories' – to which Art 85 GDPR arguably applies.[48] Popular actors, athletes and politicians have been licensing and thus commercializing their names, images and other aspects of their identity for decades. It remains open for debate how such licensing of economic parts of personality rights[49] will be treated under the GDPR. The answer is not trivial nor of only theoretical interest.[50]

3. *Courts as bridge builders*

The analysis of the GDPR and the DCSD reveals fundamental conflicts that were not solved by the legislator. According to Art 3(1) sentence 2 DCSD consumers are granted similar rights irrespective of whether they pay a monetary price or provide personal data instead. Consequently, the DCSD – at least partially – achieves its aim to create a level playing field for providers irrespective of the nature of remuneration. However, as personal data is not accepted as counter-performance, the DCSD lacks detailed remedies once the contract is terminated and given consent is withdrawn. In contrast, Art 3(8) stipulates that the DCSD shall be without prejudice to the GDPR. Similarly, Art 16(2) DCSD demands that providers of DCS shall comply with the obligations applicable under the GDPR as far as personal data of consumers are concerned.

Instead of providing detailed rules for obvious legal conflicts, the DCSD points to the GDPR, a regulation that deliberately turns a blind eye to the *de facto* commercialization of personal data. As if the relationship between GDPR and DCSD was not already complex, recital 40 DCSD leaves the contractual consequences of a withdrawal of consent entirely to the national laws of the Members States. The respective European institutions were well aware of the conflicts during trilogue proceedings. However,

---

6.2.2019, B6-22/16 – *Facebook* (a short summary is available in English: <https://www.bundeskartellamt.de/SharedDocs/Entscheidung/EN/Fallberichte/Missbrauchsaufsicht/2019/B6-22-16.pdf?__blob=publicationFile&v=4)> accessed 5 August 2019.

48 Rec. 153 para 7 GDPR.

49 In US American law such business models are facilitated by a broad right to publicity. See for a comparison: James Q.Whitman, 'The Two Western Cultures of Privacy: Dignity Versus Liberty' (2004) 113 Yale Law Journal 1151, available at: <http://www.yalelawjournal.org/article/the-two-western-cultures-of-privacy-dignity-versus-liberty> accessed 5 August 2019.

50 An application of Art 6(1)(b) provides no convincing solution. See below IV.2.

they could not strike a reasonable compromise. Consequently, the task of synchronizing has – like a hot potato – been passed on to the courts. Fundamental economic policy decisions were delegated to the realm of the CJEU.

IV. Alterative options for synchronization

Prior to proposing a two-tier interpretation of Art 6(1) it is sensible to briefly illustrate the alternative options and describe their disadvantages. One option could be to interpret providing access to personal data as a mere condition (1). The second option relies on a flexible interpretation of Art 6(1)(b) combined with a strict control of General Terms and Conditions (2). The third option relies on an extensive application of Art 6(1)(f) GDPR (3).

1. Personal data as condition

Ever since *Lawrence Lessig* coined the phrase 'Code is Law'[51] it is accepted that software (code) can partially substitute enforceable legal duties. Even without entering into the specifics of current research on so-called smart contracts based on blockchain technologies, it is easy to imagine simple transactions that are performed by software and subject to technical requirements. Access to DCS can depend on the technical requirement that access to personal data is granted also. Leaving aside the actual complexity of modern contracts, it is possible to code a basic exchange of digital objects as technical conditions (if x then y). Such software-based transactions help to avoid some of the risks which were traditionally solved through contract law. Technology can reduce the need for mutual trust and thus substitute expensive precautions that would otherwise be necessary when dealing with strangers over long distances (i.e. insurance coverage, securitization, clearing agencies or a trustee as intermediary). Code is particularly effective in eliminating the risks triggered by duties of pre-performance.

It is convincingly argued that many of the products provided by GAFAM and BAT are based on numerous micro exchanges of bits and bytes. From a legal perspective, such micro transactions can be interpreted as performances based on mutual legal conditions. Technical code and le-

---

51 Lawrence Lessig, *Code and other laws of cyberspace* (Basic Books 1999).

gal conditions correspond.[52] Indeed, usage of search machines or a social networks usually depend on an enabling of tracking tools either by accepting cookies or by logging on to an user account. In brief, code provides access to DCS and access to personal data concurrently.[53]

The main advantage of an interpretation of such technical access to personal data as a legal condition is its conformity with the GDPR and the DCSD.[54] According to a mnemonic that every German undergraduate student is taught: A condition suspends, but is not enforceable (German: '*Die Bedingung suspendiert, zwingt aber nicht*').[55] Therefore, if granting access to personal data is a mere legal condition, such an interpretation is consistent with both the right to withdraw consent at any time according to Art 7(3) and the reluctance to denote personal data as counter-performance or commodity. As remarked by *Michael Grünberger*, the right to withdraw consent at any time and without cause facilitates competition as it provides a strong incentive for providers to offer 'good value for data'.[56]

However, such congruence of technical code and legal condition poses many legal challenges. This article will focus on two aspects, which indicate that the option of perceiving access to personal data as a legal condition is insufficient. *Firstly*, relying on micro transactions based on technical code and legal conditions will benefit a particular business model. If processing of personal data is merely based on a condition and not subject to contractual duties, this incentivizes an immediate and exhaustive exploitation of person-

---

52 Philipp Hacker, 'Daten als Gegenleistung: Rechtsgeschäfte im Spannungsfeld von DS-GVO und allgemeinem Vertragsrecht' [2019] ZfPW 148, 172ff.

53 Art 3(1) of the Commission's proposal required the consumer to 'actively provide' personal data. For criticism of such wording: EU Parliament, 27.11.2017, COM (2015) 634 – C8 – 0394/2015 – 2015/0287 (COD); Axel Metzger, Zohar Efroni, Lena Mischau and Jakob Metzger, 'Data- Related Aspects of the Digital Content Directive' 9 (2018) JIPITEC 90, paras 25–28; Axel Metzger, 'Verträge über digitale Inhalte und digitale Dienstleistungen: Neuer BGB-Vertragstypus oder punktuelle Reform?' [2019] JZ 577, 579.

54 The European Parliament has mentioned such interpretation of access to personal data as condition. However, the concept was not elaborated on: Report of the European Parliament, 27.11.2017, 8 ('The report deletes the term "counter-performance", criticized by the EDPS, and replaces it with the term "condition"'), available at: <http://www.europarl.europa.eu/RegData/etudes/BRIE/2018/614707/EPRS_BRI%282018%29614707_EN.pdf> accessed 5 August 2019); the term is repeated by the EDPB in its Guidelines 2/2019 (n 15), para 27 ('conditional').

55 *Savigny*, System des heutigen Römischen Rechts III, 1840, § 128, p. 231; as cited by: Philipp Hacker, 'Daten als Gegenleistung: Rechtsgeschäfte im Spannungsfeld von DS-GVO und allgemeinem Vertragsrecht' [2019] ZfPW 148, 196.

56 Discussion at a workshop on 'rights in data', 22.2.2019, University of Bayreuth.

al data. The right to withdraw consent is intended to provide data subjects with control and thus protect privacy. In practice, the option of access to personal data as a condition plays into the hands of GAFAM and BAT or more generally, dominant platforms.

The disadvantages of micro transactions based on coded conditions will be borne by those market entrants who cannot afford to treat their customers as 'walled gardens' and who need to plan ahead when establishing their business model. Enterprises who take privacy seriously and seek to build a basis of mutual trust, might require a more reliable foundation for their business model, and therefore depend on a secured stream of personal data. Such stability is typically delivered by contractually binding temporal duties to perform.

While Art 20 GDPR (right to data portability) is supposed to reduce lock-in effects and assist at switching providers, it also reinforces such unpredictability. Art 20 enables data subjects to combine the right to withdraw consent and the right to migrate personal data to a new provider. As the preparation for and the actual performance of data portability causes costs for providers, all data controllers need to earn that money in advance. They are well advised to collect and exploit personal data prior to providing access to digital content or digital services. As withdrawal of consent has only relative effect, it encourages data controllers to obtain a consent that includes processing by third parties and thereafter immediately provide the personal data to such third parties. Once consent is withdrawn, data controllers are merely obliged to inform subsequent data controllers, if such notice does not cause disproportionate efforts. Whenever controller and data subject are of differing opinions on the interpretation of what amounts to 'disproportionate efforts', it will be for the data subject to enforce the right to information – according to Art 15(c) and Art 19 sentence 2 GDPR – against each subsequent controller and thereafter request the data to be erased. Rational apathy will deter data subjects from such a 'scavenger hunt' that follows the chain of data processing initiated by the original consent.

Secondly, in the words of *Martin Schmidt-Kessel*, such conditioned micro exchanges recall 'the stone age of the law on obligations'.[57] Although it is correct that the law on data contracts is still in its infancy, nevertheless, it is crucial to realize that such streams of independent and subsequent micro transactions tend to evade strict legal control. Businesses that rely on continued access to personal data for a certain period and are willing to

57 Discussion at a workshop on 'rights in data', 22.2.2019, University of Bayreuth.

provide a high level of privacy would not even be able to rely on consent for a short period due to the unstable and elusive nature of consent.

2. *Option: extensive application of Art 6(1)(b) GDPR*

According to Art 6(1)(b) processing of personal data shall be lawful only if and to the extent that it is necessary for the performance of a contract to which the data subject is party. Art 6(1)(b) does not provide an implied consent.[58] In contrast, it stipulates a statutory basis for the processing of personal data that is accessory to a contract. Art 6(1)(b) can justify a process that uses a customer's postal address and contact details when delivering parcels ordered by a customer or to issue an invoice.[59] However, it is not for the parties to agree on a 'data license' which defines the processing of personal data or targeted advertising as the main contractual performance. Consequently, Art 6(1)(b) is subject to a strict proportionality test[60] that is, therefore, inflexible and leaves little room for interpretative reasoning.

When comparing the wording of Art 3(1) sentence 2 DCSD and Art 6(1)(b) it becomes obvious that the DCSD is not applicable if personal data provided by the consumer is exclusively processed by the trader for the purpose of supplying DCS.[61] Therefore, it is unlikely that Art 6(1)(b) provides an option to synchronize the DCSD and the GDPR. However, the relationship between Art 3(1) sentence 2 DSCD and Art 6(1)(b) is less clear than the respective wording suggests. The interpretation of the term 'necessary for the performance' is key to its application. As one would expect, data protection authorities suggest the most restrictive interpretation. According to the 'Guidelines 2/2019 on the processing of personal data under Art 6(1)(b) GDPR',[62] published by the EDPB, Art 6(1)(b) is not available for negotiation. Instead, it only allows auxiliary or supportive processing if required for the performance of a different contractual purpose.

58 However, in practice it can be very difficult to distinguish between data processing based on Art 6 (2)(b) and on consent, in particular as Art 6 (2)(a) does – in contrast to Art 9 (2)(a) – not require explicit consent.

59 EDPB, Guidelines 2/2019 (n 15), para 11.

60 EDPB, Guidelines 2/2019 (n 15), para 25.

61 Furthermore, the DCSD is not applicable if the processing can be based on Art 6(1)(c) GDPR (Art 3(1) sentence 2 DCSD: 'for allowing the trader to comply with legal requirements to which the trader is subject'). Presumably the DCSD is not applicable if the processing can be based on Art 6(1)(d) GDPR (necessary to protect the vital interests of a natural person) as it has no link to contract law.

62 EDPB, Guidelines 2/2019 (n 15), para 54.

Of course, it is the core contractual purpose of a social network to allow a customer to connect and communicate with other customers of the network. In other words, there can be no doubt that the processing of huge volumes of personal data is 'necessary for the performance' of a contract aimed at connection based on names, pictures, geographical locations and interests. Nevertheless, the EDPB has made clear – or rather unclear – that Art 6(1)(b) should not be applicable if a business model relies on targeted advertising for funding. It argues that 'personal data cannot be considered as a tradeable commodity. Even if data subjects can agree to processing of their personal data, they cannot trade away their fundamental rights'.[63]

People with a background in law could interpret such language as a proposal to interpret the wording of Art 6(1)(b) in the light of Art 8 ECHR/Art 16 TFEU and thus reduce its scope, specifically to contracts for the use of networks such as *Facebook* or *LinkedIn* which are seemingly 'for free', simply because they are paid for by advertisers on the back end of the platform. However, the EDPB's assessment remains vague, as it also admits 'that personalization of content may (but does not always) constitute an expected element of certain online services, and therefore may be regarded as necessary for the performance of the contract with the service user in some cases'.[64] That reasoning could, of course, also be applied to social networks as average users expect that their messages, 'likes' and timelines on these platforms are to be received by accepted 'friends' and 'connections' rather than a random bunch of strangers.

In summary, while it is very likely and reasonable that the DCSD will not apply in case the processing of personal data is based on Art 6(1)(b) GDPR, it is less clear how the latter will be applied as the number of business models that rely on some form of personalization soar.

3. *Option: Extensive Application of Art 6(1)(f) GDPR*

According to Art 6(1)(f) processing of personal data shall be lawful only if and to the extent that it is necessary for the purposes of the legitimate interests pursued by the controller or by a third party, except where such in-

---

63 EDPB, Guidelines 2/2019 (n 15), para 51 as regards 'Processing for online behavioural advertising'.

64 EDPB, Guidelines 2/2019 (n 15), para 54 as regards 'Processing for personalisation of content'.

terests are overridden by the interests or fundamental rights and freedoms of the data subject which require protection of personal data.

As mentioned above, several institutions have proposed very restrictive interpretations of the legal preconditions required for valid consent or processing based on a contract. If these interpretations of Art 6(1)(a) and (b) were correct and thus upheld by the CJEU, consequently most current business models, which are based on the processing of personal data, would have to rely on Art 6(1)(f). General clauses are well known as flexible tools, not only in administrative law but in private law too. They work as an overpressure relief valve, to be applied when detailed legal rules are overstrained by technical, economic or social development. However, they function only for safety and as a mechanism of last resort. When applied too often, the case law becomes vague and poses a danger to legal certainty. Consequently, while offering a technology neutral and flexible basis for the processing of personal data, Art 6(1)(f) places the burden of striking the right balance on data controllers (*ex ante*). Multiple data protection authorities and hundreds of national administrative and civil courts will decide *ex-post* whether these attempts of synchronization meet their respective interpretation of European and national laws. The person who is least involved in that entire process is the data subject itself.

Art 6(1)(f) does not require the conclusion of a contract and it would suffice to inform data subjects of their right to object to the processing (Art 21 GDPR) in a controller's 'Privacy Policy'. Viewed from the perspective of empowering individual autonomy, the right to object provides a weak tool. Eventually, it will be for data protection authorities and courts to balance all interests involved and thus arrive at a decision whether a business model is legal or illegal. This task requires assertive judges, who presume that they know the preferences of data subjects best. In short, individual autonomy is replaced by balancing of interest performed by businesses and courts, thus facilitating heteronomy.[65]

V. *Proposal for a two-tier interpretation of Art 6 GDPR*

The most promising option is both extremely unpopular and – perhaps surprisingly – very old. It is based on three prerequisites:

65 It is very likely that most decisions on Art 6(1)(f) will be based on complaints logged by not-for-profit bodies, organizations or associations according Art 80(2) GDPR.

First, those working in the legal professions must focus on what they do best: Differentiation. Currently, the GDPR follows the model of 'one size fits all', an approach that has a tendency towards hubris. At least according to data protection authorities and the German Federal Competition Agency, the GDPR compromises notions of anti-trust law below the traditional threshold of anti-trust law[66] and adopts instruments traditionally perceived as consumer protection law, while it also applies to entrepreneurs. Furthermore, the GDPR has been constructed to provide a leverage in international trade conflicts with a clear focus on regulating foreign corporations, in particular the platforms of GAFAM and (in the future) BAT. Ever since its applicability after May 2018, and driven by major 'data scandals', public opinion and some politicians have started to misinterpret data protection law as a tool to avoid so-called 'echo chambers' and the manipulation and radicalization of opinions, especially prior to general elections. In short: Being overambitious itself, the functions assigned to the GDPR are in a danger of overblowing it completely. It is time to re-focus on the objectives stipulated in Art 1 GDPR.

Secondly, personal data – like personality rights – are special in that they contain an unalienable linkage to a human being. Due to that linkage to human dignity, personal data will not develop into a new type of immaterial property right.[67] However, despite that linkage personal data can be commercialized and is thus a *de facto* commodity comparable to the economic parts of traditional personality rights.[68] Consequently, personal data

66 According to such understanding Art 7(4) GDPR lowers the requirements otherwise stipulated by Art. 102 TFEU (abuse of a dominant market position), see Bundeskartellamt (German Federal Competition Agency), Beschl. 6.2.2019 (B6–22/16) paras 621ff and para. 646. Against such interpretation and rejecting the decision of the Bundeskartellamt: OLG Düsseldorf, 1. Kartellsenat, Beschl. 26.8.2019 – VI-Kart 1/19 (V), BeckRS 2019, 18837 para 67 – Facebook I („[…] es handelt sich um eine rein datenschutzrechtliche, nicht um eine kartellrechtliche Bestimmung" [engl.: Art. 7(4) concerns data protection law, not competiton law].

67 On such discussion: Herbert Zech, 'A legal framework for a data economy in the European Digital Single Market: Rights to use data' (2016) 11(6) Journal of Intellectual Property Law & Practice 460, 463; for the US: Shyamkrishna Balganesh, 'Quasi-Property: Like, But Not Quite Property' (2012) 160 University of Pennsylvania Law Review 1889; Pamela Samuelson, 'Privacy as Intellectual Property' (1999) 52 Stan. L. Rev. 1125.

68 Huw Beverley-Smith, Ansgar Ohly and Agnes Lucas-Schloetter, *Privacy, Property and Personality* (Cambridge University Press 2005) 94ff; Franz Hofmann, 'The Economic Part of the Right to Personality as an Intellectual Property Law? – A Comparison between English and German Law' (2010) 2 Zeitschrift für Geistiges Eigentum/Intellectual Property Journal 1ff.

can be traded, but not transferred.[69] Rather than denying it altogether, legislators should start to manage such commercialization actively.

Thirdly, any interpretation of the GDPR should focus on strengthening autonomy rather than heteronomy. Despite the difficulties of tagging sets or even streams of personal data with a price, it is nevertheless fundamental to allow data subjects the ability to choose. Although consent is imperfect and compromised due to information asymmetries, biases, negative externalities and other market failures, it remains the best option to account for individual preferences, and thus incentivize data-based innovations valued by data subjects. Of course, there is a crucial need for icons according to Art 12(7), (8). If these are not delivered soon, the European Parliament or Council needs to take back control according to Art 92(3). As regards enforcement these icons – if developed rigorously – can complement the potentially high financial penalties.

As has been illustrated above, data as a condition and an extensive application of Art 6(1)(b) and (f) would be detrimental to the target of strengthening autonomy. Therefore, the following figure classifies the available options according to the opposite tendency to support autonomy or heteronomy:

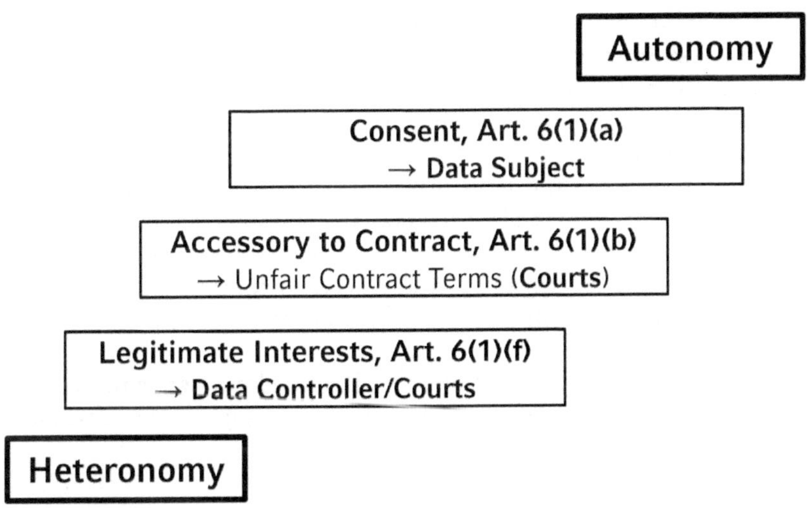

69 Andreas Sattler, 'Personality to Property? – Revisiting the Fundamentals of the Protection of Personal Data' in Mor Bakhoum et al (eds), *Personal Data in Competition, Consumer Protection and Intellectual Property Law – Towards a Holistic Approach?* (Springer 2018) 27, 39ff.

The case of celebrity merchandising illustrates the need to strengthen autonomy. It is obvious that such merchandising should be based on a celebrity's consent according to Art 6(1)(a). However, as the GDPR applies irrespective of whether a data subject is a consumer or an entrepreneur, such celebrity merchandising would be subject to Art 7(3), too. However, if Art 7(3) is mandatory law irrespective of the status of the data subject, the fate of these contacts would be subject to the right to withdraw consent at any time, and without cause as well. In short, if Art 7(3) is interpreted as strictly as most legal scholars and data protection authorities propose, this would jeopardize the long-established contractual basis of celebrity merchandising. Thus, it is suggested that the legal requirement for valid consent is interpreted in a more flexible manner. The fundamental right to protection of personal data could be guaranteed while striking a proportionate balance with other fundamental freedoms granted to individuals and businesses.

Such an interpretation can be based on an assessment that the definition of consent in Art 4 no. 11 only provides the minimum standard under European law. This interpretation has a crucial impact: Art 4 no.11 would continue to exclude silence of a data subject or a pre-ticked box as a declaration of will and consent.[70] If Art 4 no.11 provides only the minimum standard required according to Art 8 ECHR, it does not preclude national contract laws from accepting forms of consent that reach beyond such a minimum standard. As a consequence of such interpretation, Art 7(3) should be construed as to refer only to such a minimum standard of consent. In applying legal doctrine, the (too) far reaching wording of Art 7(3) should be reduced to situations in which consent reaches only the minimum threshold as required by Art 4 no. 11. Above this minimum standard and following such a teleological reduction of its wording, Art 7(3) would have dispositive character and is thus subject to agreement.[71] Such interpretation would generally extend the options of consent, allowing for a tiered approach.

Consequently, the term 'consent' could be developed into a much more sophisticated European concept than currently envisioned. The subsequent

70 Recital 32 sentence 3 GDPR.

71 For details on the doctrinal methodology and its consistency with EU-Law: Andreas Sattler, 'Personenbezogene Daten als Leistungsgegenstand' [2017] JZ 1036, 1041ff.

figure – which is based on German law[72] – resembles the emancipatory route that the term 'consent' might travel as societies progress:

Potential Interpretations of Consent
(Germany)

Strict right to withdraw consent
Any contractual limitation (due cause / time) to withdraw is void.

Limited right to withdraw consent
Withdrawal prior to start of performance / if hereafter → right to damages.

Enhanced consent (temporally binding, but including sunset clause)
Withdrawal of consent is dispositive → (extra-)ordinary rights to termination.

Assignability of right in personal data (copyright as a model?)
- **Dualism**
  Right to privacy and right to publicity / personality rights and economic rights.
- **Monism**
  One single right without an option to differ between personality right / privacy and economic rights / right to publicity.

While the wording of Art 7(3) seems to support only the first level of a strict right to withdraw consent, some authors have suggested that in cases that amount to an abuse of such right, data subjects might be obliged to compensate data controllers.[73]

Bearing in mind that contract law and consumer law provide many instruments to protect data subjects who are consumers, a third level of consent should be considered. As has been shown, it is likely that the wording of Art 7(3) reaches too far and should not apply in cases of celebrity merchandising. While celebrities tend to have legal advisors and might there-

72 On the German concept of consent: Ansgar Ohly, *Volenti non fit iniuria – die Einwilligung im Privatrecht* (Mohr Siebeck 2002).

73 Wolfgang Kilian, 'Strukturwanddel der Privatheit' in Hansjürgen Garstka and Wolfgang Coy (eds), *Wovon – für wen – wozu? Systemdenken wider die Diktatur der Daten – Wilhelm Steinmüller zum Gedächtnis* (Helmholtz-Zentrum für Kulturtechnik, Humboldt-Universität zu Berlin 2014) 195, 212; Wolfgang Kilian, 'Personal Data: The impact of Emerging Trends in the Information Society. How the marketability of personal data should affect the concept of data protection law' (2002) 28 Computer und Recht International 169ff; Jan Henrik Klement, in Spiros Simitis, Gerrit Hornung and Indra Spiecker (eds), *Datenschutzrecht* (Nomos 2019) Art 7 para 92; Carmen Langhanke and Martin Schmidt-Kessel, 'Consumer Data as Consideration' (2015) EuCML 218 (221: 'justified breach').

fore be entrepreneurial data subjects, the same reasoning applies if ordinary data subjects provide personal data for commercial advertising and become 'the face to a product'. Although all these cases are within the scope of the GDPR, it is very unlikely that Art 7(3) will be applicable, if celebrities, models and freelancers provide personal data for money.

There might be reasons why the deliberate commercialization of personal data for money is not comparable to data subjects providing personal data for access to DCS.[74] However, it is worthwhile considering whether the right to withdraw consent could be suspended for a short and pre-fixed period of time (for example as sunset clause of two months[75]), thus allowing more stable relationships between data subjects and data controllers. Of course, there should be no automatic extension of consent,[76] such General Terms and Conditions would be subject to transparency and fairness control and would not preclude any cause for an (extra)ordinary termination right of both contract and consent. Despite the proposed option to suspend the right to withdraw consent according to Art 7(3) for a certain period, the link between a human being and personal data remains unassailable and can itself provide a cause for extraordinary termination. Merged into a two-tiered model this leads to the following options of processing personal data under private law.

Obviously, such an interpretation of the GDPR requires further research and a more synchronized approach towards contract law, consumer protection law and data protection law.[77] If this article can stimulate such research on a European concept of 'consent', it has achieved all the author could hope.

---

74 When exchanging data for data it is particularly difficult to determine a value and fairness of a transaction.

75 In contrast to the original consent that is – in general – not limited in time (German Federal Court of Justice (BGH), 1.2.2018, ZR III 196/17 para 31), such deviation from the right to withdraw consent should be for a limited period, thus, requiring active renewal.

76 Thus, it would require a stricter rule than provided by no.1(h) of the Annex ('Terms referred to in Article 3(3)') to Council Directive 93/13/EEC of 5 April 1993 on unfair terms in consumer contracts, OJ L95, 21.4.1993, 29–34.

77 For an overview see the conference volume: Mor Bakhoum, Beatriz Conde Gallego, Mark-Oliver Mackenrodt and Gintare Surblyte-Namaviciene (eds), *Personal Data in Competition, Consumer Protection and Intellectual Property Law – Towards a Holistic Approach?* (Springer 2018).

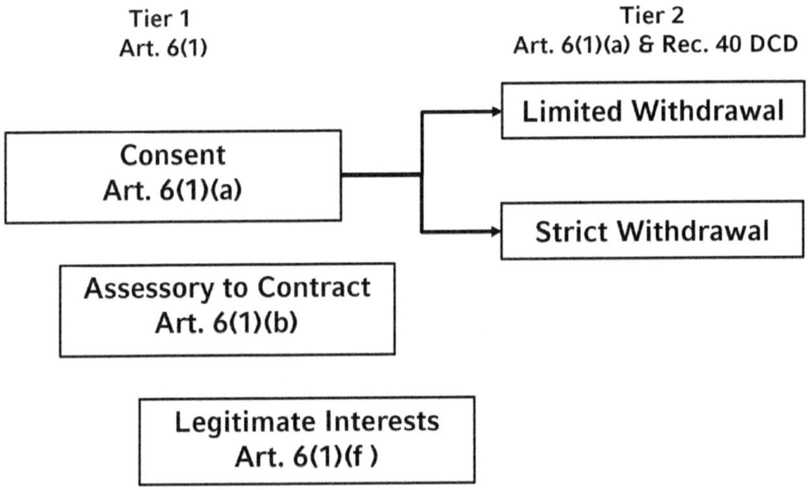

VI. *Conclusions*

Instead of a summary, this article will conclude with ten theses. As it is the ultimate expectation that all theses will eventually be falsified, it is hoped that each thesis will give cause for criticism.

1. Personal data is a commodity: Famous actors and athletes have been exploiting the economic parts of their personality rights for many decades. Ordinary data subjects provide access to personal data and receive access to DCS in reverse. Thus, personal data has been and will be commercialized despite the utopian proclamation in recital 24 DCSD ('no-commodity').
2. Personal data is tradeable, but not transferable: In contrast to many other commodities, personal data cannot be transferred. Personal data is defined by an unassailable link to a data subject. This link is guaranteed by Art 8 ECHR and it justifies (extra)ordinary rights to terminate a contract. However, it does not preclude data subjects and controllers from concluding contracts to process and thus economically exploit personal data.
3. The processing of personal data is an ideological battlefield: The European legislator was unable to provide legal solutions to a fundamental conflict. While the Commission's proposal accepted personal data as counter-performance and corresponded with economic reality, Parliament and the European Data Protection Supervisor rejected such con-

cept. The legislator was unable to reconcile the fundamental right to the protection of personal data with other fundamental rights such as freedom to choose an occupation (Art 15 ECHR), freedom to conduct business (Art 16 ECHR) and the general principle to conclude contracts (Art 6(3) TEU).

4. The EU legislator opted for evasion through delegation: In order to reach political compromise, the DCSD is based on the lowest common denominator. The national laws that implement the DCSD will be applicable if a consumer provides access to personal data in order to obtain access to DCS. However, as regards the conflicts that follow from Art 3(1) sentence 2 DCSD, the legislator points towards the GDPR (Art 3(8) and Art 16(2) DCSD) and national contract law (Recital 40 DCSD). Legal conflicts that are both essential and obvious are thus delegated to the courts of Member States and the CJEU.
5. Synchronization of the DCSD and the GDPR based on the interpretation that access to personal data is a mere condition corresponds with the right to withdraw consent according to Art 7(3) GDPR. However, such understanding leads to streams of micro transactions that benefit the current business models of already dominant platforms. If binding contractual relationships are precluded, many innovative business models will not occur.
6. Synchronization based on an extensive interpretation of Art 6(1)(b) GDPR (accessory to a contract) seems to be excluded by the wording of Art 3(1) sentence 2 and recitals 24 and 25 DCSD. However, when considering the drafted guidelines of the EDPB on the interpretation of Art 6(1)(b) GDPR – and recital 26 DCSD – this is less clear.
7. Synchronization based on an extensive interpretation of Art 6(1)(f) GDPR (balancing of interests) is an option. As such, balancing of interests will be performed by the data controller (*ex ante*) and national data protection authorities and courts (*ex post*). Such a general clause is a flexible tool and works as a safety net. Despite the right to object contained in Art 21 GDPR, Art 6(1)(f), nevertheless, facilitates heteronomy. It will be judges who decide what is best for controllers, data subjects and other natural persons involved.
8. When arranged on a staircase that starts at heteronomy and ascends to autonomy, Art 6(1)(f) is at the lowest level. Further up and at the second level follows Art 6(1)(b). Consent is placed on the top level. Art 6(1)(a) can be interpreted to contain different levels of consent. As no European concept of 'consent' exists, it is worthwhile considering the different levels of consent accepted according to national laws of the Member States.

9. Viewed from a German perspective, Art 4 no. 11 can be interpreted to contain the minimum standard of consent as required according to Art 8 ECHR. However, the definition does not preclude agreement on a type of 'consent' that reaches beyond this European minimum standard.
10. Art 7(3) can be interpreted to be only applicable to such minimum standard of consent as defined by Art 4 no. 11 GDPR. Such a teleological reduction of the (too) extensive wording of Art 7(3) is supported by the fact that personal data has been the object of contractual performance for decades. A right to withdraw consent at any time and without cause would jeopardize the long-established licensing practice in the area of celebrity merchandising. Consequently, Art 7(3) is dispositive. Data subjects and data controllers can generally contract out. However, European law will have to provide a strict framework – including a sunset clause – for such deviation from Art 7(3) if data subjects are consumers.

Data as Counter-Performance in B2B Contracts

Martin Fries[*]

I. Introduction

It is one of the foundation stones of the leading social media business models in the 21st century to realize that goods and services might be paid not only with money but also by making data available to the other party. In spite of that, paying with data has only recently come to the attention of lawmakers. And so far, the regulatory debate on this topic has been conducted from a special angle: Even though it is not necessarily consumers who pay goods or services by providing data, most contributions in this field mainly focus on the special needs of consumers dealing with businesses.[1]

Against this background, the present contribution examines the phenomenon of data as counter-performance with a specific focus on B2B contracts. After describing the prevailing regulatory approach towards allowing data as a payment method (II.), it examines three examples for such phenomena in the B2B world (III.). From there, the contribution derives demands for the future design of contract law, platform law, and data protection law (IV). The final section concludes (V.).

II. Data as counter-performance as a regulatory topic

Where data is provided as contractual counter-performance, the crucial questions are about payment awareness and decision-making power. In other words: As long as contracts are perceived to be the result of au-

* Private Lecturer at the Ludwig-Maximilians-University, Munich (LMU).

1 See, eg, Carmen Langhanke & Martin Schmidt-Kessel, 'Consumer Data as Consideration' (2015) 1 EuCML 218; Axel Metzger, 'Data as Counter-Performance: What Rights and Duties Do Parties Have' (2017) 8 J. Intell. Prop. Info. Tech. & Elec. Com. L. 2; Natali Helberger, Frederik Zuiderveen Borgesius & Agustin Reyna, 'The perfect match? A closer look at the relationship between EU consumer law and data protection law' (2017) 54 Comm. Mkt. L. Rev. 1427.

tonomous decisions by both parties,[2] the party paying with data should know that, by allowing usage of her data, she is indeed providing a good of substantial economic value, and she should find herself in a position where she does not depend on the good or service she is paying for but agrees to an entirely voluntary deal.

This is a demand that can be supported not only by principles of contract law but also from the perspective of data protection law. Namely the European General Data Protection Regulation 2016/679 (GDPR)[3] ties the usage of personal data beyond the direct fulfilment of the contract to the consent of the data subject.[4] In cases in which the data is not necessary for the execution of the contract, Art 7(4) GDPR rarely provides for the voluntary consent of the data subject to any data usage. This regulatory approach was recently confirmed by the European Directive 2019/770 on certain aspects concerning contracts for the supply of digital content and digital services[5] which, in the event of contract termination by a consumer, does not prohibit the trader to spontaneously refrain from the use of personal data provided as counter-performance,[6] but at least maintains the rights of the data subject set out by the GDPR.[7]

As the GDPR confines itself to the provision of personal data, it is important to note that there is no regulatory means to prevent people from providing *non-personal* data even where they – along the key needs for provisions of contract law – are not aware of providing an asset of value or do not feel able to negotiate the requirement to provide data away from the incipient contract. Quite the opposite: Outside the realm of personal data, the regulatory credo is the free flow of data. Non-personal data is perceived to usually be a non-rivalrous and non-exclusive, ie to a large extent a *public* good that adds to societal welfare where as many market participants as

---

2 This is the predominant approach in European contract law, see Stefan Grundmann, 'Information, Party Autonomy and Economic Agents in European Contract Law' (2002) 39 Comm. Mkt. L. Rev. 269.

3 OJ L119/16.

4 See Art 6(1)(a), 7 GDPR. The exceptions set out in Art 6(1)(b)f do not play an equal role here. Against this background, Beata A Safari, 'Intangible Privacy Rights: How Europe's GDPR Will Set a New Global Standard for Personal Data Protection' (2016/17) 47 Seton Hall L. Rev. 809, speaks of 'intangible privacy rights' – a perspective that is everything but uncontroversial, see below (n 27).

5 OJ L136/19.

6 Art 16(4)(a) of the preceding Directive Proposal, COM (2016) 634 final, was more consumer-friendly, in this regard.

7 Art 16(2) of the Directive 2019/770, referring to Art 12f GDPR.

possible are granted access.[8] The new Regulation (EU) 2018/1807[9] on a framework for the free flow of non-personal data in the EU points in that direction.

Thus, where market participants unreflectedly pay with non-personal data, there is no legal safety net that allows them to claim their data back. Obviously, the EU assumes that such incidents will rarely occur as players who provide non-personal data and are thus not covered by the GDPR are usually businesses who know what they do and do not need special regulatory protection. However, this perspective is questionable as even in the B2B market, there are considerable power imbalances that may lead less mighty market participants to provide data as counter-performance without a proper legal basis and without a legal option to reverse this transaction. Does this observation call for a special legal regime on businesses providing non-personal data as counter-performance?

III. Three examples on data as counter-performance in B2B contracts

A view on three subsets of cases where businesses provide data as contractual counter-performance accounts for a better assessment of the need for regulatory action.

1. Data trading platforms

The growing Internet of Things has brought to light a vast array of digital items and machines which collect data and exchange data between contractual partners in the regular course of business. In most cases, that kind of data exchange does not constitute the core performance and counter-performance of the executed contract, however, it is performed as a give and take, and if the data flow stopped in one direction the reverse flow would most likely be stopped as well.

Whereas the legal problems associated with this type of data exchange are usually limited to questions of data security, things get more complicated as soon as the data exchange is managed and supervised by some third party, such as data trading platforms. Such platforms have recently

8 Martin Fries & Marc Scheufen, 'Märkte für Maschinendaten: Eine rechtliche und rechtsökonomische Standortbestimmung' (2019) MMR 721, 725.

9 OJ L303/18.

emerged in Europe, America, and Asia. They aim at facilitating data exchange by providing a framework for the conclusion of data purchasing agreements, the subsequent data transfer, and the resolution of conflicts that arise from these business relationships.

The difficulties which data traders face when trading over such a platform are quite similar to those well-known from other trading platforms: The platform operators often set contractual rules which not only maximize platform sales, but also give the platform exceptional discretion in the event of a conflict, up to an exclusion of unpleasant dealers from the platform. They might as well use a trader rating system giving ranking preference to those market participants who are willing to pay the largest brokerage fee. The fact that these phenomena occur in *data* trading platforms in the same way as in the established online marketplaces has not yet been empirically proven; however, experience with other platform types points in this direction.

2. *Social networking services*

The second example of data as counter-performance comes from an unexpected direction: At first sight, social networking service providers like *Facebook* or *Instagram* target only private individuals who upload their personal data – like text messages, photos, or videos – to interact with their friends and simultaneously pay the service provider for their networking services by providing analyzable and thus valuable insights into their thoughts, feelings, and preferences.

However, modern social networks have always also worked as a platform for self-marketing by business people and companies: So-called *influencers* make a living from their social network accounts by promoting themselves or advertising products through professional photographs, video clips, and related texts. Little surprising in such a people business, influencers upload massive amounts of personal data to their social network account. And even if they do it for business reasons, they are, in this respect, protected by the GDPR because the law does not tie up with a consumer status here.

Nevertheless, providing personal data is not the only issue for influencers as they are mostly regarded as persons of public life anyway. They also have reason to worry about their business strategy which is visible for the social network provider like an open book. Their whole business depends on the network, which makes them extremely vulnerable for an increase in prices and leaves them no bargaining power as to scheduled modifications of the network appearance.[10]

3. *Free online services*

A third example for data as counter-performance in the B2B market concerns free services that are primarily aimed at consumers, but on a regular basis also used by small and medium enterprises with limited needs for data processing capacities. For instance, the cloud service provider *Dropbox* offers a Basic Version with a storage volume of 2 GB, and the translation service *DeepL* provides a free online translator with the caveat that all entries are stored and used for business purposes.[11]

Above all, these business models lead to problems in the field of data protection and data security. For example, *DeepL* requires its users not to upload personal data so that the extensive data processing be not dependent on their consent.[12] It is, however, questionable whether using the service without a proper assessment of its privacy statement already constitutes consent in unlimited data processing according to Art 6(1)(a), 7 GDPR. Meanwhile, the cloud service provider *Dropbox* allows users to upload personal data and sets on the fact that the consent pre-formulated in its privacy statement satisfies the requirements of the GDPR.[13] Especially in the B2B sector, services of both types regularly store information concerning the clients of their users which might be subject to special laws on the handling of trade secrets.[14] It is doubtful whether the security measures

---

10 See, eg, the policy change by *Instagram* in mid-2019 to start hiding likes from other users; <https://www.nytimes.com/2019/07/18/world/instagram-hidden-likes.html> accessed 22 April 2020.

11 It is questionable whether the provider of such an online service and its users are already concluding a contract; otherwise, there is a similar problem with regard to pre-contractual obligations.

12 *DeepL* Privacy Statement <https://www.deepl.com/privacy.html> accessed 22 April 2020, sub No. 4.

13 *Dropbox* Privacy Statement <https://www.dropbox.com/privacy> accessed 22 April 2020.

14 For Germany, this would be § 4 of the Trade Secrets Protection Act (*Gesetz zum Schutz von Geschäftsgeheimnissen*, GeschGehG) and § 202a of the Criminal Code (*Strafgesetzbuch*, StGB).

taken by free online services providers sufficiently account for these legal requirements.[15]

IV. Substantial challenges for legal policy

What are the consequences of these actual findings for the proper design of contract law, platform regulation, and data protection law?

1. Contract law: wait and see

One of the main regulatory objectives of contract law is an informed decision by all persons involved.[16] Where the legal capacity of the parties is not at stake, the main issue is transparency on the content and the consequences of an incipient contract. In this respect, the core objective of all regulatory efforts has been to make people paying with data aware of the fact that this data bears a value they lose to the other party.[17]

In its attempts to capture the phenomenon of data being provided as contractual counter-performance, the European Union has so far focused on consumers. The hidden rationale behind this regulatory approach is the assumption that businesses know what they are doing when providing data to their counterpart, especially if they do so in return for an otherwise free good or service. It is questionable whether this holds true for founders of new businesses or small enterprises.[18] Nevertheless, it is conclusive that the main focus is on B2C constellations here, as the law can still be amended if empirical findings show that the legal measures should rather be extended beyond the B2C range.

---

15 In early 2017, *Dropbox* had to admit that they had stored data up many years after their apparent deletion; see <https://www.bleepingcomputer.com/news/software/dropbox-kept-files-around-for-years-due-to-delete-bug/> accessed 22 April 2020.

16 See above (n 2).

17 In this regard, the legal means enacted in Art 16 of the Directive 2019/770 on certain aspects concerning contracts for the supply of digital content and digital services seem, however, quite faint; see above sub II.

18 Whereas European private law does not contain special rules for founders of new businesses, the German Civil Code (*Bürgerliches Gesetzbuch*; BGB) treats start-ups in certain situations like consumers because of their lack of business experience; see §§ 513, 655e (2) BGB.

2. *Platform law: observe the effects of new regulation*

In a B2B relationship, many businesses will agree to a contract being fully aware that the obligation to pay with data resulting from this contract is the consequence of the sheer bargaining power of a platform monopolist. This calls for legal solutions in the field of antitrust law as soon as empirical findings show that a monopolist has used her market power to push unfair conditions into contracts. Right now, this is first and foremost a question of the individual case which is handled by Art 101 and 102 TFEU.

The European Union has recently added the Regulation 2019/1150 on promoting fairness and transparency for business users of online intermediation services (P2B Regulation)[19] to this framework. Its Art 9 requires platforms not to shield the personal or non-personal data of customers or merchants, but to grant free data access to any merchants operating on the platform.[20] Aside from that, platforms also have to give reasons where they restrict, suspend, or terminate the contract with a trader (Art 4)[21], they have to disclose the main parameters of their ranking mechanism (Art 5), and they have to create transparency as to any differentiated treatment of their business users including price discrimination (Art 7).[22]

These rules do not solve the question of how a sound data pricing mechanism for B2B contracts might look like. None of them actually aims at data being provided as counter-performance, and most of them are not even data-specific. However, the implementation of the P2B Regulation will allow an insight into some crucial parts of the predominant platform business models, open up a more intense discussion on data handling, and in general leave less space for unfair commercial practices. This might also alleviate problems arising from data cluelessly provided as contractual counter-performance.

---

19 OJ L186/19.

20 In the event of a collision with GDPR rules, Art 1(5) of the P2B Regulation gives priority to the GDPR. See also Heike Schweitzer & Martin Peitz, 'Ein neuer europäischer Ordnungsrahmen für Datenmärkte?' (2017) NJW 275, 279–280; Heike Schweitzer, 'Datenzugang in der Datenökonomie: Eckpfeiler einer neuen Informationsordnung' (2019) GRUR 569.

21 However, the law does not set rules for admissible or inadmissible reasons für restriction, suspension, or termination of the contract.

22 The regulation approach that the EU followed with the P2B Regulation could be further developed in a so-called Digital Services Act, which might in a couple of years replace the E-Commerce Directive 2000/31/EC.

3. Data protection law: the enforcement challenge

The third considerable challenge for legal policy relates to data protection. Here, new regulation is already in place. Applicable since May 2018, the GDPR was indeed a wake-up call for many players to reconsider their data handling policies and to create transparency as to where personal data is stored and processed.[23] At the same time, mistrust has remained regarding the question to what extent data protection is now only a public confession of data-processing companies that is hardly matched by their actual behavior.

With special regard to data being provided as contractual counter-performance: Given the anecdotal insights mentioned above[24] it seems quite likely that social media platforms store and process influencer data far more than permitted by voluntary consent. And there is much to suggest that free online services use the data entered into their online tools for purposes of machine learning regardless of whether it is about personal data triggering the compulsory application of the GDPR and whether they got the respective consent of the concerned person.

The crucial problem here is, however, the mere knowledge about violations of data protection rules. The fact that a company stores or uses personal data without legal authorization may be discovered accidentally in individual cases in the course of a search triggered elsewhere. At the same time, the vast majority of cases remains unreported. Sometimes, a business might have reason to doubt the proper handling of their personal data. But the possibilities for competitors to defend themselves against breaches of data protection with means of competition law are quite limited.[25] Thus, most people expect the public authorities to enforce the GDPR,[26] which makes it unlikely for violations of data protection law to be discovered and

23 There is empirical evidence that online communication and e-commerce have slowed down since the GDPR is applied in May 2018; Samuel Goldberg, Garrett Johnson & Scott Shriver 'Regulating Privacy Online: The Early Impact of the GDPR on European Web Traffic & E-Commerce Outcomes' (2019) <https://ssrn.com/abstract=3421731> accessed 22 April 2020.

24 See above sub III.

25 Fabian Uebele, 'Die Durchsetzung des Datenschutzrechts über UWG und UKlaG auf dem Prüfstand von Rechtsprechung und Gesetzgeber' (2019) GRUR 694, 695–699.

26 This was highlighted by *Benjamin Görs* at the Colloquium on EU Law and the Digital Economy on 17 May 2019, in Münster.

sanctioned.[27] Exceptions confirm the rule.[28] A more effective approach would include more room for maneuver including the possibility to impose higher fines as well as more staff for data protection authorities.

V. Conclusion

There are two considerable challenges regarding contracts obliging one party to provide data as counter-performance: The first one is to make this party understand that her lunch is not free but paid with her data. The second one is to make her contractual partner handle the data confidentially and in accordance with the statutory data protection provisions. Both questions emerge not only in consumer contracts but also on the B2B level; however, the comprehension question seems less urgent here, so it was with good reason that the EU has limited the Directive on the supply of digital content and digital services to B2C transactions. To the benefit of both consumers and businesses, the new P2B Regulation accounts for more transparency in data handling and data processing. However, the last step – the enforcement of existing data protection rules – remains difficult for the time being. Especially with respect to large trading platforms, the EU would have to tighten the sanctions for data protection violations in Art 83 GDPR if the careful handling of other people's data is not to remain just a lip service.

---

27 Thus, Peter Gola & Christoph Klug, 'Die Entwicklung des Datenschutzrechts im zweiten Halbjahr 2018' (2019) NJW 639, 642, recommend to take data protection in one's own hands ('Selbstdatenschutz'). For a much more fundamental critique on the GDPR which comes to a similar conclusion ('the emperor is naked') see Winfried Veil 'The GDPR: The Emperor's New Clothes – On the Structural Shortcomings of Both the Old and the New Data Protection Law' (2019) <https://ssrn.com/abstract=3305056> accessed 22 April 2020.

28 See the list of GDPR fines and penalties imposed by data protection authorities of EU Member States at <http://www.enforcementtracker.com> accessed 22 April 2020.

Discussion Panel

Statement

Benjamin Görs[*]

By the adoption of the so-called 'digital package', consisting of the Digital Content Directive 2019/770 and the new Sale of Goods Directive 2019/771, the EU legislature is breaking new ground in several respects. Both from a contract law and a consumer protection point of view three aspects have to be highlighted:

I. Rules for goods with digital elements

The market for connected goods, which encompasses a broad spectrum ranging from smartphones to smart homes to smart cars, is growing rapidly. The two new directives provide for a far-reaching EU-wide set of contract law rules for this market and establish new consumer rights. These new rules for goods with embedded digital content were a crucial point for the success of the trilogue negotiations of both directives. Without these rules, the package would have remained incomplete.

II. Update obligations

According to both directives the trader or seller is obliged to provide security updates and updates keeping the digital content or the good in conformity with the contract. This even applies to one-off supply situations such as sales contracts where – according to current German law – the seller's primary contractual obligations generally end after the delivery of the good. So the two new directives have created sales contracts with a continuous supply element. From a dogmatic point of view this is a really significant innovation. The new right to demand updates from the trader or seller is likely to become the pivotal remedy for the consumer and will also contribute to an enhancement of IT security in general.

---

* German Federal Ministry of Justice and Consumer Protection.

III. Economic value of data

The Digital Content Directive is recognizing the economic value of personal data by expanding contractual rights and remedies also to contracts where the consumer – instead of or together with paying a price – 'provides or undertakes to provide' personal data. In view of the conceivably narrow scope for action which data protection law leaves to contract law here (as spelled out in the Legal Opinion 4/2017 of the European Data Protection Supervisor[1]), the EU lawmakers seem to have found a reasonable and practicable solution: the Digital Content Directive will be applicable where the trader processes personal data provided by the consumer, except in cases where the processing is based on article 6(1)(b), (c) or (e) of the General Data Protection Regulation.

The two directives have to be transposed into national law by 1 July 2021. In view of the next election to the Bundestag in autumn 2021, the German legislative procedure must therefore probably be completed by the beginning of 2021.

1 The Opinion can be found here: <https://edps.europa.eu/data-protection/our-work/publications/opinions/contracts-supply-digital-content_en> accessed 5 July 2019.

Data as a Counter-Performance

Anne Riechert[*]

I. What are the challenges in the context of 'Data as a Counter-Performance'?

Value of Data

There are many difficulties to determine the value of data despite the – in the meanwhile – corny phrase that data is the new oil. In this context it should also be mentioned that according to *v. Lewinskis*' studies the value of one person could be less than 1 cent or up to a sum which is equivalent to the price of a used car (he himself points out, however, that this range is based on information that is not methodologically reliable).[1] Furthermore – as *Bokor* points out – the economic exploitation of the right of personality has so far been a privilege of a small number of people who has gained sufficient recognition.[2] Even the literature on the subject of customer loyalty systems primarily highlights the tax treatment of these programs and not the use of data or their economic compensation vis-à-vis the people concerned.[3] Nevertheless, consumers have more than an interest in data protection: they also have an interest in being involved in the value creation process of data.[4] For that reason, *Specht* suggests allowing the consent

* Professor of Data Protection Law and Law of Information Processing, Frankfurt University of Applied Sciences; scientific director of the Stiftung Datenschutz (Foundation for Data Protection).

1 K v. Lewinski, 'Wert von personenbezogenen Daten' in Stiftung Datenschutz (ed), *Dateneigentum und Datenhandel* (Erich Schmidt 2018) 211.

2 J Bokor, 'Die Richtlinienvorschläge der Kommission zu Verträgen über digitalen Inhalt und Online-Warenhandel' 2, available at <https://www.bundestag.de/resource/blob/422554/6f0bd347b413226ad2ffe992dc5cfa9f/bokor-data.pdf> accessed 13 November 2019.

3 Bokor (n 2).

4 L Specht, 'Rechte an Daten – Regulierungsbedarf aus Sicht des Verbraucherschutzes' in Stiftung Datenschutz (ed), *Dateneigentum und Datenhandel* (Erich Schmidt 2018) 315.

as a contractual counter-performance.[5] This proposal is now covered by the Digital Content Directive.[6] But this directive does not set a value for data either.

In summary, it can be said that we have an unclear legal situation concerning the exploitation of data. The European Data Protection Law does not solve the problem either because it has a dignity-based approach and no price tags for data and in this context *v. Lewinski* also explains that market privacy is the deliberate blind spot of the European Data Protection Law.[7] Therefore, the deliberate commercialization of certain aspects of the right of personality through binding rules for everyone would be something new.[8]

New legal framework?

Is a new legal framework really necessary? The market is fully functional and we do not have a market failure. But apart from this economic point of view a further question that is also being discussed is whether it could be advantageous to the data object and if it includes a simplification for the trading of data if the data subject has an exclusive right which ensures him or her a power of disposition. This seems promising at first sight – despite the fact that a contractual disposition does not necessarily need exclusive rights.[9]

The right of informational self-determination (Article 1(1), Article 2(1) GG) – in a German context – is a defensive right and does not standardize an absolute right of control over data: Since the census judgement of the German Federal Constitutional Court (*Bundesverfassungsgericht*),[10] it has been acknowledged in jurisprudence and literature that the 'data subject

5 L Specht, 'Datenverwertungsverträge zwischen Datenschutz und Vertragsfreiheit – Eckpfeiler eines neuen Datenschuldrechts' in RG Briner and A Funk (eds), *DGRI Jahrbuch 2017* (Otto Schmidt 2018), 35ff.

6 Directive (EU) 2019/770 of the European Parliament and of the Council of 20 May 2019 on certain aspects concerning contracts for the supply of digital content and digital services [2019] OJ L136/1.

7 v. Lewinski (n 1) 215.

8 Bokor (n 2).

9 Specht (n 5) 37. With regard to exclusive rights -with further references- see also A Riechert, 'Dateneigentum – ein unauflösbarer Interessenkonflikt?' [2019] DuD 353ff.

10 BVerfGE 65, 1, 43ff – *Volkszählung*; from the jurisprudence of civil courts see for example BGH, DuD 2009, 565ff – *spickmich.de*.

has no absolute, unrestricted control over his or her' data, since he or she develops his or her personality within the social community. In this social community the information, even to the extent that it is personal data, represents a part of social reality that could not be attributed exclusively to the data subject alone.

Beyond that, it is argued that data has no capacity for property and that the rules of intellectual property rights shall not apply accordingly.[11] Data is seen as a new commodity that is close to the property and close to intellectual property. However, data ownership is not regulated by law: Data is not classified as an object and the classification of data as intangible property is also not possible according to the prevailing legal view, since a numerus clausus is assumed in intellectual property law and for this reason only cases already regulated by law are recognized.[12] Consequently, if there is a need for a data ownership or for exclusive rights for the data subject it is necessary to pass a law or to develop the law by court. The legal situation in other European Member States is similar: *Schefzig* points out, for example, that the French Civil Code provides for civil and criminal mechanisms on the part of the data holder to prevent or eliminate the misuse of data and French criminal courts have confirmed that downloading data without theft of the medium can nevertheless mean theft, but that in Spain there are neither judgments nor laws concerning the ownership of data.[13]

However, there are many concerns regarding an exclusive right, like for instance the monopolization and the selling off fundamental rights.[14] Moreover, a data ownership would not be enough and a parallel legislative action would be necessary in order to protect consumers – which are two

---

11 cf W Kilian, 'Personenbezogene Daten als schuldrechtliche Gegenleistung' in Stiftung Datenschutz (ed), *Dateneigentum und Datenhandel* (Erich Schmidt 2018) 199–200; K-H Fezer, 'Digitales Dateneigentum – ein grundrechtsdemokratisches Bürgerrecht in der Zivilgesellschaft' in Stiftung Datenschutz (ed), *Dateneigentum und Datenhandel* (Erich Schmidt 2018) 135.

12 Kilian (n 11) (who points out a 'numerus clausus').

13 J Schefzig, 'Brauchen wir ein Recht an Daten?' [2017] 3 Deutscher AnwaltSpiegel 3ff, available at <https://www.deutscheranwaltspiegel.de/wp-content/uploads/2017/02/1_Schefzig_DAS_03_2017.pdf> accessed 13 November 2019.

14 According to *Buchner*, however, it is just copyright law which demonstrates that even exclusive rights provide sufficient scope to strike a balance between the exclusive rights on the one hand and the freedom and communication interests of the general public on the other (B Buchner, 'Is there a Right to One's Own Personal Data?' [2017] Zeitschrift für Geistiges Eigentum, Intellectual Property Journal, 416ff, 417).

very different things.[15] Therefore, a new legal framework for data is often demanded which also comprises consumer protection regulations – a law of obligation especially for data (‘*Datenschuldrecht*’).

II. Consumer protection and data protection

Consumer Rights

The ‘Directive on contracts for the supply of digital content and services’ (Digital content Directive)[16] covers reality by explicitly allowing data as a counter-performance.[17] So it seems that a basic decision for the aforementioned new legal framework is already made – at least regarding consumer rights.

Nevertheless, a lot of questions arise and have to be answered: What about the legal consequences of a withdrawal of consent, the prohibition of coupling or the question of (lacking) enforceability? According to recital 40 the Directive does not regulate the consequences for the contracts in the event of the consumer withdrawing the consent for the processing of the consumer's personal data. Such consequences should remain a matter for national law. In this context, *Specht* suggests that the withdrawal of the consent should not be touched, even if the consent in the context of a contractual obligation as a counter-performance is given.[18] Therefore, the situation is comparable to the exceptional right of termination: The contractual relationship ends – according to the explanations of *Specht* – ex-nunc if the service of the data processor is also provided within the framework of a continuing obligation.[19] This corresponds to recital 39. *Specht* further argues that alternatively, a claim for compensation could also be justified which would, however, require legislative action.[20] But in this context the interests of data subjects have to be taken into account additionally and to be checked if such compensation could lead to a restriction to the right of withdrawal and the right to self-determination.

15 *v. Lewinski* (n 1) 215 points out the contractual fairness.

16 Directive (EU) 2019/770 of the European Parliament and of the Council of 20 May 2019 on certain aspects concerning contracts for the supply of digital content and digital services [2019] OJ L136/1.

17 Specht (n 5) 38.

18 Specht (n 5) 42.

19 Specht (n 5) 52.

20 Specht (n 5) 53, 42.

Legislative action would also be required regarding enforceability of a declaration of consent, although – as *Specht* points out as well – the possibility of exercising a permanent 'dolo-agit-argument' exists.[21] With regards to another relevant point, the prohibition of coupling, *Specht* argues that this is an expression of the principle of the voluntariness and should therefore protect the person concerned, above all, (merely) from being subjected to the external control of a third party. Nevertheless the legal transaction makes it possible – within the scope of exercising private autonomy – to bind and *Specht* states in this context that it is not telos of the coupling prohibition to protect from this commitment.[22]

Therefore, it seems that proposals for solutions already exist that are worth taking into consideration.

Data Subject

Nevertheless, if we talk about the consumer rights we also have to talk about the data subject and privacy matters in order to find the best solution. There are a lot of concerns regarding the feared sale of fundamental rights.

But what are the facts? There is, in reality, another significant factor that needs to be taken into consideration: We all know that companies would not have any data base without the contribution of the data subject, in particular the users and consumers. Currently, we have the situation which is called 'factual property' or 'de-facto property'. *Kerber* explains this kind of situation by using the example of car data, where the car manufacturers have the exclusive control due to the fact that the data is on their proprietary servers. He remarks that this actual control can cause problems of access in the context of networked driving, as other services (just need) require access to this data.[23] *Kerber* refers to the TRL-Study of the EU Commission and the analysis how to ensure a fair solution, for example by re-

21 Specht (n 5) 54.

22 Specht (n 5) 47.

23 W Kerber, 'Dateneigentum und Datenhandel kompakt. Wem unsere Daten künftig gehören (können)', Seminar on 22.11.2018; W Kerber, 'Data Governance in Connected Cars – The Problem of Access to In-Vehicle Data' [2018] Jipitec 316.

ferring to an 'on-board application platform' or a 'shared server'.[24] A 'shared server' shall guarantee an anti-discriminatory access to data for all relevant service providers participating in the field of a connected car. This is the economic point of view which also requires a legal basis. From the legal point of view this solution includes the exercise of the right to self-determination by the data subject on the one hand and a neutral organization on the other hand which is allowed to make a relevant decision. Regarding the latter a comparison could be drawn to the establishment of data trusts which are already discussed in literature, e.g. by *Buchner*. He remarks that data subjects are no longer in a position to effectively control his or her right of self-determination due to the lack of experience as well as the complexity of data processing.[25] Therefore, he suggests data trusts.[26] This proposal is also made by other authors, e.g. by *Fezer*, who recommends a neutral agency which sets rules and negotiates on behalf of the consumers but in the sense of a democratic systems so that all parts of society are represented in such an organization.[27] Furthermore, *Fezer* refers to a so called 'Datensondervermögen' which means putting all values in one big pool as separate property of data – in the sense of a separate asset of data.[28]

The establishment of data trusts or data agencies could even be a necessary requirement regarding the protection of data subjects. This is especially true since the future data processing often ends as a black box, particularly due to AI applications. But the main concern regarding this suggestion is the 'selling off' of fundamental rights and it is criticized that such models do not recognize that we are talking about a human right and the risks to renounce it. *Schneider* remarks in this context on the one hand the positive aspect due to the easing burden in regards to the data subjects so that in combination with the right to withdrawal, the purpose limitation and the principle of transparency the status of data protection could be increased.[29] If a trust is established in compliance with these principles the

---

24 European Commission, 'Access to In-vehicle Data and Resources' (Final Report), <https://ec.europa.eu/transport/sites/transport/files/2017-05-access-to-in-vehicle-data-and-resources.pdf> accessed 23 November 2019), in particular 149ff.

25 B Buchner, 'Eigentumsrechte an persönlichen Daten?' in H Redeker and P Hoppen (eds), *DGRI Jahrbuch 2011* (Otto Schmidt 2012) 51, 58.

26 Buchner (n 25) 58.

27 Fezer (n 11)115, 154ff.

28 Fezer (n 11) 159.

29 I Schneider, 'Regulierungsansätze in der Datenökonomie' 9, available at <http://www.bpb.de/apuz/292347/regulierungsansaetze-in-der-datenoekonomie?p=all> accessed 13 November 2019.

data subject retains control due to his or her freedom to decide which companies may access which personal data for which purposes. On the other hand, *Schneider* stresses that it remains open which government agency would exactly authorize the trustee and that is has to be clarified how the participation of the data subjects could be realized democratically and, if necessary, transnationally, whereas another important questions finally would lead to the old question who monitors the guards? [30] A trust may not pursue its own interests and must be trustworthy, whereby the independence of the Trustee vis-à-vis state or economic authorities must be ensured in the long term and a focus on the public good must be guaranteed.[31]

Therefore, we are currently all facing a very important issue and must decide how best to defend the rights of us all in the future because – finally – we are all data subjects. The GDPR alone – unfortunately – does not seem to be sufficient.

This raises the following questions:

According to the aforementioned and as a whole, there are different questions which have to be answered and to be unified: (1) Do we need more distributional justice according to the currently existing 'de-facto property' and in which way could a financial participation of users be conducted in practice? (2) Do we need more regulations or does the GDPR sufficiently protect the data subjects and, on the other hand, also give them sufficient opportunities to exercise their rights in a digitalized world? (3) Is she or he able to understand the consequences in case of allowing the consent (and data) as a contractual counter-performance and is it possible at all to draw up an agreement that transparently reflects the consequences? (4) Could a trust be a helpful organizational instrument or does a trust rather entail a threat to the rights of data subjects?

30 Schneider (n 29) 9.
31 Schneider (n 29) 9.

III. 'Directive on contracts for the supply of digital content and services' (Digital content Directive)

Could the Directive shed light on the situation?

Well, the Directive does not apply where the provided data is solely used to provide the digital content and the trader does not process that data for any other purpose (e.g. for marketing purposes). Apart from that, the Directive does not specify any value of data either.

In addition, there are some inconsistencies or ambiguities. As mentioned before, the Directive should not apply to situations where the trader processes personal data exclusively to supply digital content or a digital service.[32] According to the European Data Protection Board the processing for 'service improvements' or 'recommendations' (e.g.) cannot be regarded as necessary for the provision of the service.[33] Does this mean that the Directive applies because the provided data is not solely used to provide digital content or does the Directive not apply because the related data is exclusively provided to supply just that kind of service? Is this an event of a conflict and the GDPR (or rather the interpretation of the GDPR) should prevail (see recital 37)? What about the contractual freedom? This question is also relevant for all other (possibly conceivable) products or offers combining a bundle of services. In a nutshell: It is necessary to answer the question of how to distinguish between the various services within a complex contract which may be based on different legal bases. In some cases the provided data can be based on a legitimate interest which is currently also reflected in the terms of a contract. Therefore, the question is one the hand whether data will be used by the trader for *other purposes* when, for example, it is processed for recommendations or for a customized, person-

32 According to Article 3 '[t]he Directive shall also apply where the trader supplies or undertakes to supply digital content or a digital service to the consumer, and the consumer provides or undertakes to provide personal data to the trader, *except* where the personal data provided by the consumer are exclusively processed by the trader for the purpose of supplying the digital content or digital service in accordance with this Directive or for allowing the trader to comply with legal requirements to which the trader is subject, and the trader does not process those data for any other purpose.' (emphasis added).

33 European Data Protection Board, 'Guidelines 2/2019 on the processing of personal data under Article 6(1)(b) GDPR in the context of the provision of online services to data subjects' <https://edpb.europa.eu/sites/edpb/files/consultation/edpb_draft_guidelines-art_6-1-b-final_public_consultation_version_en.pdf> accessed 13 November 2019.

alized and localized content. On the other hand the consequences have to be examined, in particular whether legitimate interests can be covered by the Directive at all: Normally within a contract a deliberate decision-making of the contracting party is necessary. It may therefore be necessary to amend the contractual agreement and define the services and the counter-performance differently, unless this would be not allowed for reasons of consumer protection or data protection.

In this context it might also be helpful to specify the term 'provided', as already demonstrated by the controversial guidelines on data portability (Article 29 Working Party).[34] The term 'provided' according to Article 20 GDPR (Data Portability) is restricted as it refers to data which is necessary for the performance of the contract or based on consent. Other legal bases are excluded. It must also be mentioned that in opposite to the former draft of the Directive an activity by the consumer is not required any more. This is all the more important if we consider the discussions around article 20 GDPR and the question whether the term 'provided' requires an active participation of the data subject, e.g. that only this data should be covered which the data subject controls and accesses on its own.[35] Therefore, despite the deletion of the term 'actively' in Article 3, it does not seem obvious whether the interpretation of the Directive is now final and distinct.

Furthermore, the Directive refers to metadata but it is also not clear in which extent usage data shall be included. According to the draft of the ePrivacy Regulation metadata may also reveal very sensitive and personal information and means data for the purposes of transmitting, distributing or exchanging electronic communications content, i.e. usage data. So it could be examined whether the definition of the draft of the ePrivacy Regulation also applies to the Directive or if a common definition is possible. Beyond that, the meaning of recital 25 of the Directive could be discussed in whole. The Directive should not apply to situations where the trader *only* collects metadata, *such as* information concerning the consumer's device or browsing history, except where 'this situation' is considered to be a contract under national law. Regardless of the question whether 'this situation' is allowed under GDPR it seems not entirely clear

34 Article 29 Data Protection Working Party, 'Guidelines on the right to data portability', WP 242 rev.01, <http://ec.europa.eu/newsroom/document.cfm?doc_id=44099> accessed 13 November 2019.

35 More information: Stiftung Datenschutz (ed), 'Practical Implementation of the Right to Data Portability', available at <https://stiftungdatenschutz.org/fileadmin/Redaktion/Datenportabilitaet/kurzversion_studie_datenportabilitaet.pdf> accessed 13 November 2019.

in which cases the protection of the Directive is denied. However, according to the 'factual digital situations' and since we are all confronted with this every day when using information on websites, it is necessary to find sufficient regulations for cookies or other technologies which are able to track us. The 'DSK' (Datenschutzkonferenz) already decided that cookies (except cookies which are technically necessary) need the consent of the data subject.[36]. The former draft of the Directive explicitly excluded cookies according to recital 14.[37] But the final version of the Directive leaves this situation unclear and does not mention that even cookies and other tracking methods are important tools to gain and gather valuable data. Overall, the question remains to which extent there is a need to regulate metadata, respectively cookies.

IV. Conclusion

The actual question that arises in this context as a whole is to what extent it is possible for a data subject to exercise 'data sovereignty'. Is he or she in a position to make a self-determined decision and able to evaluate the value of his or her data? Wouldn't the data subject be overwhelmed, especially considering AI – where decisions often resemble a black box? These questions are already raised in the aforementioned explanations but can not be answered by the Directive.

---

36 Position of the Conference of data protection authorities on the applicability of the TMG (Telemedia Act) to non-public bodies as of 25 May 2018 (adopted on (26 April 2018) <https://datenschutz.sachsen-anhalt.de/fileadmin/Bibliothek/Landesaemter/LfD/PDF/binary/Konferenzen/Nationale_Datenschutzkonferenz/Unterlagen_der_DSK/95._Konferenz/Positionsbestimmung-TMG.pdf> accessed 13 November 2019; Guidance from data protection authorities for service providers (March 2019) <https://www.datenschutzkonferenz-online.de/media/oh/20190405_oh_tmg.pdf> accessed 13 November 2019. This is also in accordance with the proposal of the ePrivacy Regulation of 10 January 2017 (European Commission, Proposal for a Regulation of the European Parliament and of the Council concerning the respect for private life and the protection of personal data in electronic communications and repealing Directive 2002/58/EC (Regulation on Privacy and Electronic Communications) COM (2017) 10 final of 10.1.2017). An overview of the current state of negotiations of the ePrivacy Regulation is provided by the Bavarian State Commissioner for Data Protection, <https://www.datenschutz-bayern.de/0/eprivacyVO.html> accessed 13 November 2019.

37 Proposal for a Directive of the European Parliament and of the Council on certain aspects concerning contracts for the supply of digital content, COM(2015) 634 final of 9.12.2015.

The consequence is if we discuss the possibility of data as a counter-performance the right to self-determination has also to be discussed.

However, only the legal system can provide a response to changes in the facts of a new digitalized world. Digital reality cannot be ignored.

Data as Counter-Performance & the Digital Content Directive – The End of a Debate?

Rebekka Weiß[*]

Data is undoubtedly one of the cornerstones of today's economy, industrial developments and innovation. Many data driven services, platforms and products are offered free of charge to users. However, innovation and improvement of existing services, be they data driven or not, require investments. If a service is offered without monetary counter performance, the financial aspect of the contractual equation needs to be covered from another side. As data can be used in a variety of ways, can be monetized and has an intrinsic value, it was soon discovered as a new way for monetization in the data driven environment. Especially ad-driven services use data to personalize their services and tailor ads to their users. User platforms, social networks, search engines, software functions are therefore offered free of charge and are financed through advertisement that uses the data the user provides or the information gathered from the user when he is using the service. The system benefits all sides: the user gets access to a lot of web based and free services (and the system caters to the fact that many users would not be willing to pay for websites and services they have grown accustomed to using for free), the advertisers gain access to a highly specified group of potentially interested people and the provider gets to monetize his service without having to bill the user himself.

The controversy and political debate around data driven free services is often explained by a perceived disproportionate advantage of the providers. From a consumer and data protection standpoint it is often argued that the user does not have the power to renegotiate the terms of these contracts, does not get enough contractual remedies and should be included in the value added to his data. This discussion led to different political and legal approaches that all argued for more 'fairness' and an improvement of the user's position. Some even argued that a data ownership should be developed. Apart from contradicting the General Data Protection Regulation (GDPR), which explicitly allows for data processing in cer-

* Head of Trust & Security, German Federal Association for Information Technology, Telecommunication and New Media (Bitkom).

tain cases without the users consent and does not view right to data as absolute, data ownership could not be brought into conformity with the existing legal framework.

The proposed Directive on Digital Content turned the discussion in another direction and introduced a legal framework for data as counter performance, manifesting the commodity status of data into law.[1] The Directive´s aim is to provide consumers with contractual remedies if the digital content or the digital service is not in conformity with what was agreed upon or can reasonably be expected by the consumer (Article 6 and 6a Digital Content Directive). The scope of the Directive with respect to contracts where the consumers provides data in exchange for the possibility to use the service, however, refers not to Article 6(1)(b) GDPR but to the other legal grounds of the GDPR (in practice, Article 6(1)(a) and Article 6(1)(f) will probably be the most important cases). This leads to an interesting conundrum: Article 6(1)(b) GDPR provides for a legal basis for processing if such processing is necessary for the performance of the contract to which the data subject is party. One could argue (and it has indeed been argued) that this 'necessity' could also be seen in the provision of a service free of charge, making the provided data necessary for the fulfilment of the contract: monetizing data instead of charging for the service in order to provide a service for free. This would constitute exactly the situation the Digital Content Directive wants to regulate: a contract where the user provides data in exchange for using a service. With not referencing Article 6(1)(b) GDPR the new Directive passed on the chance to create symmetry.

The proposal furthermore introduces a more restrictive approach to the question, which processing is necessary in a contractual relationship.[2] The legal assessment will be further complicated once the e-Privacy Regulation[3] will enter into force as it introduces another phrase into the mix as Article 8(1)(c) provides that processing of data shall only be allowed of it is

---

1 The Digital Content Directive follows a long line of Digital Single Market Dossiers that all follow the same aim: ensuring a harmonized internal market and drive innovation, ensure consumers protection and the growth of the European Market.

2 Article 6(1)(b) GDPR: 'processing is necessary for the performance of the contract' and Article 3(1) Digital Content Directive: 'data exclusively processed for supplying the digital content'.

3 European Commission, Proposal for a Regulation of the European Parliament and of the Council concerning the respect for private life and the protection of personal data in electronic communications and repealing Directive 2002/58/EC (Regulation on Privacy and Electronic Communications) COM(2017) 10 final of 10.1.2017: <https://ec.europa.eu/digital-single-market/en/news/proposal-regulation-privacy-and-electronic-communications> accessed on 26.08.2019.

'necessary for providing an information society service requested by the end user'. Attorneys, courts and data protection officers will sure discuss the scope and differences between 'necessary for the performance', 'necessary for providing a service' and 'exclusively processed for supplying content' in order to determine which legal framework will have to be complied with. In a time where companies are still in the process of implementing the GDPR, reacting to new Guidelines from the Data Protection Authorities and Court decisions (having to adapt to an ever-changing landscape of legal opinions on how to implement the GDPR requirements) the Digital Content Directive will not only generate additional costs but also increase legal uncertainty.

Apart from legal uncertainty the possibility to freely withdraw consent will lead to practical uncertainty, as the contractual consequences of the consumer withdrawing his consent are not described in the Directive. And there is yet another interesting loophole in the regulatory framework: The Digital Content Directive only covers B2C and not B2B contracts, although businesses are using the same services as consumers (influencers and fanpage operators come to mind). If the Digital Content Directive comes into effect, the contractual remedies an influencer has will differ from the rights available to a consumer, even though the business user might depend considerably more on the service.

When analyzing the practical consequences the new rights will have, the right to withdrawal raises important questions as well. The current framework provides that in case a consumer makes use of his right of withdrawal the contractual partner has to refund him the amount already paid for the product or service. If under the Digital Content Directive the user provides data as counter performance it is still unclear what the consequences of a withdrawal will be with regard to the obligations of the provider.[4] Will he have to 'refund' the data as in transferring it back to the consumers or will it suffice to simply delete it? Would the provider have to delete the data as well if he has a legal basis to keep the data for another purpose (the discussion regarding whether controllers are allowed to process data if the user provided it on the basis of an 'unnecessary' consent because the controller has another legal basis for processing will undoubtedly come up again in situations such as these). Another open question that needs careful consideration is whether the contractual withdrawal will at the same time constitute the withdrawal of the consent under the GDPR.

4 Recital 12 makes it clear that the right to withdrawal following the Consumer Rights Directive 2011/83/EU will apply to contracts regarding digital content.

Seeing that the member states might choose different ways to implement the Directive with regards to their national contract law, harmonization will not be achieved and lead to additional legal uncertainty.[5] As the Digital Content Directive is so closely connected to many still debated GDPR questions we might end up in a situation where even the harmonization of the interpretation of the GDPR might be endangered by the newly introduced framework.

The discussion about data driven services and their contractual and data protection implications are therefore far from over. The Digital Content Directive might have put an end to the debate whether free services are considered contracts with a counter performance on the user's part but did not provide answers to the bigger question: Is the Digital Single Market regulatory framework coherent and comprehensive enough to drive innovation for digital services in the EU, does it depict reality and will it be possible to harmonize the frameworks enough to ensure a stable European Market?

5 See Recital 22 Digital Content Directive.

Contributors

Sergio Cámara Lapuente

Professor of Civil Law, University of La Rioja

Sjef van Erp

Professor of Civil Law and European Private Law, University of Maastricht

Martin Fries

Private Lecturer, Ludwig-Maximilians-University, Munich

Benjamin Görs

German Federal Ministry of Justice and Consumer Protection

Philipp Hacker

AXA Postdoctoral Fellow at Humboldt University of Berlin and Associated Member at the Centre for Law, Economics and Society, UCL

Václav Janeček

Research and Course Development Fellow in Law and Technology, University of Oxford

Sebastian Lohsse

Professor of Roman Law, Comparative Legal History, Civil Law and European Private Law, University of Münster

Gianclaudio Malgieri

Doctoral Researcher at the Law, Science, Technology & Society (LSTS) Research Group, Free University of Brussels

Axel Metzger

Professor of Civil Law and Intellectual Property Law, Humboldt University of Berlin

Anne Riechert

Professor of Data Protection Law and Law in Information Processing, Frankfurt University of Applied Sciences; Scientific Director of the Stiftung Datenschutz (Foundation for Data Protection)

Andreas Sattler

Senior Lecturer, Ludwig-Maximilians-University, Munich

Martin Schmidt-Kessel

Professor of German and European Consumer Law, Private Law and Comparative Law, University of Bayreuth

Reiner Schulze

Professor of German and European Civil Law, University of Münster

Juliette Sénéchal

Associate Professor of Private Law, University of Lille

Dirk Staudenmayer

Head of Unit 'Contract Law', DG Justice and Consumers,
European Commission. Honorary Professor at the University of Münster

Rebekka Weiß

Head of Trust & Security, German Federal Association for Information Technology, Telecommunication and New Media (Bitkom)

Christiane Wendehorst

Professor of Civil Law, University of Vienna